Ideology and the Theory of Political Choice

Michigan Studies in Political Analysis

Michigan Studies in Political Analysis promotes the development and dissemination of innovative scholarship in the field of methodology in political science and the social sciences in general. Methodology is defined to include statistical methods, mathematical modeling, measurement, research design, and other topics related to the conduct and development of analytical work. The series includes works that develop a new model or method applicable to social sciences, as well as those that, through innovative combination and presentation of current analytical tools, substantially extend the use of these tools by other researchers.

GENERAL EDITORS: John E. Jackson and Christopher H. Achen

Keith Krehbiel
Information and Legislative Organization

Donald R. Kinder and Thomas R. Palfrey, editors
Experimental Foundations of Political Science

John Brehm
The Phantom Respondents: Opinion Surveys and Political Representation

William T. Bianco
Trust: Representatives and Constituents

Melvin J. Hinich and Michael C. Munger
Ideology and the Theory of Political Choice

Ideology and the Theory of Political Choice

Melvin J. Hinich and Michael C. Munger

Ann Arbor

THE UNIVERSITY OF MICHIGAN PRESS

Copyright © by the University of Michigan Press 1994
All rights reserved
Published in the United States of America by
The University of Michigan Press
Manufactured in the United States of America
⊗ Printed on acid-free paper

1997   1996   1995   1994   4   3   2   1

A CIP catalogue record for this book is available from the British Library.

Library of Congress Cataloging-in-Publication Data

Hinich, Melvin J.
    Ideology and the theory of political choice / Melvin J. Hinich and
Michael C. Munger.
        p.   cm. — (Michigan studies in political analysis)
    Includes bibliographical references and indexes.
    ISBN 0-472-10198-6 (alk. paper)
    1. Elections.   2. Voting.   3. Social choice.   4. Ideology.
I. Munger, Michael C.   II. Title.   III. Series.
JF1001.H56   1994
324.6'01—dc20   94-12209
                                                              CIP

To
Joseph and Sarah Hinich and
Herbert and Marjorie Munger

Contents

Preface

It is unorthodox for a statistician and an economist to write a book about politics. This is particularly true when one realizes that our thesis involves the consequences for a science of political choice of something so amorphous and ill-defined as ideology. In truth, it is the very fact that ideology has remained amorphous and ill-defined in the study of political choice that provoked us to begin this work.

There are two mains themes in this book. The first is the claim that ideology is the conceptual answer to the problems and contradictions in much of modern political economy. The second is the specification and exposition of a particular model of political choice in which ideology is imbedded. Though these two themes are related, it is important to keep them distinct. Readers interested primarily in one of these themes may find other sections tedious or overlong; for this we apologize in advance. To answer the questions we have in mind, we must cut too many corners as it is.

Formal political theory has reached a critical juncture, where internal contradictions and the lack of interesting or useful new results have set members of the discipline to casting about for alternatives. Several approaches have gained adherents, the most important of which are the study of ideology and the study of lobbying, rhetoric, and political communication as signaling games. We do not claim that the signaling approach is wrong, or that it is not valuable. Instead, it is argued that a complete understanding (which, by the way, this book will not provide) of the role of ideology as the answer to problems of cooperation will subsume the signaling approach in a broader context. The signaling game method is a means of conducting microanalysis on the patterns of messages and language we expect to see in politics. Further, the signaling theory is the only way of identifying patterns of communication that are credible and internally consistent, and therefore have survival value. Unless it ultimately turns out that ideologies do more than specify ethical or moral principles, and that they actually make adherence to those principles consistent with purposive behavior, our enterprise will not have been successful.

That said, the goal of this book is to work downward from macro-level phenomena. In chapter 1, we give an overview of a theory of political choice rooted in ideology. The goal of this approach is to explain and predict the patterns of dynamic political strategies, historical movements of party platforms, and the nature of political disagreement and debate. The theoretical linkage between the micro and macro analyses remains to be worked out, but the two approaches must be mutually reinforcing.

Theme two, the devising of a formal model in which the developing theory of ideology can find representation, provides the book with its organization. Chapter 2 reviews the foundations of the classical spatial model of political choice by citizens, and considers the origin of that body of work in public choice economics of the 1960s and 1970s. We review the theory of public goods and the public finance perspective on political choice, and present reasons why this approach turned out to be less useful than it appeared at first. Chapter 3 reviews the classical spatial model, and introduces the quadratic utility function, which will be used for most of the remainder of the book to represent citizens' preferences. Though the quadratic is a restrictive functional form, it has great expositional advantages, because it is intuitive and easily manipulated. Chapter 4 is a synthesis of the substantive challenges to the classical spatial/public choice model, and makes some preliminary arguments about why ideology can answer these challenges. Chapter 5 relates the concepts of party and ideology, and draws distinctions between them.

Chapter 6 is the simplest version of the formal theory of ideology. This chapter adapts Downs's theory of ideology and correspondence to the policy space that interests voters. We correct and flesh out this insight by drawing on developments in spatial theory of the early 1980s. It is important to point out that much of this chapter is devoted to the first theme of the book: the establishment of ideology as an analytically useful representation. The reader may or may not agree with our particular formulation of the theory of ideology, but the problems the model is set up to address require a perspective that only a theory of ideology can provide.

Chapter 7 provides empirical perspectives on how our conception of ideology can be measured and made more explicit. This chapter is designed not to test competing hypotheses about political choices, but to illustrate ways such testing might be accomplished. Chapter 8 puts together the full model of political choice by citizens. The formal theory of ideology is melded with the probabilistic theory of voting, a means of accounting for abstention and uncertainty of the theorist/observer about the decision rule of the voter.

Chapter 9 digresses to pick up the last remaining component of the unified model, the role and function of interest groups in the campaign. Although there has been a wealth of theory on this subject, it has never before been possible to specify completely, or even accurately, the role of groups in the campaign. Without a theory of ideology, there is no campaign; with a theory of ideology, we can advance a more complete theory of groups. Finally, in chapter 10, the disparate strands of voter choice, candidate strategy, ideology, and interest groups are united in a model of the campaign. We assume probabilistic voting and specify a Bayesian model, where new information from candidates (financed by campaign contributions from interest groups) influences voter perceptions of candidates. The results allow us to describe the likely equilibria, and nonequilibria, of more complex political contests than have been possible before. Chapter 11 is more speculative, concentrating on the impact of negative campaigning on the political system. In our model, negative campaigning is rational from the perspective of a candidate who wishes to win an election. But it damages the political system, and makes all voters worse off. We show that the equilibrium result, if negative campaigning is allowed, is not a Pareto optimum. Voters get no informational gain, and suffer from increased variance in the distribution of expected candidate positions, but candidates obtain no electoral advantage from the negative campaigning that causes this difficulty.

Credit for completion of the book is shared by many. Vickie Carroll and Julie Daniel showed more patience and fortitude in the hurry-up-and-wait process of typing and retyping the manuscript than they should have had to. The ideas contained in the manuscript owe much of whatever coherence they possess to comments in seminars at California Institute of Technology, Carnegie Mellon University, George Mason University, University of North Carolina, University of Rochester, Princeton University, University of Texas, Texas A & M University, and Washington University. Particularly useful responses were given by David Austen-Smith and Jeffrey Banks (who still question the value of the whole thing!), Dennis Coates, Roger Congleton, Arthur Denzau, John Freeman, Kevin Grier, John Ledyard, Peter Ordeshook, William Riker, A. Raoul Rutten, Norman Schofield, and Robert Tollison. William Keech read the whole manuscript and made innumerable important and useful suggestions. Douglass North, both through direct comments and his work of the past fifteen years, showed the way toward establishing the need for a better understanding of ideology and its role in shaping human activity; our debt to him cannot be overestimated.

Research assistance and in-depth criticisms were offered by Sergio Berenzstein, Janet Box-Steffensmeier, Han Dorussen, Julia Davidson, Scott DeMarchi, Jay Dow, James Endersby, Jorge Gonzalez, Laureen Hartnett, Victoria Heid, Jonathan Hubschman, Megan Koch, DuJuanna Massenburg, Hallie Schenker, David Scocca, and Joseph TenBarge. Whatever quality this work possesses is due in large measure to the quality of the comments we have received and tried to respond to; on the other hand, the responsibility for shortcomings lies with the authors alone.

Finally, we thank our families for putting up, for the past five years, with our need to write in the middle of the night, to fill floors with papers and open books, and to seem even more distracted and confused than usual in conversation. We didn't always thank you enough at the time.

CHAPTER 1

Ideology and Politics

I tell you folks, all politics is applesauce.
— Will Rogers, *The Illiterate Digest*, 1924, 30

Politics has got so expensive that it takes lots of money to even get beat with.
— Will Rogers, Syndicated Newspaper Article, June 28, 1931

Most scholarly research on elections appears to accept Professor Rogers's first insight as true, and the second as inexplicable. The "politics" of the campaign, the speeches, the persuasion, the posturing, and the symbolism, are just applesauce, a minor side dish to the main course of issue stew. Consequently, it is hard to explain why enormous resources of money, time, and energy are dissipated in this unimportant and unexamined aspect of elections. For some reason, actual participants seem to take the process very seriously.

The way citizens make political choices affects more than just the immediate distribution of resources. The institutions, or "humanly created rules of the game,"[1] of the society help to determine its long-run prosperity, the ideas that are important for political debate in future contests, and the ability of citizens to cooperate and trust each other. Ultimately, the ideas institutions promote, and the ethical restrictions institutions place on individual actions, are the most important determinants of the very definition of a society and how it performs.[2]

Yet, the classical spatial theory of electoral competition among parties and candidates consciously abstracts away from institutions and ideas. Formal theories of political choice are explicitly *designed* to focus on strategic movements by candidates to increase their expected vote share, given the expected platform of their opponent(s). This analysis relies on the correctness of an analogy drawn from economic spatial location theory, an analogy that has systematically misled political theorists. The alternative proposed here is a concept that, while hardly new, captures concisely what current theory omits. That concept is ideology.

---

1. This definition of institutions comes from North (1990b).
2. Two authors who have argued this point at much greater length are North (1981, 1990a) and Harrison (1992).

In the following pages, a theory of ideology is spelled out, and its implications for political choices in a community are explored. Our first task is to convince social scientists that this conception is important, and that its incorporation into existing work is valuable. We begin by arguing that the present notion of political interaction, particularly the theory of elections, can be greatly improved by being modified to account for ideology. Then, the theory of public goods, voting, and interest group influences on elections are reviewed. Finally, we present a unified model of purposive political action, incorporating voters, candidates, parties, and interest groups in the face of immanent uncertainty. Along the way, we hope to persuade the reader of two things. First, rigorous formal models of politics may someday account for emotion, history, and the idiosyncrasies of human cognition. Second, adding such factors to existing models will strengthen their power to predict and explain.

As noted above, this formal perspective on ideology is not wholly new. Many points addressed in this work were advanced in Anthony Downs's seminal 1957 book, *An Economic Theory of Democracy*. But this work has been misinterpreted; the orthodox "Downsian" model of elections is different from what Downs intended. The main goal of Downs's theory was accounting for the pervasive atmosphere of uncertainty and limited information in which political decisions are made. Downs advances the rudiments of a spatial model in his chapters 1–4, and it is on this foundation that much of modern spatial theory, including the "median voter theorem," is built. Unfortunately, the extensions of the spatial model were accomplished mechanically, taking "issues" as the dimension(s) of the relevant space. It was precisely Downs's point that voters have too little information about parties or candidates to make such a detailed analysis. In fact, the attenuated incentives for voters to learn much about politics prompted Downs to develop his theory in the first place. The spatial theory of Chapters 1–4 in Downs was a man of straw, and it is time to begin to analyze men of flesh and blood.

In constructing a formal theory of policy formation, we reprise Downs's original motivation for using spatial theory: to represent political preferences in the face of uncertainty, where "represent" takes on the technical meaning given it in microeconomic theory. We require a theory that focuses on the simplified, abstract left-right "ideological" dimension Downs constructs, but that is still based on voters who care about policies. Downs speaks of his spatial theory as if this were his goal, but presents no model that can represent choices by rationally uninformed voters. Later work in political theory has confused Downs's simple model with his ambitious goal, and has accepted "issues" as the space where political choice takes place. This focus conflicts with the simple, symbolic, and viscerally evocative messages of real campaigns. Until now, spatial theory has not accounted for ideology.

Downs defines ideology as "a verbal image of the good society *and the chief means of constructing such a society*" (1957, p 96; emphasis added). Note that this definition has two parts: identifying the ends toward which society should strive, and then specifying policies that are means to these ends. The reason that ideologies serve a vital purpose in politics is the uncertainty that suffuses political decisions. The decision rules political actors use to select specific policies are hard to gauge. Perhaps more important, the causal link between means and ends is clouded.

Downs notes that differences between parties are bereft of ideological conflicts in a world of certainty.

> When voters can expertly judge every detail of every stand taken and relate it directly to their own views of the good society, they are interested only in issues, not in philosophies. Therefore parties never need to form *weltanschauungen* at all, but can merely take *ad hoc* stands on practical problems as they arise. (1957, 98)

The situation is very different if voters are unsure of what parties will do. Voters may be uncertain because (1) they don't know the details of what the party claims as its platform, (2) they are unsure of the implications of a policy, such as a new superconducting supercollider, for their individual welfare, or (3) they find such claims less than completely credible. This is, in Downs's view, no more, and no less, than a rational reaction to the costliness of political information.

> [A] voter finds party ideologies useful because they remove the necessity of his relating every issue to his own philosophy. Ideologies help him focus attention on the differences between parties; therefore they can be used as samples of all the differentiating stands. With this shortcut a voter can save himself the cost of being informed upon a wider range of issues. (1957, 98)

Downs is hinting here at something profound: the cleavages between parties separate along simpler, more predictable lines than an n-dimensional policy space would imply, *even if what voters care about is the n-dimensional space*. A reduced-dimensional policy space represents party conflict very accurately, and at far less cost to the voters and the parties themselves. Further, the form of this cleavage is predictable from the intellectual content of the ideologies: the verbal image of good doesn't just list the dimensions of conflict, it logically *implies them*.

Consequently, parties organize themselves around ideologies, not policy positions. Platforms are more than a point in an n-dimensional space; they become abstract, even ethical, statements of what is good, and why.

Each party realizes that some citizens vote by means of ideologies rather than policies; hence it fashions an ideology which it believes will attract the greatest number of votes. . . . This ideology must be both internally consistent and consistent with the party's concrete policies . . . In our model, each party designs its ideology to appeal to that combination of social groups which it feels will produce the most support. If its design is accurate, policies chosen for their consistency with the ideology will automatically please the citizens being courted by the party. (Downs 1957, 101–2)

The point of these lengthy, repeated quotations is to establish Downs's goal in applying spatial theory to politics. The irony of crediting Downs with originating classical spatial theory in politics is that he was trying to accomplish exactly the opposite. A theory of ideology was his goal, and simple spatial theory was only the means of accomplishing this. What is now called the "Downsian" spatial model is, instead, a synthetic spatial location theory derived from economics and decision science.

Downs's earlier-cited opinion that, in a certain world, ideology is irrelevant has proved prescient: spatial theory has assumed certainty, and has largely ignored ideology. Candidates position themselves in n-dimension policy spaces in which voter ideal points are fixed and certain points. Ellipsoidal indifference curves encompassing convex upper contour sets represent voter preferences, and allow the researcher to describe the choices voters make among competing policies or candidates.

In the following chapters, we review both the contributions and drawbacks of this perspective in detail. For now, we wish only to emphasize that this picture is wrong, or incomplete: the campaign has been left out! In trying to bring the campaign back in, we are led to notice the difference between choice based on issues and choice based on campaigns. Real campaigns designed to attract votes are dominated by symbolism and a few simple messages or themes. Scholarly spatial analysis of voting has emphasized issues, and positions on issues may be what voters ultimately value most. We are left with a challenge: how are we to depict the relation between ideology, the realm of real political discourse, and the complex n-dimensional space that real voters care about? In other words, how are ideologies projected or mapped onto predictions about policy?

The answer Downs gives is vague and confused, which probably explains why little has been made of this connection until now. He claims: "voters are ultimately interested in actions, not ideologies, so each party must frequently check its actions directly against the voters' preferences" (Downs 1957, 102).[3] But how are these preferences expressed? How can a party

---

3. Downs's claim that voters are " . . . interested in actions, not ideologies . . . " is a claim that may, itself, be wrong. Downs conceived of ideologies as devices that reduce transaction and

measure policy preferences when political rhetoric, and the very construction of an individual's political outlook, is expressed in ideological terms?

The fact that the two spaces are separate requires some correspondence between them. Downs recognizes this, and offers the following explanation:

> This dualism can be depicted on our graph of political space. . . . Each party takes stands on many issues, and each stand can be assigned a position on our left-right scale. Then the party's net position on this scale is a weighted average of all the particular policies it upholds. . . . Each citizen may apply different weights to the individual policies, since each policy affects some citizens more than others. (1957, 132–3)

The ideas embodied in this nascent theory of ideology have not been extended, or even much noticed, by students of politics. Political scientists have either rejected Downs or embraced only chapters 1–4. In part, the explanation lies in the fact that Downs's correspondence, or mapping, between ideology and policy is not workable. If the ideological dimension is a weighted average of policy positions, where the weights differ across voters, there is no coherence in ideological messages, and therefore no information (even on average) in ideological positions. Consequently, ideology (as Downs defines it) might be a shorthand rule or heuristic for individual voters, but it is not a means of communicating in groups or organizing parties.

The thesis advanced in this book is that ideologies are quite different from personal belief systems or heuristics to guide individual choice. Ideological messages contain coherent statements of how to choose and what to do. Citizens can, on average, agree on the content and meaning of these statements, though their evaluation of the worth of the statements may differ. As a result, ideologies are the basis for choice in group decisions, and provide the language in which groups debate and disagree.

In the following pages, Downs's fundamental insights on the importance of uncertainty in political discourse are reformulated in a more general theory of ideology. It is useful, before we begin, to contrast a model of choice based on ideology with the best-known of the voting models of choice under certainty, the "median voter theorem." Various versions of the median voter theorem (MVT) are identified with Downs (1957), Black (1958), Davis and Hinich (1966, 1967), and Plott (1967). The MVT is a highly abstract theoretical approach to voting behavior. Nonetheless, the MVT purports to make important predictions about practical political interaction. The central point of

---

information costs. It is quite possible that the reason ideologies survive is that they reduce transaction and information costs, but that voters (if you ask them) are, in fact, "interested" in the ideologies. Strict adherence to a decision rule or heuristic is hard to distinguish from direct belief in the things that the decision rule appears to imply.

the MVT is to identify a general structural force in politics that drives candidates, parties, and policies toward the middle of the distribution of voter preferences. In its more extreme form, the MVT confers the powers of universal choice on a single actor, the median voter.

The debt owed by such spatial theory to Hotelling (1929) and Smithies (1941) is obvious. Still, as we shall soon see, this debt is really not clearly understood, and in some ways, the insights of Hotelling and Smithies have been subtly misapplied by political theorists.[4] Spatial location theory in economics generally took as its object of analysis N firms (imagine them to be hot dog vendors with wheeled carts), choosing where to locate along a straight line (imagine a boardwalk along a beach). Some fixed, exogenous distribution of potential customers along this line is assumed.[5]

Consider an example with two vendors ($N = 2$). The prediction of Hotelling and Smithies in this case is that the vendors would end up rubbing elbows at the location of the median beachgoer. Any other arrangement would mean that one vendor serves more, and the other less, than half the total market. Consequently, no other pattern can be an equilibrium, since each vendor can either (1) move closer to his rival, or (2) if already next to his rival, move around, closer to the center, and capture for himself a larger market share. More succinctly, since each vendor can guarantee himself at least half the market by locating in the center of the distribution of sunbathers, no other location makes sense. This nice result breaks down if $N \geq 3$, since if three (or more) vendors are side-by-side, the ones in the middle have zero market share. Such vendors could increase their profits by moving *anywhere* else in the space.

Consider for a moment the assumptions that underlie this model of spatial competition, and compare the situation being analyzed to political interaction. The assumptions of the hot dog game can be set out as follows:

> Vendors are identical, except for location on the boardwalk: they sell indistinguishable hot dogs and offer the same buns, napkins, and condiments; and their carts have similar appearances. People choose one over the other based solely on the concern for minimizing the walk from beach blanket to frankfurter freighter.

---

4. An exception is Sartori (1976). On pages 325–27, he critiques the "shaky" credentials of the economic basis of Downs's spatial theory.

5. Clearly, this assumption is important. If the distribution is endogenous, then the model is indeterminate. In our example, for instance, the vendors might build fixed stands instead of carts, and the beachgoers could bid on sandy spots near the stands. There would be implicit rent gradients (taking the form of queues for position when the beach opens) extending out from the stands. The steepness of the gradient would depend on the beachgoers' marginal disutility of walking.

Transactions are enforced at no marginal cost to any party to the transaction.

Movement is free, and it is clear what movement means: the physical location of the hot dog cart changes along the single dimension of the beach. The perception of relative distance is objective and shared.

The distribution of hungry sunbathers is exogenous, and does not change in response to movements or fixed locations of hot dog vendors.

Let us consider applying exactly these four assumptions to a simple political issue, say the proportion of total budget spent on education. Let voters be distributed along the 0 percent to 100 percent interval. Pick the initial positions of two candidates Theta and Psi and call these positions θ and ψ, respectively. One possible configuration is depicted in figure 1, where $\theta \neq \psi$. Assume that voters' ideal points are uniformly distributed along the 0 percent to 100 percent interval, so that the median lies at 50 percent. The question is, how directly applicable is the logic of the spatial location game?

If all hot dogs are identical, it makes sense to choose vendors based purely on their physical closeness to the hungry sunbather. Once the purchase is made, the sunbather has eaten and does not care if the vendor moves, as he can always patronize the competitor. But it is much less clear what "movement" means for a candidate in a political/policy location game. The politician is making a contingent promise, separated in time from the point when the promise is expected to be fulfilled. As a result, politicians often couch pledges in terms that both state the promise and make a commitment to carry it out.

For example, Theta might assert: "If I am elected I will, once in office months from now, work for educational proportion θ because I believe θ is the best policy." This is important because no voter cares about any one of a series of campaign promises for its own sake. Voters value only the single, final choice among mutually exclusive alternatives (the budget cannot have both θ and θ' proportions spent on education). The candidate can improve his vote share (his sole concern) by "moving" from θ to θ', since θ' is closer to the median. The promise to choose θ was incredible.

Voters must therefore assess not just the platform, but also the candidate. More accurately, voters must assess the *commitment* a candidate has to his professed platform, as well as other, more abstract, qualities.[6] The political leader must respond to unforeseeable exigencies of national crisis or international conflict. Voters, therefore, rationally value, and vote for, candidates who manifest leadership, calmness in a crisis, good character, and con-

---

6. For an empirical investigation into the importance of "nonpolicy" characteristics, such as leadership ability, honesty, etc., see Enelow and Hinich (1982b).

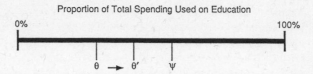

Fig. 1. One dimensional location game for candidates Theta and Psi

sistency. None of these nonpolicy characteristics have analogues in the frankfurter example, because the frankfurter purchase is a one-shot deal, with no opportunity for reneging or *ex post* recontracting. Once we have received the hot dog and examined it, we pay for it, assuming the vendor will not snatch the steaming tube steak back and run away chortling. All of these problems of reneging and *ex post* recontracting exist for politicians, however, and must be accounted for by a successful theory of political choice.

The only way a candidate can persuade voters he will do as promised is to create and maintain a reputation for probity and consistency.[7] The candidate may *want* to avoid specific promises and to maintain room for maneuver, but competitive pressures make it difficult. The campaign provides him with a series of situations where he must somehow persuade prospective voters he will behave as promised.[8] Ideally, he must convince them he will deliver as promised because deep personal beliefs prevent him from doing anything else. Returning to figure 1, this means that moving Theta's position from θ to θ' means that neither position is believable, since it is now obvious that the politician values winning more than policy. His promises were cheap talk.

This discussion raises more questions than it answers. To wit, (1) What is the meaning of equilibrium or disequilibrium in a spatial location game where a candidate must persuade voters of his position, rather than simply announcing it? (2) How do parties and potential candidates choose, or (more accurately) acquire, a reputation for a particular ideology or set of positions? (3) Most important, are these reputations chosen at all, or does the competition of politics select for the best ideologies?

To answer these questions, we need a theory of ideology that has precise

---

7. Some attempts to account for this problem in the formal literature include Bernhardt and Ingberman (1985), Lott (1987a), Dougan and Munger (1989), Lott and Reed (1990), and Banks (1990).

8. Numerous authors have noted the advantages of a "strategy of ambiguity" (Alesina and Cukierman 1987, Cukierman and Meltzer 1986, and Shepsle 1972), but this observation is incomplete and misleading. We can agree that firms in a market setting would prefer higher output prices, because the firms would earn higher profits as a consequence. It does *not* follow, however, that the firm could increase profits by raising the price of output. Similarly, the party (or candidate) who would prefer more wiggle room may not pursue it because of competitive pressures to be clear.

formal implications but preserves the intuition behind Downs's original contribution. This intuition is lost in the modern spatial theory; we bring it back. The received theorems of spatial theory do not need to be corrected in achieving this synthesis. The theorems are useful and obviously "correct," *as equilibrium conditions*. If, instead of modeling individual candidates as moving around the space, classical spatial models endogenized candidate choice and allowed parties to switch among candidates, the same results would still follow.[9] We seek not so much to modify spatial theory, as to reinterpret the intuition behind its results.

The metaphor of movement, and of fixed spatial representation of preferences, has been widely criticized by political scientists (including Stokes 1963 and Sartori, 1976). The metaphor scientists use to justify models is important, because it suggests an approach to conceiving of the problems we are investigating. Metaphors also direct the way researchers think about new solutions to these problems. Even if the models will ultimately be compared as models, with the stories stripped away, the metaphor we invoke is significant if it suggests a new model. It cannot be said that classical spatial theory is useless because the examples used to illustrate its logic are wrong. Our argument is that a slightly different "story," one based on ideology, will allow a much richer model, one that boasts both practical verisimilitude *and* theoretical rigor.

Defining Ideology: Decisions and Uncertainty

The critical power . . . tends to make an intellectual situation of which the creative power can profitably avail itself . . . to make the best ideas prevail.
—Matthew Arnold, *The Function of Criticism at the Present Time*, 1864

Of all political assets, the existence and maintenance of an ideology is by far the most fundamental. Most other strategic political activities, such as choosing candidates, issues, or coalitions, as well as tactical decisions of the campaign, such as spending money on advertising, or taking public positions, are subordinate. Day-to-day "politics" can only be understood in its broader ideological context. Association between a party, or candidate, and an ideology is logically antecedent to the political strategy of selecting a point in the n-dimensional policy space. Consequently, to understand political choice, we must learn what ideologies are and where they come from.

Settling on a definition of ideology is no mean task. Dozens of different definitions exist, each with some claim to primacy. We review three of the more prominent clusters of interpretations below.

---

9. In fact, there is precedent for taking this perspective in an approach to political choice that assumes purposive action. See Aldrich (1980).

Ideologies are collections of ideas with intellectually derivable normative implications for behavior and for how society should be organized (Higgs and Twight 1987; Reichley 1981; North 1981, 1990a, 1990c; Lodge 1976).

Ideologies are economizing devices by which individuals understand, and express ideas about, politics (Higgs 1987; Enelow and Hinich 1984; Congleton 1991; North 1981, 1990a, 1990c; Macridis 1980; Downs 1957).

Ideologies are complex, dogmatic belief systems by which individuals interpret, rationalize, and justify behavior and institutions (Higgs 1987, 1990; Domhoff 1983; Joravsky 1970; North 1990a, 1990c; Sartori 1969, 1976).

These terse summaries represent what we believe are the three major aspects of ideology emphasized by scholars.[10] Higgs (1987) emphasizes four separate aspects (cognitive, affective, programmatic, and solidary), but we will use only three, choosing to merge the affective and solidary functions.

Ideologies perform an important psychological service because without them people cannot know, assess, and respond to much of the vast world of social relations. Ideology simplifies a reality too huge and complicated to be comprehended, evaluated, and dealt with in any purely factual, scientific, or other disinterested way. (Higgs 1987, 37–38)

It is worth stressing that all notions of ideology exhibit an inherent tension between two related phenomena. The first is an anthropomorphic collection of ideas, and the second is the application of these ideas one finds in an individual's belief system; his *weltanschauung*, if not his *weltansicht*. We shall discuss this problem at some length later, but for now we will resolve this tension by decree: ideologies are collections of ideas. Individual belief systems or schema may mimic some or all parts of a particular ideology, but these beliefs are distinct from ideologies. As a practical matter, successful ideologies will find substantial correspondence across individual schema, but this is not necessary for the definition.

---

10. We have not tried to define an obviously related concept, "culture," because of its overtones of application to the entire society. Culture may well be a larger concept, in the sense that it determines the forms of the ideologies that citizens might accept. One recent definition of culture is given by Harrison (1992, 9): "Culture is a coherent system of values, attitudes, and institutions that influences individual and social behavior in all dimensions of human experience." The relation between ideology and culture is discussed at somewhat greater length in chapter 3.

It is also important to distinguish the concept of "ideological dimension" from the usage of Almond (1960), which was stated more clearly and more forcefully by Sartori (1976):

> The ideological continuum goes from the extreme of ideological fanaticism and future-oriented principledness to the opposite extreme of sheer practicalism and pragmatism. . . . When speaking of more-or-less ideology and, conversely, of more-or-less pragmatism, the implication need not be motivational but might well be cultural. That is, the ideological dimension differs from all others in that it points to a cultural factor, to the overall temper (and temperature) of politics in a given cultural setting. (Sartori 1976, 78)

This observation, and usage, is not wrong; it is simply different from our meaning. The intensity with which beliefs are held, or commitment to the ideas the ideology embodies, are, for us, matters of voter perception, not the ideas a party espouses and represents. Sartori is quite right to claim, however, that an understanding of the extent of commitment by adherents, and the reasons for it, are crucial to an understanding of any political system.

Following is the definition of ideology as it will be used throughout this book.

> Ideology: *an internally consistent set of propositions that makes both proscriptive and prescriptive demands on human behavior. All ideologies have implications for (a) what is ethically good, and (therefore) what is bad; (b) how society's resources should be distributed; and (c) where power appropriately resides.*

More simply, an ideology tells us what is good, who gets what, and who rules. Given the generality of this definition, many ideas that are not obviously political are still, in our terms, ideologies. It is no accident that these powerful ideas—including religion; seemingly simple moral precepts, such as Kant's "categorical imperative"; formal familial relations; and traditional obligations—are included. They all potentially shape the universe of political discourse and the conceptual framework individuals use to understand and debate politics. Culture, history, ideas, and emotion matter.

The definition just offered is so general and encompassing, it is important to list as illustrations some ideologies and nonideologies. Instinctual, genetically programmed, or sexual reactions are not ideological, for ideologies are always ideative. Often an ideology (such as Islam, Marxism, or Mormonism) is partly composed of ideas that serve to control or divert certain aspects of human behavior by asserting their baseness. This may lead to some subtle distinctions, of course. Is a group of men who beat and rob a passerby traveling alone in a forest behaving ideologically? One might answer no, they are simply thugs trying not to starve. Yet if we asked these men what motivates their behavior, the answer would not be "self-interest," even if they tell the truth. Instead, they would likely offer some justification (they are oppressed politically; the man they robbed is wealthy; the man they robbed is a tax-collector/Irishman/Muslim/Catholic/immigrant/Mets Fan) that implies their action is not "bad." In fact, it may even be moral! Though their actions hurt the man they robbed, their conception of "society" might dictate that society is better off after the robbery than before.

To clarify the notion of ideology, let us consider two of the best examples of well-known (if not always well-articulated) political ideologies, capitalism and communism. To illustrate the tripartite categorization, we distinguish these two in table 1, along with two other examples (fascism and the platform of the New Deal Democrats). The interesting thing about this table is that it allows us to consider the particular conflicts among these competing nations about how a society should be organized.

The "What is Good?" column has very different answers for capitalism, communism, and fascism. The latter two encourage citizens to work for the state, the welfare of their fellow citizens and country; capitalism lauds work

TABLE 1. Examples of Ideologies

	What Is Good?	Who Gets What?	Who Rules?
Capitalism	Individual achievement through work, Observance of property rights	Distribution according to output	Wealthy have more control over goods, services, and policy
Communism	Self-realization from role in society, Brotherhood of working class	Distribution according to need	Party represents general will; All are equal, so no politics
Facism	Nationalism, Racial purity, Service to fatherland	Distribution according to contribution to military/economic might of nation	Corporatist view of military-labor-industry
New Deal Democratic	Individual achievement through work, Self-respect, Self-improvement	Distribution according to output, Progressive tax structure to finance safety net whose output is insufficient	Wealthy get disproportionate power; Experts and technocrats correct for excesses of market processes

for oneself. Though the New Deal represents a mixture of these motives, its basis is closest to Capitalism. The difference is that the New Deal advocates intervention by government to help those unable to help themselves. More than a duty to achieve, New Deal ideology would claim each has a right to obtain sufficient education and wealth for self-fulfilment. A similar comparison in the "Who Gets What?" and "Who Rules?" columns shows that, while the ideologies are different across rows, the conception within each row is similar; each is internally coherent. The ideas represented are mutually supporting rather than contradictory, or just unrelated.

Imagine two further examples, an ideology that no one believes anymore, and an ideology that no one believes yet. For the first, consider the "divine right of kings." A simple description of this ideology is "the supposedly God-given right to rule formerly attributed to monarchs."[11] Two aspects of the definition are of interest, the word *supposedly* and the word *formerly*. For someone believing in the divine right of kings, *supposedly* is insulting; believing the right to be divine makes it so in fact. *Formerly* means no one believes this nonsense any longer. Surely this is not true; some minority of elderly Japanese, no doubt, still believed in Emperor Hirohito's divine right to rule, or even his outright divinity, until the time of his death in 1988. Many African and South Pacific island nations retain some vestige of a divine imprimatur on the mandate to rule.

Still, for our purposes, the condescending and western *formerly* does not eliminate the divine right of kings as an ideology, even if it is true that literally no one believes it. The set of ideas that, together, make up an ideology (the king rules with a divine mandate, revolution is blasphemy, fealty to king is fealty to God) exists, independent of whether anyone accepts them. The fact that no one finds them persuasive as a way to live, or to organize a society (both physically and intellectually), reflects on the ideology's power. But it does not change its identification as an ideology, at least in our semantic construction of ideologies as anthropomorphic entities.

The second example, an ideology that no one believes yet, is more amorphous, but in some ways more interesting. Imagine a world, or, in Plato's sense, an Order of Being, in which all potential ideologies can be mentally apprehended at once. That is, let many internally consistent sets of ideas with implications for human action and the "right" way to organize society be arrayed before us. Any individual could begin to comprehend fully only a fraction of these. The number one is persuaded by, believes in, or accepts as correct must be a small proportion of the space of *potential* ideologies. Yet one can imagine conceiving a new set of ideas with implications for political behavior. We are led to look to an ideology's origin.

---

11. *Webster's New Universal Unabridged Dictionary* (1987).

The Origins of Ideology

> The beginnings and endings of all human undertakings are untidy.
> —John Galsworthy, *Over the River*, 1933, chapter 1

How can we explain the origin of ideologies? The most basic human disputes are over property rights, rights to food, shelter, and protection of the family from aggression. At their base, these disputes are not ideological (in the sense we have defined the word as derived from abstract ideas), but any such contention possesses an ideological aspect. In the earlier example of robbers in the forest, the wealthy traveler would tell you he was attacked by unprincipled thugs. The "thugs" themselves, however, may assert, and even believe, their right to redistribute income from the rich to the poor. We will argue that, while ideologies are used strategically in this fashion, they are created out of culture, history, and emotion. Boulding gives an insight into the role of drama in the creation of ideology.

> An image of the world becomes an ideology if it creates in the mind of the person holding it a role for himself which he values highly. . . . To create a role, however, an ideology must create a drama. The first essential characteristic of an ideology is then an interpretation of history sufficiently dramatic and convincing so that the individual feels that he can identify with it and which in turn can give the individual a role in the drama it portrays. (Boulding 1964, 39; quoted in Goertzel 1992)

In terms of the three questions (what is good, who gets what, who rules) an ideology must answer, the implications of the Robin Hood myth are obvious. If the ruler behaves badly and allows illegitimate power to accumulate in the hands of the wealthy, he has violated the implicit agreement that gives him the power to rule. It is not, then, wrong to steal if the theft is from the rich and distributed to the poor (after the Merry Men deduct appropriate operating expenses, overhead, and consulting fees). Because the ruler behaves badly, an action normally proscribed (such as theft) may be encouraged. The poor get the proceeds, giving them the power to ensure that the ruler is ultimately overthrown.

We admire the stories of Robin Hood, and relate them to our children. Though simple and incomplete, the dictum of "take from the rich and give to the poor" is clearly ideological, and clearly political.[12] This tendency to use

---

12. In *Matthew* 19:21, in the Christian New Testament, believers are told: "If thou wilt be perfect, go and sell that thou hast, and give to the poor, and thou shalt have treasure in heaven." Robin Hood's innovation was simply to increase "that thou hast" by (legitimate) taking by force.

ideas to justify and give legitimacy to one's actions is well understood, its reasons for existence obvious. The choice of how to justify something one already wants to do might be thought of as strategic. Nonetheless, we must be careful not to attribute too much intellectual power, bordering on foresightedness, to people justifying primitive urges. Imagine you are hungry, and a passerby, obviously well-fed, has a cartload of food. You tell yourself he won't miss the food you will take, and it will save your life. So you take it, by force if necessary.

How far would you go? Would you injure the person if he tries to resist? Does it matter whether the food is for him alone, or if he is taking it to an orphanage? If he dies in the struggle, how will you act the next time you are similarly hungry and see someone better off than yourself? The answers to these questions become more interesting, and, for our purposes, more useful, if the "you" we are considering is part of a society of similar people, and these confrontations become routine. Consistent actions, justified in consistent ways, are the origins of ideologies. Over time, justifications that might become ideologies are tested and compared, based on whether they work. At the outset, "working" may be defined as justifying something the actor(s) wants to do anyway.

Very soon, however, more is demanded, as "success" demands two types of consistency.[13] First, the same ideology must justify the same action, and vice versa, in all similar situations. Second, as the ideology evolves over time and becomes more sophisticated, it must avoid contradictions. Consistent failure of either type of consistency can make the ideology wither away. This is not to say that perfect consistency is required, since, as Higgs (1987) notes, this is impossible.[14] Still, there exists a threshold above which contradictions in an ideology weaken its foundations of legitimacy and make it rapidly lose adherents. Proponents of an ideology are people persuaded of its correctness, its moral force, or even just its coincidence with their own private, non-ideological goals. The crucial point is that political disagreements will take the form of arguments over the moral superiority of ideologies with contradictory implications. That is, arguments will turn into debates over how the disputes *should* be resolved, not a comparison of the naked interests of the disputants.[15]

---

13. More accurately, the two types of consistency are necessary, but not sufficient, to make for a successful ideology.

14. North (1990a, 1990b) argues that the requirement of either type of consistency is very loose, and that personal belief systems, in particular, are fraught with contradictions.

15. As Milton Friedman (1953, 5) points out, the two kinds of dispute are rarely completely separate. The means of achieving a goal all agree is good is the usual rhetorical battleground, but the real disagreement is more likely on basic values, "over which men ultimately can only fight."

To summarize, we have outlined the first, and perhaps most important, origin of ideology: legitimation and justification of acts the ideology's creator(s) found desirable for other reasons. Many such justifications fail, of course, and are not heard again systemically.[16] For those that do succeed, as the acts or processes become regular and routinized, the ideological justification becomes accepted by repetition and by its utility in consistently resolving disputes. It becomes orthodox, and is widely believed if the group or individual whose power is given legitimacy does not (too often) contradict the ideology by word or deed. This orthodoxy inevitably creates an opposing, or heterodox, position. Such an observation is hardly novel, having been discussed at length by Habermas, Hayek, Hegel, Marx, and others. But our intended use of the opposition of the orthodox and heterodox ideologies, as a basis for a rational spatial theory, is novel.

Ideology Determines the Terms of Debate

Turn him to any cause of policy,
The Gordian knot of it he will unloose,
Familiar as his garter; that, when he speaks
The air, a chartered libertine, is still.
—Shakespeare, *King Henry V*, act 1, scene 1

The terms of the debate, the logic and language of the dispute, itself, in the most fundamental sense, are framed by the orthodox ideology. Dissidents are often those least advantaged by the orthodoxy, and their dissidence may be motivated by this strategic, essentially economic objection. But dissidents are also often drawn from groups the system appears to serve best, their objections fueled by a genuine moral and emotional outrage against what they perceive as inequities. The rhetorical requirements of a successful polemic ensure that any heterodox ideology must oppose the orthodox by suggesting intellectual or emotional reasons why the status quo is wrong or unsupportable. The contest is more than one of persuasion: ultimately, the contest is

---

16. Von Mises (1981) points out that there is an irreducible conflict between ideology and the policy sciences, particularly economics. But he also notes that ideology may often be the stronger force in shaping people's thinking.

Scarcely anyone interests himself in social problems without being led to do so by the desire to see reforms enacted. *In almost all cases, before anyone begins to study the science, he has already decided on definite reforms that he wants to put through.* Only a few have the strength to accept the knowledge that these reforms are impracticable and to draw all the inferences from it. Most men endure the sacrifice of their intellect more easily than the sacrifice of their daydreams. They cannot bear that their utopias should run aground on the unalterable necessities of human existence. What they yearn for is another reality different from the one given in this world. (1981, 200; emphasis added)

decided by who gets to use their words, their conception, to describe the conflict.[17] This tension between two opposing sets of ideas, and statements of those ideas, creates a relevant policy space of only a few dimensions. In the most extreme, and clearest, case, the orthodox and heterodox ideologies cleave along a single dimension, as two points determine a line. As Duverger (1951) points out:

> A duality of parties does not always exist, but almost always there is a duality of tendencies. Every policy implies a choice between two kinds of solution: the so-called compromise solutions lean one way or the other. This is equivalent to saying the centre does not exist in politics: there may well be a centre party, but there is no centre tendency, no centre doctrine. The term "centre" is applied to the geometrical spot at which the moderates of opposed tendencies meet: moderates of the right and moderates of the left. Every centre is divided against itself and remains separated into two halves, left-centre and right-centre. (Duverger 1951, 215)

Sowell points out that this dichotomizing tendency is noticeable even in issues that seem unrelated:

> One of the curious things about political opinions is how often the same people line up on opposite sides of different issues. The issues themselves may have no intrinsic connection with each other . . . yet the same familiar faces can be found glaring at each other from opposite sides of the political fence, again and again. It happens too often to be a coincidence, and it is too uncontrolled to be a plot. (Sowell 1987, 6)

Sowell is quite right that there need be no "intrinisic connection" between issues. All that is necessary is that the orthodox ideology support certain positions, and the opposing ideology will automatically take the other side. Though the orthodox and the heterodox ideologies may differ on many issues, the basis for such differences derives from this reduced-dimensional contraposition. It is insufficient simply to look into who benefits and who loses from a particular policy, as this will not allow one to understand policy outcomes. What is necessary to understand any policy debate is to comprehend the ideologies that contest the status quo.[18]

---

17. The importance of the language used to describe a problem as a means of determining who wins is considered by Norton (1988) and Stone (1986).

18. Stone (1986) argues that the competition among conceptions, using symbols and arguments based on conceptual representation, is the *only* basis for policy decisions, and that there is no such thing as objective debate.

For example, any, local dispute tends to become not just one but two ideas. The first is the legitimizing ideology that justifies the resolution of the dispute in this instance, and implicitly advances reasons why similar future disputes should find the same resolution. The second is the heterodox ideology used by those who lost, or are not in power, claiming the result was not legitimate and should be reversed. Thus, although the heterodoxy may be *de novo*, it is never *ex nihilo*. Orthodoxy, because it is the first move, can be chosen from all the ideas available for justification. The heterodox position has no such latitude for choice, but must attack the intellectual and moral basis of the orthodoxy.[19]

Finally, to the extent that a heterodoxy is successful, it replaces (again, in the classic Hegelian-Marxian dialectic dynamic) the orthodoxy. The old orthodoxy is not, generally, the best response to the new. Nonetheless, the new orthodoxy will set the terms for what the new heterodoxy will look like. As a result, the latitude for genuine political strategizing of the sort routinely assumed by classical spatial models is severely circumscribed. The political process, depending as it must on the evolution of ideas, their emotional and moral appeal, and the credibility of participants on both sides, just won't allow it.

The Importance of Ideology in Politics

The test of a first-rate intelligence is the ability to hold two opposed ideas in the mind at the same time, and still retain the ability to function.
    —F. Scott Fitzgerald, *The Crack-up*, 1936, 2

Recall the standard two-candidate spatial model of voting discussed earlier, which assumes candidates locate in the feasible policy space to maximize their chances of victory. In game theoretic terms, if candidates choose strategies solely based on an objective of winning elections, if the space is unidimensional, and if all voters choose strictly according to distance, the Nash equilibrium strategy for the two candidates is to choose the median. As the MVT shows, no alternative can attain a majority over the median position. As an equilibrium condition, and a means to identify the powerful tendency in political competition for the middle to wield power, the classical spatial model has proved invaluable. Still, social science has gone too far in applying the metaphor of spatial location competition to the political process, which has, in truth, a very different set of incentives.

---

19. In a recent study of the rhetoric of the campaign to certify the U.S. Constitution, Riker (1989) advances a theoretical reason why a rational strategy may be to oppose the orthodox position. His explanation rests on the premises that (1) citizens are risk averse, and (2) rhetoric is designed to persuade, not just inform.

There are two possible remedies to the problem of representing voter choice under uncertainty over candidate intentions and future events. One is to try to adjust the classical model to account for the candidates' incentive to misrepresent and voters' consequent discounting of candidate announcements in campaigns. The most advanced work in this area is Austen-Smith (1990) and Banks (1990, 1991). This approach focuses on the role of costs of misrepresenting intentions, and the credibility of politicians. The information is specific, the issues are well known and understood; the only question is whether the candidate is telling the truth.

This work is important, and may well restore the game model of campaigns to preeminence in spatial theory, but it addresses only the narrow question of uncertainty about intentions. Worse, it assumes the same level of information that the old spatial model required, and does not address new issues at all. Candidates take separate positions on all known issues, and voters evaluate them based on their credibility. The other approach, the one we take in the following pages, though in the same spirit of correcting the standard spatial model, is radically different in its logic and application. We seek to represent voter choice directly as ideology, rather than as a spatial communication/signaling game where ideology plays a part.

We must be careful, however, lest it sound as if an ideology is a fungible resource one buys, like a consultant or a commercial. An ideology is a mechanism for transmitting information and persuading, a generally consistent set of ideas about what is the "good" in politics and social intercourse. This mechanism is evolved, not designed, and the extent of consistency among its precepts is a consequence of that evolution. Any given ideology may advance ideals that are in conflict (for example, the value of the individual and the necessity of loyalty to the state), requiring a balance of contradictory imperatives.

In real political campaigns, no party could be successful, either in electing its candidates or even in making known its platform, without some coherent and appealing ideology. Potential candidates for ideologies are sparse. The creation and popularization of a new ideology is a difficult task, requiring time, money, considerable organizational skills, and (not least) an intellectually powerful and emotionally compelling set of ideas. A nascent political party faces an almost insurmountable problem of entry. The difficulty is not one of choosing among a variety of available and well-understood ideologies and then adopting the set of positions associated with that ideology. It is generally impossible to carve out some new position in the space of ideologies, and then run campaigns against existing parties on that basis. No new ideologies exist!

The reasons are not obvious, particularly from a theoretical perspective. Consider the "space of ideologies" alluded to above. We might imagine a collection of all functional relations, or mappings, between some set of ideas and an exhaustive list of implied policies. These mappings exist to the extent that they imply a general, and largely consistent, set of policies. The means by which this implication is arrived at and widely shared among citizens is complex, but rests on some complicated, and perhaps fuzzy, cognitive process of inference. Imagining this entire space of mappings in any intuitive sense, however, is extraordinarily difficult. We can imagine a collection of ideologies that we know (socialism, communism, ritual cannibalism, free market capitalism, Christianity, or Islam). The larger set of ideologies that *could* exist, from which the smaller set of examples that we know are chosen, is quite beyond our comprehension, however. The act of creation of an ideology requires an intellectual step, a spark of recognition, of making a connection among apparently unrelated disputes or problems that no one else has ever conceived of. The question is, how large is the set of potential, or unconceived, ideologies? We can, with difficulty, conceive of the abstraction of an insensible space containing correspondences between sets of ideas and the policies they imply. There are two restrictions on the number of ideologies we might count as genuine elements of this collection of sets of ideas, and the correspondences to policy they represent.

The first is the rule of consistency, alluded to earlier. Ideologies are buffeted and reshaped by the values of the competing ethical rules they invoke. This is not a process of logic alone, but tests the emotional appeal and attraction of particular aspects of the ideology to adherents. Nonetheless, the set of ideas comprising the ideology must *causally imply* the set of policies that citizens associate with that position. It is not enough for an ideology to be a shorthand signal, a correspondence between a name and a list of actions by government.

This rule of consistency dramatically restricts the set of correspondences that qualify, in any reasonable sense, as potential ideologies. We cannot simply take a set of ideas and examine the set of policies implied: most sets of ideas have no implication, or else imply everything. We are begging the question of creation, of course, since creation recognized an implication where none before existed. Choosing a set of ideas by some arbitrary means, and then examining their implications, virtually always results in failure, because, in general, no causal implication exists.

The second problem harks back to our earlier discussion of the origin of opposition. Even if there exists a universe of potential discourse in the space of potential ideologies, the act of creation ineluctably evokes the form of its own opposition. Conceiving of a new ideology that does not address the existing orthodoxy is of little use. Thus, the space of potential ideologies is very narrow. In any practical sense, it is restricted to a choice among those ideas that justify gainsaying the prevailing ideology, or (what amounts to the same thing) attacking the justification that the prevailing ideology offers.

We can conclude that the set of feasible new ideologies at any given point is severely restricted, even before one encounters the problems of popularizing and persuading. Any aspirant, in order even to qualify for consideration, must answer or contradict the prevailing ideology, and must do so in a way that is both logically coherent and emotionally appealing. This barrier to the entry of new parties is not remotely fungible. Groups that would otherwise organize can be thwarted, permanently, by this barrier alone.

Duverger notes this tendency for orthodox, established ideologies to block the creation of new ones, particularly in the manifestation of parties as advancers of an ideology (discussed later, in chap. 5). He notes:

> The question is then to organize progressively a mass of new electors . . . the development of local [party] committees is the natural answer to this. But once this first phase is passed, once parties are firmly constituted, fresh parties as they appear beat against the barrier of the old ones: separate local movements cannot pass beyond their birthplace, and remain incapable of giving rise to a truly national party. (Duverger 1951, xxvii)

Even if the new ideology overcomes the local organizational barriers, it is also necessary that it attract the political resources to bring the idea, or basis of the organized movement, to the attention of the public. Neither idea nor money is alone sufficient for success. Both are necessary. The best ideology, in terms of internal logical consistency and emotional appeal, is as nothing without committed apostles to spread it, and financial resources to make their efforts effective. Conversely, even an enormous quantity of money, used to advertise an ideology in every conceivable forum, is of little use unless the message is effective. Money does not rule the mind, and the mind motivates political action by individuals. We must add money, or (better) political resources generally, to our list of necessary conditions for success. But we must also emphasize that while a campaign to popularize an ideology may founder on the reefs of poverty, it may not sail through on monsoons of money alone.

At the end, we will have at least summarized an argument for using ideology as the means of representing political choice. Further, preliminary conclusions of the implications for community in society, once the understanding of elections as an ideological debate is accepted, are drawn out. The ability of societies to prosper, and to create welfare for their citizens, depends on the ability of those citizens to believe in the legitimacy of the existing order. If ideologies form the basis of debate in polities, they also serve as the means by which people understand each other and themselves. Politics without ideology is Babel.

CHAPTER 2

Representing Choice by Consumers and Citizens

The fool multitude, that choose by show.
> —Shakespeare, *Merchant of Venice*, act 2, scene 9

The goal of the next four chapters is to find a means of representing political choice that is both verisimilous and scientifically sound. To represent public choices, it is useful first to briefly review the extensive work on private choice, and individual preferences over public outcomes. Two separate questions drive our consideration of voter choice among the platforms of candidates or parties in this chapter. First, how do voters actually choose? Second, how are we to represent these choices in a parsimonious, rigorous theory?

Considerable scholarly attention has been devoted to the latter question, and we review this work. A comprehensive review of the literature on representation is beyond our intentions, but even a limited overview reveals some fascinating, and largely unremarked, regularities in research from strikingly different perspectives. Important insights can be gleaned from examining the scope of alternative approaches to the seemingly obvious question of how to represent citizen's choices.

To summarize the results we will discuss:

Collective choice (which we will call citizen choice) is different, in both form and content, from choice over private goods (consumer choice). The form is different because collective choices are not aggregated individual choices, but force an individual aggregated choice. The content is different because many collective choices involve public goods.

Rules for representation of consumer choice over private goods do not apply directly to representation of citizen choice over public goods. Preference functions defined over public goods do not inherit the properties of the private goods preference functions.

Functions capable of representing preferences over public goods share certain characteristics, including linearity and the separability of consumer assessments of private good and citizen assessments of public goods.

23

There is a more general representation for preferences over public goods that derives from Hinich and Pollard (1981), and Enelow and Hinich (1984a, 1989c). The rationales for using this "predictive dimension" satisfy both the empirical (explanation) and the theoretical (representation) criteria we have established for judging citizen decision making.

Consumer Choice versus Citizen Choice

In a democracy, everyone plays two roles. The first is that of a consumer of private goods. The second is that of a citizen, one who participates in public decisions about levels of provision of public goods, the taxes used to finance these decisions, and the direction and magnitude of income redistribution. It seems tempting to assume that the same set of theories that describe consumer choice will, likewise, work for choosing public goods, with (perhaps) some minor modifications.

Those who fall prey to this temptation, however, are doomed to fail to understand politics, for they have failed to comprehend the fundamental difference between consumer and citizen choice. There are two reasons that consumer and citizen choice differ: (1) the "decisive set" and (2) the form of "goods" being chosen. It is useful to briefly consider each of these, in turn.

The Size of the Decisive Set

Although it sounds trivial, it is useful to keep in mind the fact that the number of people required to make a consumer choice is just one: the consumer. Consumption choices may have spillovers (you may not like my tie; I may not like your cigar smoke), but we all agree that individuals should be allowed to make their own choices, on at least some matters. The number of people, or the proportion of citizens, required to make a decision in a society is called the "decisive set." The size of the decisive set can range from just one (pure private choice) to the entire society (pure unanimity). The choice of the size of the decisive set determines the form of all the choices that follow, and is an important focus of constitutional social choice theory.[1]

The reason the decision is important is that, in any decisive set larger than one, the power of the individual to decide is diluted. If the decisive set is large, the incentives of the individual to participate in the collective decision process are attenuated, *regardless* of what is being decided. That is, whether the choice is over the level of consumption of private goods (how many apples

---

1. For a review of this extensive literature, see Mueller (1989). The most important entries in the literature are Arrow (1963), Buchanan and Tullock (1962), Gibbard (1973), McKelvey (1979), and Slutsky (1979).

each of us will get over the next year) or public goods (what the level of spending will be on defense of the nation), the fact that choices may be made individually or collectively means that the voluntary participation of any individual cannot be taken for granted. Thus, and for this reason alone, any useful theory of collective choice where participation is voluntary must account for abstention.

The Form of the Good: Private and Public

A private good is a product or service with two characteristics: (*a*) the marginal cost (the difference in total cost between producing K and K+1 units) is not zero; and (*b*) one person's consumption of the good precludes its use or consumption by anyone else. In fact, the very word *consumption* indicates its orientation toward private goods, because consuming something uses it up, making it unavailable for use by others. Public goods, by contrast, particularly in the extreme case of "pure" public goods (Samuelson 1954), can be provided to more people at zero marginal cost. In fact, it is impossible (or very costly) to prevent all citizens in the relevant jurisdiction from enjoying the same level of the public good, whether they pay for it or not. These two conditions for public goods, zero marginal cost of production and nonexcludability, appear to be innocuous. They are not.

In his role as consumer, the individual makes private, self-determining decisions, subject to his own wants and income, the prices he faces, and the institutions society offers to facilitate transactions. It is possible that a given individual is disenfranchised in the private goods market (i.e., has no income), but *voluntary* abstention from the private goods market makes no sense. If the individual chooses not to go to the grocery and choose among the private goods there available to him, he starves.[2]

As a citizen, analogous abstention from public good decisions has essentially no effect. In fact, in national elections, the participation or abstention of any one individual is entirely irrelevant. The reason is the nature of the collective choice process we have chosen to make public good decisions, often some form of majority rule. Decisions about public goods always affect everyone, because the decision to provide one person with a given level of the good extends that level, by definition, to all others. The canonical example of a pure public good is national defense. A given level of nuclear deterrence means that we cannot make exceptions or withhold our counterthreat to a

---

2. We thank Erik Devereux for pointing out this distinction to us. Admittedly, such "abstention" might simply result in institutionalization, where private decisions are made by the authorities. In fact, any such attempt at private nonparticipation (e.g., suicide) will result in the individual's loss of control over the private goods participation decision.

foreign nation's first strike. Citizens who did not pay their taxes and provide their share of support cannot be excluded from enjoying the national protection afforded by the public good.

The "publicness" of such goods attenuates individual incentives to participate, whether choices are collective or not. We may find that some public goods are being provided by private action, but then the problem of the "free rider" prevents the aggregation of individual decisions from satisfying anyone.[3] Though governments exist for a variety of reasons, one of the most important is the need to provide public goods efficiently. While nonparticipation in private goods consumption is irrational and destructive, abstention from a society's choice of public goods has little impact, and may be entirely rational, from the individual's perspective.

It is useful to summarize the problem outlined in this section. The theoretical machinery developed to analyze consumer choices (that is, individual choices over private goods) is not useful for analyzing citizen choices (choices that involve either collective choice processes, where the decisive set exceeds one, or public goods, where the number of consumers in common exceeds one). What is required is a theory that can account for both of these problems. The problem of abstention will be discussed later; we turn, for now, to the economic theory of public goods.

Partial and General Equilibrium for Private Goods

The essence of consumer choice is the ranking of alternative bundles of private goods, followed by the selection of the best of these bundles that is still affordable, given prices and the consumer's budget. The implications of this choice process have been extensively analyzed by economists, from the partial equilibrium approach of Bentham (Stark 1954), Pareto (1971), Edgeworth (1928), Marshall (1961), and Hicks (1946) to the still more sophisticated and elegant general equilibrium work of Walras (1954), Arrow and Debreu (1954), Debreu (1959), Arrow and Hahn (1971), McKenzie (1959), and others. The partial equilibrium approach analyzes consumer choice in one or a few markets in isolation, holding all other prices (and other agents' activities) fixed, while the general equilibrium model seeks to discover what implications a change in one price has for prices and quantities throughout the whole system.

For the most part, this work has focused on consumer choice (private goods), rather than on citizen choice (public goods). The reason is not that it is more difficult to represent preferences in one than in the other (though this is

---

3. Olson (1965) demonstrated the basic logic of this "problem of collective action." Later literature is reviewed in Mueller (1989).

true). Rather, the explanation is that the equilibrium conditions in the two settings are so different. To illustrate, let us first consider partial equilibrium consumer choice over two private goods, apples (A) and beets (B), given their respective prices, P_A and P_B and the consumer's income, I. Assuming that (1) A and B are the only two goods available, (2) the consumer exhausts his income, (3) welfare is affected only by one's own actions, and (4) certain technical conditions are satisfied,[4] we can treat the consumer's problem as if he maximizes a utility function subject to a budget constraint:

$$\max U = f(A, B) \text{ subject to } I = P_A + P_B \tag{2.1}$$

The form of the utility function, f, is intentionally left unspecified, because any one of the infinite number of functions that represent the consumer's preferences has an equal claim to being the utility function. The simple definition of representation is a matching of index numbers provided by the utility function to all possible combinations of A and B. If a particular function has the characteristic that it assigns larger index numbers to bundles the consumer values relatively more, it is said to represent those preferences. There is no requirement that the consumer actually choose according to such a function, but if preferences are represented by a function, then we know enough to predict the outcome of any pairwise comparison of all bundles. This property is called *connectedness*, or *completeness*, meaning all bundles are capable of being compared by the preferences the utility function represents. Assuming the consumer values each of the goods more than zero at the margin (i.e., more is preferred to less), the utility function is said to be *monotone*.

Another property commonly asserted for utility functions is *transitivity*, a kind of consistency of comparison without which the concept of consumer choice would be much more complex. Given three different bundles of apples and beets, X_1, X_2, and X_3, $f(A, B)$ is transitive if and only if $f(X_1) > f(X_2)$ and $f(X_2) > f(X_3)$ together necessarily imply $f(X_1) > f(X_3)$.

Assuming $f(.)$ is connected, monotone, and transitive, we can solve the consumer's problem for the necessary conditions for partial equilibrium, using the method of LaGrangean multipliers. The maximand is

$$\mathscr{L} = f(A, B) + \lambda(I - P_A A - P_B B). \tag{2.2}$$

Taking partial derivatives and setting them equal to zero yields:

---

4. Sufficient conditions for representation of consumer preferences are connectedness and transitivity. For a more complete discussion of the much weaker necessary requirements for representation, see the work reviewed in Katzner (1970), and particularly Rader (1963).

$$\partial \mathscr{L}/\partial A = \partial f/\partial A - \lambda P_A = 0 \tag{2.3}$$

$$\partial \mathscr{L}/\partial B = \partial f/\partial B - \lambda P_B = 0 \tag{2.4}$$

$$\partial \mathscr{L}/\partial \lambda = I - P_A - P_B = 0 \tag{2.5}$$

Taken together, these first order conditions imply that the consumer maximizes his welfare when:

$$\frac{\dfrac{\partial f}{\partial A}}{\dfrac{\partial f}{\partial B}} = \frac{P_A}{P_B} \tag{2.6}$$

This expression simply means that the consumer should allocate his funds for expenditures on private goods until the last dollar spent on apples provides the same marginal satisfaction as the last dollar spent on beets.

If only consumer choices (i.e., private goods, provided privately) were available to society, there would be no public choice problem, save (arguably) the initial allocation of income. Because consumption of private goods precludes their consumption by others, and assuming no spillovers or externalities in consumption, we can simply add the quantities desired by each consumer, given their respective incomes, at given prices, and determine if this summed up demand exhausts supply. If not, the price is lowered or raised until the two quantities match. If we allow producers of beets and apples to decide how to allocate their resources for production based on what prices they expect, the situation is more complex, but no more difficult in principle. We might conceive of an auctioneer who calls out a set of prices, and all consumers and producers announce their responses. If the response exceeds the supply of some or all commodities, the price(s) must be raised to entice more production and deter demand. If the response results in surplus goods, the price must be lowered to raise the quantity consumers demand and deter production. No production or consumption is allowed until the auction is over (the general equilibrium is achieved). The auctioneer (call her Goldilocks) continues the process of too high or too low in each individual market, and all markets together, until she gets it just right.

The above process, called *tâtonnement*, is clearly no more than a thought experiment. Yet it does provide (in principle) a mechanism by which the partial equilibrium responses of each individual, given prices and income, can be reconciled with the general equilibrium determination of product prices, input prices, and the consequent flows of productive resources from one sector to another. All available and required information is embodied in prices, and no individual has an incentive to misrepresent his response to Goldilocks's successive announcements. The reason is that consumption choices affect only the individual's own welfare. In the next section, we discover that attempts to apply the theory of consumer choice to citizen decision making do not turn out so well. This very elegant and mathematically precise theory can be applied to choices over the appropriate level of *public goods* only in circumstances so restrictive as to make the theory of little use.

General Equilibrium with Public Goods

The essential problem with public goods is the difficulty of establishing, even in principle, a decentralized *tâtonnement* process analogous to that for private goods. The first scholars to address the question in a general equilibrium context were Bergson (1938) and Samuelson (1954, 1977). Maintaining the previous example of apples and beets, we now add a third good, national defense (D), a pure public good. Let us also add another individual to our previous Mr. 1, whom we shall call Ms. 2. The productive capacity of society is described by the transformation function

$$T(A, B, D) = 0 \qquad (2.7)$$

where:

$$A_1 + A_2 = A$$

$$B_1 + B_2 = B$$

$$D_1 = D_2 = D$$

Bergson and Samuelson sought to answer the question of the existence of an optimal rule for determining the level of the public good.[5] This rule had to account somehow for the cost of the public good D in terms of foregone opportunities to consume private goods A and B as described by $T(A, B, D)$.

To address this question, Bergson and Samuelson appealed to a function aggregating individual utilities, which they called a *social welfare function* (SWF). An SWF takes the form of a function $w(u_1, u_2, \ldots, u_N)$, where the u_i are the utilities of the individuals who make up the society. This function was alleged to possess the same qualities as individual utility functions (connect-

---

5. Note that the equality of consumption of public goods is definitional. Public goods must be consumed in identical quantities by all citizens, regardless of the amount that they would prefer to consume.

edness, monotonicity, transitivity). Further, the SWF was ordinal, or defined only up to any order-preserving transformation.[6] Bergson and Samuelson were not interested in the form of the function, which would presumably be the output of some constitutionally guided political choice, ratified by democratic vote or other collective process. The point is that any such function, once chosen, implies a determinate and well-defined optimizing choice. To see this, consider the following maximization problem.

$$\max \text{SWF} = w(u_1, u_2) \text{ subject to } T(A, B, D) = 0 \tag{2.8}$$

or, in LaGrangean form:

$$\mathcal{L} = w(u_1, u_2) + \lambda T(A, B, D) \tag{2.9}$$

The first-order necessary conditions for the existence of a maximum of the SWF are:

$$\partial\mathcal{L}/\partial A_i = (\partial w/\partial u_i \ \partial u_i/\partial A_i) + \lambda(\partial T/\partial A) = 0, \ i = 1, 2 \tag{2.10}$$

$$\partial\mathcal{L}/\partial B_i = (\partial w/\partial u_i \ \partial u_i/\partial B_i) + \lambda(\partial T/\partial B) = 0, \ i = 1, 2 \tag{2.11}$$

$$\partial\mathcal{L}/\partial D = (\partial w/\partial u_1 \ \partial u_1/\partial D + \partial w/\partial u_2 \ \partial u_2/\partial D)$$

$$+ \ \lambda(\partial T/\partial D) = 0 \tag{2.12}$$

$$\partial\mathcal{L}/\partial\lambda = T(A, B, D) = 0 \tag{2.13}$$

The term $\partial w/\partial u_i$ represents the "weight" each citizen gets in the SWF. Assuming the SWF is ordinal, the absolute size of the weights is irrelevant; the relative size, however, is crucial. The $\partial w/\partial u_i$ term embodies the extent to which *society*, as an organic entity whose preferences are embodied in the SWF, values increments in the utility of each *individual*. It is these weights, then, that represent the essential collective choice problem. Bergson and Samuelson clearly emphasize that such a choice is beyond their analysis, though of course the feasibility of the choice is crucial. Given these weights (they are left unspecified, and general, in Samuelson's analysis), we can proceed to the next stage.

For the two private goods A and B, these conditions imply that, just as in equation 2.6 before, for each individual:

---

6. This claim turns out to be more controversial than it appears. For a discussion, and citations to the relevant literature, see Mueller (1989), chapters 19 and 20.

$$\frac{\dfrac{\partial w}{\partial u_i} \dfrac{\partial u_i}{\partial A_i}}{\dfrac{\partial w}{\partial u_i} \dfrac{\partial u_i}{\partial B_i}} = \frac{\dfrac{\partial T}{\partial A_i}}{\dfrac{\partial T}{\partial B_i}} \qquad (2.14)$$

The only differences between this expression and equation 2.6, the analogous condition for pure private goods, are that (1) prices are now stated in costs of other goods foregone instead of in monetary terms and (2) each marginal utility is now multiplied by the weight that the individual receives in the SWF. The rationale for the indeterminacy of the weights is now clear: they are not relevant to individual marginal decisions (notice the $\partial w / \partial u_i$ terms cancel in equation 2.14), but matter only for distributional (i.e., political) questions. Thus equation 2.14 is true for *any* arbitrary SWF, and therefore, for all possible SWFs.

The situation for the public good D is more complex. Choosing to consider only Mr. 1 and private good A (the other cases are symmetric), the necessary condition for a social optimum is:

$$\frac{\dfrac{\partial w}{\partial u_1} \dfrac{\partial u_1}{\partial D} + \dfrac{\partial w}{\partial u_2} \dfrac{\partial u_2}{\partial D}}{\dfrac{\partial w}{\partial u_1} \dfrac{\partial u_1}{\partial A_1}} = \frac{\dfrac{\partial T}{\partial D}}{\dfrac{\partial T}{\partial A}} \qquad (2.15)$$

This result is one of the most fundamental in all of the study of political theory. In equation 2.14, we saw that consumer choice on private goods is independent of the SWF chosen, but is determined, as in 2.6, solely by prices and income. In equation 2.15, the $\partial w / \partial u_i$ terms do not cancel: *the choice of the optimal level of the public good depends on the relative weights each person is given in the SWF*. In addition, the choice of the optimal amount of defense for Mr. 1 depends on the preferences of Ms. 2! We cannot talk about private choice, as consumers of public goods, without immediately becoming concerned with our political choices, as citizens.

Expression 2.15 has another implication, no less important. Whereas equation 2.14 shows that the ratio of marginal utilities must equal the price ratio for a consumption optimum, the numerator in equation 2.15 is the *sum* of the marginal utilities for all citizens in the jurisdiction enjoying the public good. Put another way, the optimal quantity of the public good is determined by the marginal evaluations of all consumers, because all consumers must, definitionally, enjoy (or detest) the same amount of D. For private goods, auctioneer Goldilocks could announce a price and let individuals vary the amount they produced or consumed, until an equilibrium was reached and the auction ended. How could such an auction be conducted if the *quantity* was fixed, as it must be for a pure public good?

Vary price, of course. Wicksell (1958) and Lindahl (1939) suggest that the optimum for public goods will be reached when each person pays exactly his marginal value for the fixed quantity of the public good, and the total revenues exactly cover the cost of producing that quantity. For example, Goldilocks announces a certain level, D', of national defense, and Mr. 1 and Ms. 2 respond with their willingness to pay. If the sum of the two bids exceeds the cost of D', Goldilocks says, "This national defense is too small," and announces $D' + 1$. This process continues until the sum of bids match the costs at "just right": D^*. In standard economic terms, this process equates social marginal benefits and marginal costs by *vertically* summing the demand curves of each individual. This Lindahl tax price system is illustrated in figure 2: each of the tax shares, t_1 and t_2, is precisely the consumer's marginal evaluation of the optimal quantity D^*, and $t_1 + t_2 = t$, the total cost of the program.

It would appear that this procedure establishes, at least in principle, the possibility of a disaggregated, individualistic solution to the public goods problem. Once an SWF is established by some means, we are able to follow a *tâtonnement* process that yields a determinate, Pareto-optimal solution. This appearance is false, however, for three separate reasons: (1) No SWF possessing even minimally desirable characteristics exists, in general, (2) there are incentives to misrepresent preferences, and (3) it is impossible to isolate public goods in general equilibrium models. We discuss each of these briefly below.

Problem 1: Impossibility Theorems

The original work in this area was done by Arrow (1963), who demonstrated that no Bergson-Samuelson SWFs exist. More precisely, Arrow showed that any social welfare function that obeyed certain apparently innocuous conditions must be dictatorial. That is, the decisive set for all decisions has to be one, and it is always the same one: the dictator. Relaxing the conditions somewhat has allowed dictatorship to be expanded to oligarchy, but no SWF can, in any realistic sense, be called democratic. Arrow's results have been extended using alternative proof techniques (Blau 1972; Vickrey 1960), in slightly different institutional settings (Kemp and Ng 1976; Parks 1976; Schwartz 1981), and with weaker or alternative assumed properties of the desired SWF (Sen 1970; Brown 1975; Roberts 1980).[7] The basic result has only been reinforced by the later work, and it largely negates Bergson and Samuelson's early enthusiasm: no SWF exists that is not imposed (dic-

---

7. For an excellent discussion of the evolution of the social choice literature, see Mueller (1989).

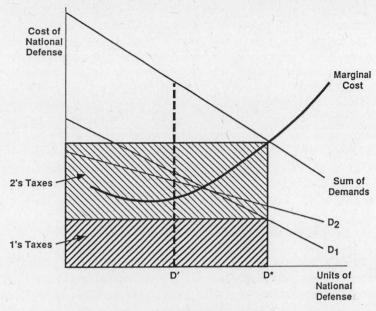

Fig. 2. *Tâtonnement* **with public goods: Lindahl tax shares**

tatorial), so no democratic mechanism can truly solve the problem of representing and satisfying citizen desires for public goods.

Problem 2: Demand Revelation and Misrepresentation

Consider the Wicksell-Lindahl solution to the public goods problem: fix quantity and vary price according to the taxpayers' own, self-reported marginal
evaluations. Rather than an honest evaluation, however, the more likely result
is misrepresentation. The direction of the bias in the revealed demand for
public goods will be determined primarily by the institutional link between the
taxpayers' announced demand and their tax share. If individual i wants more
of the public good, and taxes are equally shared, he should overrepresent his
demand, since he pays only a small share of the incremental cost. If, instead,
we adopt a Lindahl scheme where announced demands are *exactly* one's tax
share, citizen i should declare a zero evaluation, or at least considerably
understate his preference, since he can free ride on whatever level of the
public good is financed by the tax payments of others. Again, we confront the
fundamental difference in theorizing about public goods: it is easy to imagine
that citizen i is better off with zero taxes and a level of public good well below
his ideal, than at his ideal and paying his honestly revealed Lindahl tax share.

Numerous authors have sought to solve the demand revelation problem, including Clarke (1971), Groves (1973), Tideman and Tullock (1976), Strauss and Hughes (1976), and Groves and Ledyard (1977). But once more, the early optimism about a promising approach has been cruelly dashed by the further progress of theory. Though there do exist *in principle* means of arriving at Lindahl equilibria (Slutsky 1977a, 1977b, 1979; Denzau and Mackay 1979), other researchers (Roberts 1977; Rubenfeld 1977; and Shapiro 1973) have demonstrated versions of impossibility results ending any cause for optimism in this direction. There does not exist an incentive-compatible (i.e., honest demand revelation inducing) tax mechanism for public goods. Gibbard (1973) and Satterthwaite (1975) show that, in fact, there is no scheme relying on voting that can solve the problem without creating opportunities for manipulation.

Problem 3: "Induced" Public Sector Preferences

An obvious, and commonly used, strategy is to ignore the public goods problem in a general equilibrium context and treat public goods as a separate subsector of the consumer choice problem. This approach appears to be sensible when the public decision to be made is truly separable from economic concerns (e.g., moral decisions on abortion, freedom of speech or religion, etc.), and it is widely used in the literature on spatial theory. Preferences are represented by positions in policy space, with departures from these "ideal points" implying lower utility.

The difficulty is that few public issues are truly separate from economic, private good decisions. The reason is that even if preferences are separable (the ideal level of public goods does not depend on the level of private goods consumed), the "induced" preferences may not be. For example, it makes no sense to speak of an ideal level of public good separate from the mechanism for financing it. The tax cost of the public good determines the quantity of private goods foregone, so that induced preferences may depend strongly on tax share. As noted in the discussion of incentive compatibility above, free-riding and enjoying a diminished level of the public good may be preferable to one's ideal level and a full tax share. We must be very careful to define what ideal even means in this induced preference context.

The first attempt to imbed public sector preferences in a model with both public and private goods, given a particular tax system, was by Barr and Davis (1968), who claimed to have solved the problem of induced public sector preferences. The resulting empirical implications for the "median voter" have been widely recognized (Borcherding and Deacon 1972; Bergstrom and Goodman 1973; a more detailed discussion is given in chap. 3) and accepted. But there are difficulties with accepting such results unreflectively. The response in later work (including Denzau and Parks 1975, 1977, 1979, 1983; Slutsky 1977b) has demonstrated that only under certain strict conditions does the concept of induced preferences for public goods make useful sense for theory. The most general statement, summarizing the inherited properties for public sector preferences derived by Slutsky (1977b) and Denzau and Parks (1977, 1979) and proving necessary and sufficient conditions for single-peaked preferences, is Coughlin and Hinich (1984). Single-peakedness has long (since Black 1958) been recognized as a sufficient condition for the existence of equilibrium, *provided the policy space is unidimensional*. Unless preferences possess this property, however, it may be impossible to say anything about general equilibrium in a spatial model. This, in itself, is neither good nor bad; rather, it is a result. It underscores once again the differences between consumer and citizen choice. Determinate equilibria exist, and are Pareto optimal, in consumer theory, but the same is simply not true for decision theories that reflect aggregations of individual choices. Individually complete, monotonic, and transitive preferences do not, in general, lead to determinate, or even rational (i.e., Pareto optimal), social choices.[8]

Slutsky, and Denzau and Parks, demonstrate that if personal preferences follow some standard microeconomic assumptions (reflexivity, connectedness, transitivity, regularity, weak convexity, and convexity), these attributes are inherited by the associated public sector preferences. Other commonly assumed attributes, including monotonicity, homotheticity, and circular or ellipsoidal individual public sector indifference curves are not derivable from "economic preferences." Coughlin and Hinich demonstrate that if preferences are economic, a necessary and sufficient condition for single-peaked public sector preferences is that the mapping from the space of possible public policy alternatives into fully described policy states is either (1) constant or (2) linear, over the relevant range. If the policy space is unidimensional, the necessary and sufficient condition is that the mapping is either constant or strictly monotonic.

Though the Slutsky-Denzau-Parks and Coughlin-Hinich results are not optimistic about the usefulness of traditional representations of citizen preferences, they are of crucial importance to the study of social choice. The existence of a necessary and sufficient condition means that equilibrium may exist in a spatial representation of citizen's public sector preferences. The result is essentially a negative one, because we now know where *not* to look. In general, one of two sets of conditions is required to undertake any general analysis of both consumer and citizen choice:

---

8. Becker (1983) would dispute the existence of non-Pareto public decisions, at least in equilibrium, based on a Coasian bargaining process. The existence of such cooperative collective solutions is problematic, as we shall discuss later.

1. Consumer and citizen preferences must be strongly separable, so that changes in prices don't change demand for public goods, and changes in taxes don't change demand for private goods. This means more than just that the issues must be considered on the agenda separately (though this is true). The issues must be *truly* separable, in voters' utility functions, so that their preference for one of the goods is independent of the level they expect to receive of all others.

2. *a.* Explicit account of the tax distribution and cost of public goods must be made, and must be part of citizen choices. There must be some linkage between taxes and prices of private goods.

   b. The mapping from policy choice to public policy outcome must be (almost) constant or linear.

Criteria for a Theory of Representation

In discussing the state of our knowledge of the representation of citizen choice, we must conclude that this work is not yet at the same level as that for consumer choice. Worse, the approach of adopting the model of private choice has reached several definitive dead ends. Any successful theory of representation must provide two things: (1) a plausible empirical description of actual choice, and (2) a useful theoretical characterization of choice, where useful is taken to mean capable of generating falsifiable predictions. To the extent that the research reviewed in this chapter has not produced a theory of citizen choice that is defensible on either of the above grounds, the results are negative. Yet these results also represent a significant achievement of unqualified progress in clarifying the issues in one of the most complicated and vexing problems in all of social science.

The positive results point primarily to a more integrated theory of citizen choice, since, in every case, seeking a partial equilibrium solution has produced a dead end. We saw that Bergson and Samuelson's approach foundered on the nonexistence of a social welfare function. But the results of Arrow and others in rejecting the SWF approach are not hard to understand: we cannot make political choices without accounting for the institutions by which political choices are made. The fact that no tax scheme engenders honest revelation of preference means only that no decentralized process that ignores negotiation and compromise can accurately represent actual political interaction. Similarly, the apparently limiting research of Slutsky, Denzau-Parks, and Coughlin-Hinich indicate that we cannot sustain a dichotomy between consumer and citizen choice. Instead, each citizen consumes and each consumer sees his choices circumscribed by political events and public policies.

Taken together, these results are at once daunting and encouraging. Daunted because we are denied a simple partial equilibrium representation, we are simultaneously encouraged by the fact that these results suggest a set of boundaries within which a more useful theory of political choice can be constructed. The next chapter reviews the classical spatial theory of voting behavior. Chapter 4 then presents the foundation of an alternative means of representing political choice by citizens, based on the concept of ideology.

CHAPTER 3

The (Amended) Classical Spatial Theory of Elections

Any discussion of classical spatial theory applied to politics must begin with Downs (1957). In the next chapter, we will focus on Downs's theory of ideology; for now we examine his theory of voting. Because many of Downs's fundamental insights have been ignored or only partially developed, his model of voting is presented at length. But before we begin, it is useful to make some distinctions and establish just what we mean by a *spatial* model of voting. After all, this book seeks both to establish ideology as a useful analytic concept and to advance a coherent and rigorous representation of that concept. The structure of the model we use is spatial, because only a spatial model can answer both of the fundamental questions a complete theory of political choice must answer.

Question 1: Why are citizens presented with the alternatives they are presented with, and not some others? For example, why are some important things "issues," and other, equally important, things not?

Question 2: Given the choices presented, (*a*) why do citizens vote or participate in politics at all, and (*b*) why do they make the choices they make?

The spatial model of ideology is uniquely suited to answer both questions simultaneously, and in a logically recursive fashion. The classical (Downsian) spatial model based on rational choice among issues is only capable of addressing parts of the two questions. The psycho-social model is a very powerful tool for explaining the individual actions in question 2, but has no applicability to the first question at all.

Later chapters will outline a theory of the origin of the alternatives among which citizens can choose. Our present goal is to consider the second question, the role of individual choice. As noted above, the question must be decomposed into two parts: (1) why do citizens vote at all? (2) Once in the polling place, how do citizens decide among candidates and parties? The "why do people vote" question is one of the most vexing and important questions facing social scientists, and has been the subject of an enormous quantity of scholarship. For the most part, this corpus of work is beyond the scope of our inquiry, but it is important to briefly review what conclusions have been reached, however tentatively.

With only a few exceptions, the literature on voting has conflated the "why vote?" and "for whom?" inquiries.[1] The two major approaches have been (1) the rational choice perspective, and (2) the psychological determinants of turnout. Downs's model influenced both schools, but had its greatest impact (not surprisingly, given Downs's economic viewpoint) on the rational theory of voting. Downs, himself, does not clearly distinguish the "why" and "for whom" questions, as we shall see.

In Downs's view, candidates (or parties) compete with one another in seeking reelection. The relation between voter and candidates is complex and recursive:

> How a voter casts his ballot depends upon what actions the government takes and what actions the opposition says it would take were it in office. . . . The actions a government takes depend upon how the government thinks voters will cast their ballots. These statements delineate a relationship of mutual interdependence. . . . (Downs 1957, 72)

Actually, Downs's view is that voters evaluate both incumbents and challengers based not just on what they have done, but also on what voters anticipate they will do.[2] Actions in the past are one guide, but promises made during the campaign about future actions also influence expectations. The model Downs propounds appears, on its face, to be easily formalizable, a function of the difference between the utilities associated with the two candidates, the costs of participating, and the likelihood that one vote will influence the outcome. We choose to present a more familiar form of the rational model, from Riker and Ordeshook (1968). An individual will decide to vote if and only if:

$$P*NCD + D \geq C \tag{3.1}$$

where, for each voter:

---

1. Some exceptions are Burnham (1965); Kelley, Ayres, and Bowen (1967); and Cox and Munger (1989).

2. The argument has repeatedly been made that voters' best guide to what a candidate will do is what he has done. Beginning with Fiorina's (1981) seminal work, an extensive literature on "retrospective" voting has grown up. In a series of papers, McKelvey and Ordeshook (1985, 1986, 1987) have sought to establish the amount and types of information voters require to make "good" choices.

P = the probability that this individual's vote will affect the outcome of the majority rule election.

NCD = perceived net benefits of one candidate over another in the eyes of the individual (net candidate differential in Downs's parlance).

D = the individual's sense of civic duty. This is the utility derived from voting, regardless of the outcome.

C = costs associated (at the margin) with the act of voting, including opportunity cost of time spent, chance of inclement weather, and so on.

The logic of this model is the simplest kind of cost-benefit analysis: if the (expected) benefits exceed the costs, the citizen becomes a voter for the candidate he most prefers. Otherwise, he abstains. But notice how complicated the model truly is. The decision of whether to vote is made simultaneously with the choice of for whom. Assume for the moment the duty term is negligible ($D \approx 0$); then the citizen votes if and only if $P*NCD > C$. Assuming $C > 0$ (i.e., that voting entails some costs), we know at a minimum $P*NCD \geqslant 0$ is a necessary condition for voting.

An alternative way to put this point is that if either P or NCD is zero, the simple Downsian model predicts abstention. The P term is the individual's belief (in probability terms) that his vote will transform a loss into a tie, or a tie into victory, for his preferred candidate. If an individual knows how all the others will vote, P is either 1 or 0; the effect of the vote is certain, and the only question is whether or not it affects the outcome. Such a perfect information outcome is highly unrealistic, even in small electorates, for (a) the information on how others will vote is hard to come by, and (b) even if everyone tells our voter how they will vote, he still has to decide if they are telling the truth. Finally, even if such informational demands can be met, they can be met for only one voter! That is, only one voter can go last, and all the others must vote while there is still, effectively, some uncertainty.

There is yet another problem, as a simple example shows. The number of cases where $P = 1$, assuming perfect information, is vanishingly small. Suppose that the individual conceives of the actual electorate (that is, those who actually vote, rather than those who are eligible) as a random sample from the eligible electorate. Suppose, further, that the polls show that the election is a dead heat between candidates Theta and Psi. The probability of an actual tie in any realization of the random variable "margin" (V_θ, or vote for Theta, minus V_ψ, or vote for Psi) then has an error determined by the sample size. Let N be the individual's guess as to the number of people who will vote, not counting himself. Then a rational model of the personal probability is that $P = C(N, N/2)2^{-N}$, where $C(.)$ is the "combinations" operator. $C(N, N/2)$ is the number of possible outcomes that are ties, or where $V_\theta = V_\psi$

$= N/2$. For example, if $N = 10$, there are $(10!)/[(5!)(5!)] = 252$ possible tie outcomes. To get the probability, we divide by the total number of $2^{10} = 1024$ outcomes: $P = 252/1024 = .246$. That is, in an electorate of ten, there is approximately one chance in four that a rational voter will believe her vote will influence the outcome, assuming the polls predict a dead heat *ex ante*, and that each of the voters is in fact equally likely to vote for either candidate. As N grows, P falls rapidly: $N = 109$ implies $P = .05 \times 10^{-20}$; $N = 1000$ (still a small electorate, after all!) implies $P = .019 \times 10^{-251}$. This number, which has 251 zeroes between the decimal and the "19," has another name. Any rational person would call it "zero" for the purposes of predicting the chance of influencing the election.

The probability gets even smaller even faster if the election is not perceived as "too close to call" *ex ante*. The candidate who has the lead is almost surely going to get a majority if (1) most people have decided how to vote by the time of the poll, and (2) the poll itself is statistically accurate. If either candidate is ahead in the polls, the parameter ρ in the binomial distribution is $\rho \neq .5$, which implies that the probability of influencing the outcome is trivial. As we showed above, when $\rho = .5$ (the case where the binomial takes its maximal value), the probability is still below the threshold where it has implications for action, or even realistic measurement. So, the conclusion goes, why would anyone vote? The "rational" voter should not vote.

Several scholars (Ledyard 1984; Palfrey and Rosenthal 1985) have noted that this conclusion cannot be quite right: P is not given exogenously but is determined precisely by what each voter believes others will do, and by how others view him.[3] To see this, note that if $P = 0$ no one votes, so that one vote determines the election. But then P "really" isn't zero, at least *ex post*; in fact, it is one! Ledyard demonstrated that this game among voters has a mixed-strategy equilibrium, where turnout exceeds zero. This was an important achievement, because turnout was rationalized, and participation was shown to be consistent with purposive, self-interested behavior. Palfrey and Rosenthal showed, however, that as the size of the electorate rises, equilibrium turnout shrinks, even in Ledyard's game. In the limit, as the potential electorate goes to infinity, the rational turnout goes toward zero. The only conclusion we can draw is that, while interpreting the P term is difficult because of its endogenous and strategic determination, at the margin, it is likely to play the role Riker and Ordeshook envision for it: larger P's imply larger turnout.[4]

Returning to the $P*NCD$ product in the Riker-Ordeshook model, we now

---

3. It might be argued that this conclusion came much earlier, from Barzel and Silberberg (1973) and Ferejohn and Fiorina (1974).

4. Cox and Munger (1989) offer several more complex reasons for the empirical regularity that turnout and electoral closeness may be positively correlated.

consider the "net candidate differential," term *NCD*. Using Downs's notation, we can define *NCD* as follows:

$$NCD = E(U_\theta) - E(U_\psi) \tag{3.2}$$

where *U* is the voter's utility function, Theta and Psi are parties/candidates, and *E* is the expectations operator. Notice that if $E(U_\theta) = E(U_\psi)$, $NCD = 0$, and the citizen has no reason to vote. It is worth repeating this: The voter has *no reason* to vote, even if he is certain he is the only voter!

To summarize, we have two complementary necessary conditions (assuming *D* is negligible) for voting: $P > 0$ and $NCD > 0$. Even if Satan runs against the archangel Gabriel, in a very large electorate (each member of which might vote) voting is useless. And if the candidates are clones (Gabe against Gabe, or Beelzebub against Beelzebub), voting is without purpose, even if the citizen is the only voter.

Problems with the Simple Downs-Riker-Ordeshook Model

There are several important problems with the rational model, as presented in the previous section. Even allowing for the endogeneity of *P*, the predicted equilibrium level of turnout is less than 5 percent. This suggests that the level of turnout we actually observe, on the order of 10–60 percent of eligible voters, must be explained by pure consumption, either out of a sense of duty or the avoidance of guilt.[5] A difficulty with this reformulation is that it implies citizens, *all* citizens, vote if and only if $D \geq C$, since *P* is vanishingly small. This leaves unexplained the empirical regularity that turnout is quite closely correlated with actual (and, presumably, expected) closeness of the election, which, of course, determines the probability of being the pivotal vote.

One answer might be that *D* or *C* are, themselves, functions of expected closeness. Another is that voters systematically overestimate the level of *P* (Kahneman and Tversky 1973, 1979; Lichtenstein and Slovic 1971), but are reasonably well informed about marginal or incremental changes. Yet a third possibility is that offered by Cox and Munger (1989): political elites and owners of resources allocate those resources based on their expected return, which varies with the expected closeness of the race.

---

5. The D term assumes a social, interactive aspect of the citizen's utility function. In its simplest form, the D term is a reaction to the assessments of others: we feel better if others approve of our actions, and worse if they scorn us. Participation in a group activity, such as voting, causes a social reaction, which is why the pure rational choice theory of turnout has had such a difficult time explaining behavior.

All three answers are surely candidates for further consideration, but we must step back for a moment and consider the fundamental issue. The questions of how citizens decide whether to vote, and for whom, rest on a specification of what citizens want. A possible representation of citizen goals is the utility function used in public finance economics. We saw in chapter 2, however, that unreflectively applying the utility function representation in inducing public sector preferences leads to problems. A more useful representation is the spatial model of politics hinted at in Downs (1957) and Black (1958), and formalized in Davis and Hinich (1966, 1967), Plott (1967), and Davis, Hinich, and Ordeshook (1970). It is from this model that the "median voter theorem" (MVT, already discussed in chap. 1) is derived, and it is a variant of the spatial model that we will use throughout the remainder of this book. The spatial model seeks to represent citizen preferences in terms of distance. The units in which this distance is measured may be actual units of public goods and services, or Lancasterian units of the characteristics of the resulting bundle of public policies.[6] The reason that spatial theorists can be vague about the issues or goods over which these preferences are defined is that the preferences are taken as primitive, not induced, representations of voter utility functions.[7]

Downs's Model of Voters

The logic underpinning the model is that citizens choose to vote, if at all, for the candidate (party) "closest" to them. If there is more than one public good (i.e., both military protection and education), or more than one dimension (i.e., safety and health), the concept of closeness is more complicated because each dimension may have a different weight in voters' evaluation of its utility. This is simply to say that the citizen may value an improvement in health more than an equivalent improvement in safety. Once this set of weights is established, however, the spatial model is capable of representing citizens' preferences and allowing us to make predictions about the proportion of the total vote a candidate or set of policy choices commands.

The classical spatial model operates on several assumptions whose nature it is important to clarify at the outset. For now, we will assume that all citizens vote, though we will drop this assumption as soon as possible. First we present Downs's functional version of the complete model, and then we will turn to the assumptions underlying the Davis-Hinich version that gives specific (weighted Euclidean distance) forms to the functions.

Downs (1957, chap. 3) advances a general model of government and

---

6. The reference is to Lancaster's (1966) "new approach to consumer theory."

7. We are grateful to Norman Schofield for a conversation clarifying our understanding of this point.

voter behavior in the form of five abstract structural equations. In simplified notation, we define the following:

V = actual votes for incumbent party
$\hat{V}$ = votes expected by incumbent party
a = actions of incumbent party
U = voters' evaluation (utility) deriving from government action
s = strategy or platform of challenging party
f_i = an abstract functional relationship

Given these definitions, we can specify the assumptions of the model in the form of structural equations.

$$a = f_1(\hat{V}, s) \tag{3.3}$$

$$\hat{V} = f_2(U, s) \tag{3.4}$$

$$V = f_3(U, s) \tag{3.5}$$

$$U = f_4(a) \tag{3.6}$$

$$s = f_5(U, a) \tag{3.7}$$

In words, these equations can be summarized as follows:

(3.3) What the government (incumbent party) does while in office is a function of expected vote and the platform of the challengers. It is presumed that a is chosen to maximize $\hat{V}$.

(3.4) Expected vote for the government is a function of the utility citizens actually enjoy and the platform of the challengers, which citizens use to forecast what their utility would be if the government were changed.

(3.5) Actual vote received by the incumbent party is, similarly, a function of U and s. This means that the incumbents are correct in their identification of the arguments of $\hat{V}$, but it need not be the case that $f_2(.) = f_3(.)$. Actual and expected vote may differ; Downs does not make clear if this difference is just a random error or some structural bias in forecasting.

(3.6) The utility of the voter is a function of the actions of the government. The only thing that the voter cares about is what the government actually does, so that voters are not "ideological," but are purely, narrowly, self-interested.

(3.7) Finally, just as the government's action is determined by expected vote and the challenger's strategy (3.3), the challenger's strategy is determined by expected vote and the government's strategy.

Downs blithely notes that "This set of five equations has five unknowns: expected votes, actual votes, opposition strategies, government actions, and individual utility incomes" (Downs 1957, 73). He identifies the "circularity of our analytical structure: votes depend upon actions, and actions depend upon votes" (73). The unmistakable implication is that an equilibrium, or expected, stable, and predictable result, is associated with this system of equations. To the extent that such a result actually exists, it is the "median voter" theorem of classical spatial theory.

The assumptions of classical spatial theory are four. First, voters possess complete and transitive preferences over the set of policies. Second, voters use certain indices to measure policy, both for expressing their own preferences and for evaluating candidates' positions. Third, all voters use the same index or set of indices for evaluation, and only these indices. Finally, voters evaluate candidates based on a *loss function*, related to the spatial distance between the candidate's proposed platform and the voter's ideal point.

To fix notation and establish the important concepts, we can assume the following:

M = voters (indexed i = 1 to M)
L = candidates (indexed p = 1 to L)
n = policy dimensions in the policy space Ω (indexed j = 1 to n)
U_i = the ith voter's utility function
$\mathbf{x}_i$ = the n × 1 column vector of dimensional ideals in Ω for the ith voter
(so $\mathbf{x}_i$ is his "ideal point")
$\boldsymbol{\omega}_p$ = the n × 1 vector of policies in candidate p's platform in Ω, with a
point denoted by the ordered n-tuple ($\omega_1, \omega_2, \ldots, \omega_\xi, \ldots, \omega_\nu$)

For simplicity of exposition, let us assume $M = 3$ (Messrs I, II, and III), and that $L = 2$ (Theta and Psi). Further, let $n = 1$, so that the vector definitions above are all scalar for the sake of example. We then have the simple classical single-dimensional model depicted in figure 3, with a specific kind of assumption made for the form of U_i for I, II, and III. That form is the quadratic function, adapted for use as a representation of utility. The one-dimensional form for the quadratic is:

$$U_i = C_i - a_i(\boldsymbol{\omega}_p' - x_i)^2 \tag{3.8}$$

where C_i and a_i are arbitrary constants, $-\infty < \{C_i, a_i\} < \infty$. Figure 3 is an

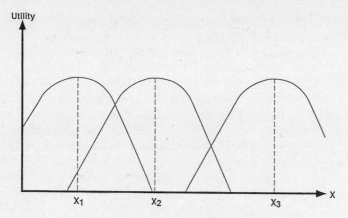

Fig. 3. Classical median voter model

example of how the utility functions of the three voters I, II, and III might look.

In general, it need not be true that C_i or the a_i be identical across voters, but we assume it for the sake of our example. The single-dimensional policy space is spending on the only known public good, education. Assume that tax shares are fixed at one-third for all voters, and that there is a requirement for a balanced budget.

Under these circumstances, we can predict the outcome of any electoral contest between Theta and Psi, so long as they choose platforms in the available policy space, and so long as voters have quadratic utilities. A moment's reflection suggests why this model is associated with "the Median Voter," or voter II in our example. A median is defined as an ideal point that has *both* of the following characteristics: (*a*) $N/2$ of the ideal points are less than or equal to it, and (*b*) $N/2$ ideal points are greater than or equal to it. The ideal point x_{II} has 2 ideal points less than or equal to it (x_I and x_{II}), and 2 ideal points greater than or equal to it (x_{II} and x_{III}). Since $N/2 = 3/2 = 1.5$, and $1.5 < 2$, x_{II} is a median point. Since it shares this characteristic with no other points, in this example x_{II} is a *unique* median.

As is clear from figure 3, all of the utility functions are depicted as having the same shape, but with different ideal points. To make the example concrete, let us assume the following three utility functions:

$$\text{I. } U_I = 100 - .5 (20 - \omega_p)^2 \tag{3.9}$$

$$\text{II. } U_{II} = 100 - .5 (30 - \omega_p)^2 \tag{3.10}$$

$$\text{III. } U_{III} = 100 - .5 (50 - \omega_p)^2 \tag{3.11}$$

These utility functions are all examples of quadratic loss functions, and have the following characteristics:[8]

1. Increasing Marginal Loss, or Disutility. The three ideal points are $x_I = 20$, $x_{II} = 30$, and $x_{III} = 50$. At these points, and only there, is utility maximized (in our example, maximum utility is 100, but this constant is arbitrary). Since only a single level of policy can be chosen, at most one voter can have $U_i = 100$. The other two evaluate proposed positions based on how far they diverge from their ideals, and this evaluation is nonlinear. The further away, the worse off the voter is, and disutility increases as the square of distance.[9]

2. Symmetry. For each voter, departures from his ideal are associated with equivalent utility losses, regardless of whether they represent moves to the left or right. In figure 3, we see for voter i that the two proposals ω_p' and ω_p'' yield identical levels of utility, because they are equidistant from x_i. Voter i's preferences are symmetric about his ideal point x_i if and only if his utility function is symmetric. In symbols:

$$U_i(\omega_p') = U_i(\omega_p'') \text{ iff } |\omega_p' - x_i| = |\omega_p'' - x_i| \qquad (3.12)$$

where "iff" means "if and only if" and $|\omega_p - x_i|$ is the simple Euclidean distance between two points. Along one dimension, this distance is the absolute value of the difference between the two points.

3. Single-peakedness. The final important characteristic of quadratic utilities is their simplicity for theorizing about social choice. Quadratic utilities have a single, central maximum. Departures from this maximum imply lower utility, so that if one starts at an ideal point and moves away in either direction, utility falls monotonically. This characteristic rules out several plausible types of preferences, and is therefore a substantive restriction on the set of preferences our theory can

---

8. The assumption of quadratic utilities is a technical convenience, but it is also restrictive. There are many plausible patterns of preference other than the quadratic. Nonetheless, for all its restrictiveness, the quadratic is very useful for theoretical work linked with the statistical concept of variance. That is our reason for choosing it here.

9. This is easily demonstrated using calculus: Assume for simplicity $x_p < x_i^*$. Then:

$U = C - b (x_p - x_i^*)^2$

$dU/dx_p = -2b(x_p - x_i^*) \leq 0$

$d^2U/dx_p^2 = 2b > 0$

Thus utility decreases at an increasing rate as x_p and x_i^* diverge, though $dU/dx_p = 0$ at the utility-maximizing $x_p = x_i^*$.

TABLE 2.   Two Examples of Voter Choice over Candidates θ and ϕ

Voter Utility Functions:

Voter	Utility Function
I	$100 - .5(20 - \omega_p)^2$
II	$100 - .5(30 - \omega_p)^2$
III	$100 - .5(50 - \omega_p)^2$

Panel A: $\omega_\theta = 20$, $\omega_\psi = 50$

Voter	Ideal Point	Utility if Theta Wins	Utility if Psi Wins	Votes For
I	20	100	-350	Theta
II	30	50	-100	Theta
III	50	-350	100	Psi

Winner: Theta (2/3)

Panel B: $\omega_\theta = 30$, $\omega_\psi = 33$

Voter	Ideal Point	Utility if Theta Wins	Utility if Psi Wins	Votes For
I	20	50	15.5	Theta
II	30	100	95.5	Theta
III	50	-100	-46.5	Psi

Winner: Theta (2/3)

represent, at least in the single-dimensional case. As we shall see, in the multidimensional case the assumption is less restrictive.

It is important to emphasize that the results we present do not depend on the assumption of quadratic utilities for their validity. In fact, in only a few cases will the results even require a symmetric utility function. Usually, we will need no more than differentiability (which is somewhat stronger than continuity) as a characteristic for utility functions.[10]

We are now in a position to consider two examples of voter choice, given the ideal points and utility functions listed for I, II, and III. Table 2 lists two

---

10. For a more complete, and technically rigorous, discussion of the necessary conditions for representation of citizen preferences, see Schofield (1985*b*).

sets of candidate position ω_θ and ω_ψ, and uses the ·configuration of voter preferences outlined earlier. In panel A, $\omega_\theta = 20$ and $\omega_\psi = 50$. Clearly, I votes for Theta and III for Psi, since the two candidates have pledged these voters' ideal points and provided a utility of 100, compared to the opponent's pledge of -350. The interesting question is how II will vote. If we compare the utility of $\omega_\theta = 50$ and $\omega_\psi = -100$, we see II votes for Theta. Rejecting Psi seems obvious, because 20 (ω_θ) is closer to 30 (x_{II}) than 50 (ω_ψ) is. This conclusion is general for voters with symmetric preferences: you vote for whomever is closer (closest, if more than 2 candidates).

Panel B considers the outcome when $\omega_\theta = 30$ (the median preference) and $\omega_\psi = 33$ (the mean preference). This example is more interesting, because the decision is a closer one (the candidates are not very different) and we are comparing two important measures of the central tendency of citizen desires, the mean and the median.[11] Once again, the decision for I and III is easy because any separation of the candidates on education spending matters more the further away from the ideal point the candidates are. A difference of just 3 units (33–30) is a utility difference of 35.5 for I (in favor of Theta) and 56.5 for III (in favor of Psi). The same difference for II implies a utility difference of only 4.5. Still, he votes for Theta, and Theta again wins the election.

The median position, $x = 30$ deserves our attention, because it possesses two extremely important characteristics. First, it is a "Condorcet Winner": no other platform can command a majority against it, and the median commands a majority against all other alternatives, in a pairwise election. Second, the median position is insensitive to a variety of preference shifts by the other voters. If voter III wanted more spending than the median (30), he could advocate a centrally planned system and then claim $x_{III} = 5,000$, not 50. If we relied on a centrally planned system that sought to serve the mean preference, this strategic move by III would raise the mean from 33 to 1683.33. But the median does not suffer from this susceptibility to individual strategizing: the median is 30 whether $x_{III} = 50$, $5,000$, or 5 billion.[12] Voter III *could* affect the median, of course, by claiming $x_{III} = 20$, or 10, or any amount less than 30. But this would hurt III, not help him. In some measure, this example provides an insight into why voting is such a pervasive phenomenon as a

---

11. We have noted before that the mean and median compete as conceptions of the "general will" that democratic means are supposed to discover. Rousseau was vague in his description of how the general will might be determined, and in fact admitted in *The Social Contract* (1762) that "In the strict sense of the term, a true democracy has never existed, and never will exist" (book 3, chap. 4).

12. For recent extensions and refinement of the "median" concept, see Koford (1982, 1993) and the review in Mueller (1989). In particular, Koford contrasts the median with "competitive equilibrium," a concept which *is* sensitive to the placement of the ideal points away from the median.

choice mechanism: it solves social choice problems by stripping away opportunities to register the intensity of preferences. With these opportunities come the chance for manipulation. Voting's central focus on median preference appears to reduce (though it certainly does not eliminate) the incentive and opportunity for strategic manipulation.[13]

We are now in a position to state the central result of the simple theory of deterministic voting, the Median Voter Theorem (MVT) and an important corollary:

Median Voter Theorem:
Suppose ω_{med} is a median position on the single political dimension for the society, preferences are single-peaked, and each citizen uses a monotonic distance voting rule regardless of how far or near the alternatives are located from his ideal. Then the number of votes for ω_{med} is greater than or equal to the votes received by any other platform ω_p. If the number of voters is odd, and no voters share ideal points, the median is unique.

Corollary:
Suppose that each voter's utility function is symmetric, and a unique median ω_{med} exists for the society. Then for any two platforms ω_1 and ω_2, $|\omega_1 - \omega_{med}| > |\omega_2 - \omega_{med}|$ if and only if ω_2 beats ω_1 in a majority rule election.

These two theorems are offered without proof (very similar statements are proved by Enelow and Hinich 1984a, 12–13), but the reader can appreciate the intuition behind them and the power they have for understanding elections. The MVT result tells us that if the assumptions hold, if one candidate adopts the median position and the other does not, the one at the median will either win, if ω_{med} is unique, or will tie. If both candidates are free to adopt any position on the ideological dimension, then there is no reason, under the condition of the MVT (for a candidate who wishes to win!), to adopt any position other than ω_{med}. This outcome is an equilibrium, or stable situation with no inherent tendencies to change, because once it is achieved, no other platform can beat it.

Suppose that the candidates cannot quickly move to the median. Assume that moving is costly and slow, but the candidates have time and the ability to move. Does the MVT or its corollary say anything about whether there is any tendency for them to move to ω_{med} if neither of them start at the median? The MVT corollary tells us that if (1) all voters chose among two candidates

---

13. The susceptibility of voting rules, and other decision rules, to manipulation was analyzed by Gibbard (1973) and Satterthwaite (1975).

strictly according to the distance from their ideal points, (2) candidates know the locations of ω_{med}, and (3) both candidates want to win a majority of votes cast, then the candidate closer to ω_{med} will win. Thus, if the candidates can reposition themselves in an incremental manner, they will move toward ω_{med}.

Together, these results appear to provide all the motivation and theoretical underpinning one would need to go out and test the theory in a variety of contexts. The prediction of this simple model is that winning candidates should be at or near the median of the distribution of voter ideal points, and that candidates should converge toward the median, as a consequence.

Problems with the Median Voter Theorem and Classical Spatial Theory

Spatial theorists have now moved beyond the simple MVT outlined in the previous section. A number of improvements and corrections have been offered, for the most part in a piecemeal fashion, with little regard for integrating the various components. In this section we offer a brief overview of these improvements. Later, in chapter 8, the full model, as amended, will be outlined. Unfortunately, but not surprisingly, with these improvements come a marked increase in the mathematical complexity of the exposition. Part of the beauty of the MVT is its simplicity and elegance, but this simplicity is a failing as well, as the MVT abstracts from numerous details important to the study of real-world politics.

The extensions we discuss are (1) Abstention, or Endogenous Turnout; and (2) Multiple Dimensions with Nonseparable Preferences. We examine each of these lacunae in classical modeling in turn.

Endogenous Turnout: Allowing for Abstention

The model presented thus far has assumed 100 percent turnout, a useful initial abstraction, but a very limiting assumption if we desire to use the model to predict and understand real-world events. The spatial model is quite capable of handling abstention (Hinich and Ordeshook 1970; Hinich, Ledyard, and Ordeshook 1972; Enelow and Hinich 1984a), though, as we shall see, making turnout endogenous is accomplished only at a considerable price in complexity.

The basic concepts of abstention can be incorporated quite easily into our intuition about voting. There are (at least) two reasons why voters might choose not to vote within the simple framework we have advanced thus far: (1) Indifference (as described by Downs (1957) and Riker and Ordeshook(1968)), and (2) Alienation (Hinich and Ordeshook (1968) and Ordeshook (1967)). Indifference would imply that the voter is equally satisfied with all alternatives, or (more weakly) has no preference for either candidate strong enough to justify (costly) voting. Indifference would imply abstention whether the voter is disgusted or wildly enthusiastic about the choices offered him. Alienation has to do with how "relevant" or, in our terms, close, the candidates are. Even if one of the candidates is closer than the other, the voter has little sense of political efficacy because neither candidate appears to believe that voter's, or that segment of the voting population's, opinion is worth paying any attention to.

It is easy to portray indifference and alienation graphically. In figure 4, panel A depicts a single voter's ideal point, and two sets of candidate positions ω_θ and ω_ψ. Notice that the voter is indifferent between ω_θ' and ω_ψ', as well as between the much closer ω_θ'' and ω_ψ''. (further, we have now set $n = 2$, so that the example is no longer one-dimensional). Of course, if the candidate positions were ω_θ' and ω_ψ'', the voter would choose the candidate Psi. But paired as the platforms are, he finds himself indifferent in each case, though at two very different levels of utility.

Panel B gives the analogous diagram for alienation. Imagine that here $|\omega_\theta' - \omega_\psi'| = |\omega_\theta'' - \omega_\psi''|$ (the absolute differences between the two platforms are the same in terms of simple Euclidean distance). That is, the voter has a strict preference, by the same relative amount, for both ω_θ' over ω_ψ' and ω_θ'' over ω_ψ''. But if the race is between ω_θ' and ω_ψ', both alternatives are so far away the voter sees no point in participating. More generally, abstention from alienation assumes that beyond some distance (defined here as δ), the voter loses interest in the election, or perceives himself as lacking efficacy because he is so far from the political debate he hears and sees in the media and in campaign rhetoric. More formally, define $[\mathbf{q} - \mathbf{z}]^2$ as the Euclidean distance between points $\mathbf{q}$ and $\mathbf{z}$. Then the voter is alienated (and therefore does not vote at all) if no candidate p has a platform in the set of points in Ω such that $[\omega_p - \mathbf{x}_i]^2 \geq \delta$.

Enelow and Hinich (1984a) present an integrated two-dimensional example worth reproducing here. In figure 5 we see the two policy dimensions ω_j and ω_k, as well as two candidate positions $\omega_\theta = (\omega_{j\theta}, \omega_{k\theta})$ and $\omega_\psi = (\omega_{j\psi}, \omega_{k\psi})$. Rather than reproducing a voter or set of citizen ideal points and predicting whether they will vote or abstain, because of either indifference or alienation, Enelow and Hinich use simple set theoretic representation. They depict regions where citizens (if any exist with those preferences) vote or abstain. In our terms, any citizen more than δ away from both candidates abstains out of alienation, where δ is the radius of the two circles. If the candidates are close enough so that the two circles intersect, there is also a group of citizens who abstain out of indifference. This group need not be depicted as a narrow line, but (as we present it here) can be a region with nontrivial area, provided an "almost" indifferent citizen does not vote, perhaps because the small (though

Panel A: Indifference

$$|x_i - \omega_\theta'| = |x_i - \omega_\psi'|$$
$$|x_i - \omega_\theta''| = |x_i - \omega_\psi''|$$

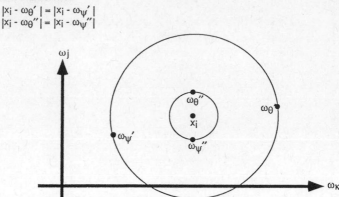

Panel B: Alienation

$$|x_i - \omega_\theta'| - |x_i - \omega_\psi'| = |x_i - \omega_\theta''| - |x_i - \omega_\psi''|$$

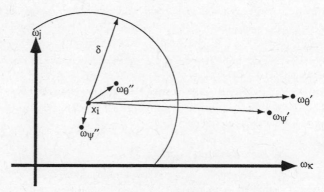

Fig. 4. Indifference and alienation as explanations for abstention

nonzero) difference between the candidates does not offset his costs of voting.[14]

Each of the two causes, indifference and alienation, is sufficient for abstention. To obtain a better logical grasp of voting and nonvoting, we can restate the information contained in figure 5 in set-theoretic terms. This is useful, both because it clarifies the logic of voting in the spatial model and because it introduces concepts we will need later on. Let {.} denote a set, or

---

14. We thank David Scocca for clarifying the diagram, and this discussion, considerably. In particular, Scocca made precise the curvature of the region of indifference, whereas the earlier Enelow and Hinich diagram made the borders of the region linear.

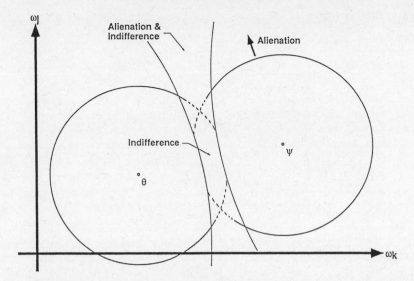

Fig. 5. Integrated indifference-alienation example for voting decisions

collection of elements; let $\cap$ mean *intersection* and $\cup$ mean *union*. Finally, let the superscript c denote *complement*, or the set of all elements of the universal set *not* elements of the superscripted set. Then we can identify nonvoting citizens (identified by their ideal points) as members of one or more of the sets A (alienation) or I (indifference):

$$A = \{[\mathbf{x}_i \text{ such that } |\boldsymbol{\omega}_\theta - \mathbf{x}_i| > \delta]$$

$$\cap [x_i \text{ such that } |\boldsymbol{\omega}_\psi - \mathbf{x}_i| > \delta]\} \tag{3.13}$$

$$I = \{\mathbf{x}_i \text{ such that } |\boldsymbol{\omega}_\theta - \mathbf{x}_i| \approx |\boldsymbol{\omega}_\psi - \mathbf{x}_i|\} \tag{3.14}$$

Let us call $\S$ the set of voters; then $\S^c$ is the complement of the set of voters, or citizens who abstain. We can now define $\S^c$ and $\S$:

$$\S^c = A \cup I \tag{3.15}$$

$$\S = A^c \cap I^c \tag{3.16}$$

Citizens who abstain are either alienated, indifferent, or both. Conversely, those who vote are not indifferent and are within δ of one or both candidates.

Multiple Dimensions: The Breakdown of Graphical Analysis

It became clear fairly early in the spatial analysis of elections that the single-dimensional model we have focused on to date could be adapted to multiple dimensions. The obvious question to ask was whether the MVT, or at least some analogous result, could be proven in the multiple-dimension case as well.

The answer is, in general, no. The conditions under which a unique stable spatial voting equilibrium exists, even under the classical assumptions, are so specialized and the likelihood of their occurrence is so remote as to cause the theorist to despair. To see why, consider figure 6, which depicts the ideal points x_i of three voters I, II, and III. For simplicity, we assume that the goods for which the two-dimensional space is defined (total budget on education and total budget on defense) are, in citizens' minds, exact substitutes, and units are defined so that simple Euclidean distance (SED) again represents preferences. This assumption gives rise to the very convenient result that indifference sets are circular, and the entire indifference map of each citizen is the set of concentric circles centered on x_i), with greater radius implying lower satisfaction.

We have established a status quo position at the platform (ω_θ) of the incumbent (Theta). The indifference curve of each citizen through ω_θ establishes the "preferred to" sets of I, II, and III. Any point inside the indifference curve, and hence closer to x_I, x_{II}, or x_{III}, is preferred by that citizen to ω_θ. Is the status quo ω_θ, or any other possible platform ω_ψ of the challenger Psi, an equilibrium? Just as before in the single-dimensional case, an equilibrium is a Condorcet winner, or platform that beats all other feasible proposals in pairwise majority rule elections.

Let us first consider ω_θ. Since there are three citizens (let us assume all three vote, to focus our attention on one thing at a time), a necessary and sufficient condition for a platform to be an equilibrium is that there does not exist a point that two or more voters prefer to the present status quo. If two or more do prefer a proposal to the status quo, that point becomes the new status quo and must then face new proposals. Our assumptions give us a simple and very elegant way to determine whether ω_θ is an equilibrium. We need only discover whether the voters' indifference curves through ω_θ intersect.[15] If they do, the set of platforms preferred to ω_θ by one voter shares some elements with the analogous set for at least one other voter. We can therefore use our set notation to define a majority rule equilibrium (MRE). The following theorem is adapted from Shepsle and Weingast (1981).

---

15. By intersect, we mean cross with different slopes, not simply share a single point of tangency.

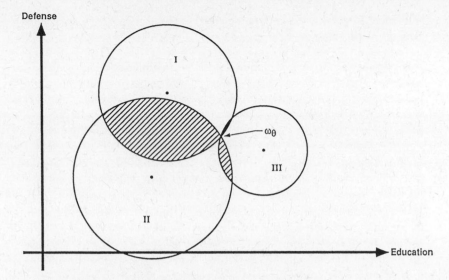

Fig. 6. Spatial competition in two dimensions

Majority Rule Equilibrium Theorem: *Let:*

> ω_p *be an arbitrary platform in the policy space;*
> ω_o *be the status quo, either arbitrarily chosen initially or the result of a series of majority rule comparisons;*
> $c(S)$ *be the number of voters in a defined subset S of the set of voters § (including the whole set §);*
> $W_i(\omega_o)$ *be the set of points preferred to ω_o by voter i.*

Then: For three voters, ω_o is an MRE if and only if there does not exist a platform ω_p such that two or more of the three voters prefer it to ω_o. In symbols:

$$(W_I(\omega_o) \cap W_{II}(\omega_o)) \cup (W_I(\omega_o) \cap W_{III}(\omega_o)) \cup (W_{II}(\omega_o) \cap W_{III}(\omega_o))$$
$$= \varnothing, \text{ or the empty set.}$$

For any arbitrary electorate §, where $c(§) = N$, ω_o is an MRE if and only if there does not exist a platform ω_p and a set of voters S such that:

1. $c(S) \geq (N/2) + 1$ *(S comprises a majority of §), and*
2. $\omega_p \in \{\cap_s W_i(\omega_o)\}$ *(all members of S prefer ω_o to ω_p).*

It might be more accurate to consider the MRE theorem a definition, since the latter part of the theorem can be stated tautologically: "ω_o is an MRE if no other platform can beat it in a majority rule election." The more interesting question is, under what circumstances will an MRE exist? The work using the classical model's assumptions on this question has divided itself into two clear camps; one emphasizing the rarity of equilibria (Plott 1967, 1971; McKelvey 1979; McKelvey and Ordeshook 1976; Enelow and Hinich 1983), and the other claiming that, given the costs of outcomes that aren't equilibria, institutional arrangements will evolve that induce an equilibrium by restricting the feasible set of proposals (Tullock 1981; Shepsle and Weingast 1981).

Kramer (1972) shows that if (1) preferences are separable, and (2) issues are voted on one at a time in a fixed sequence, then the vector of median ideal points cannot be defeated in a majority rule election. The simple result underlying the logic of Kramer's find was first demonstrated by Kadane (1971). In both cases, the issue under consideration is multidimensional in only the most trivial sense, since the vote is a sequence of unidimensional decisions. Barring such an institutional arrangement (which, if it existed, would make Kramer the father of the second, or "Structure Induced Equilibrium," camp), and leaving aside the more complex institutional equilibria, even the simplest multidimensional voting scheme creates difficulties for the spatial model. Consider again figure 6. Using, as before, total budgets on education and defense as the dimensions of the policy space, we see that the median voter in one dimension (II for education) need not be the median in any other (III has the median preference for defense). What, then, is the prediction of a model using the logic of the simple Downsian median voter for multiple dimensions where issues are not voted on one at a time?

A definitive answer is available, but it is disappointing to those who consider only equilibrium results to be truly definitive. Plott (1967) demonstrated sufficient conditions for the existence of equilibrium, but these conditions (loosely, a strict ordinal pairwise balance of all voters along any vector passing through the status quo) are impossibly restrictive. Davis, DeGroot, and Hinich (1972) present necessary, as well as sufficient, conditions for the existence of a majority rule equilibrium for the case where each citizen votes for the candidate who is closest to his ideal point, where distance is the standard Euclidean measure of distance in a space. The equilibrium point is a median in all directions, which does exist for most asymmetric distributions of voter ideal points. Enelow and Hinich (1983, 1984a) proved a more general theorem demonstrating a necessary and sufficient condition for equilibrium, but this result expands only slightly the set of preference configurations that can be expected to produce a stable, determinate equilibrium.

The most extensive body of research in this area (McKelvey 1979; McKelvey and Ordeshook 1976; Cox 1987, 1990) indicates that under the assumptions of unrestricted preference configurations and free unlimited proposal power, the following set of results obtain:

1. No MRE exists.
2. For any status quo ω_o, it is possible to construct an agenda, or ordered series of pairwise majority rule comparisons, that yields a new status quo $\bar{\omega}$, where $\bar{\omega}$ is *any feasible platform* whatsoever.
3. If the agenda setter is sophisticated and possesses monopoly control over the agenda, the agenda (path) from ω_o to $\bar{\omega}$ need contain only one intermediate vote. That is, choose an ω' such that ω' beats ω_o but loses to $\bar{\omega}$. Astonishingly, such an ω' *always* exists!

These results have effectively broken the early links with the analogous economic approach of proving theorems expanding the set of conditions under which a determinate equilibrium obtains. The focus of formal political theory has turned, instead, to the arrangement of the institutions of choice (Who chooses the agenda setter? How is the "stopping rule," or last vote in an agenda, decided?), or the strategic use of agendas, and even institutions, to make disequilibrium a tool for affecting who controls political power in the society. The most forceful proponent of this view was William Riker (1980, 1982), whose view of political interaction as "heresthetics" was discussed earlier. An alternate perspective, to which we will return later, is Schofield (1980, 1985a, 1985b). Schofield claims that since MRE do not generally exist, according to the theory, the most important questions in social science involve discovering by what mechanisms political chaos is avoided. In particular, he advocates the investigation of the means by which "common knowledge" is achieved, so that credible communication and cooperation are possible. In many ways, Schofield's approach is larger, and logically antecedent, to much of social choice theory. Obviously, we believe that political ideologies are the means by which cooperation comes about, and by which chaos is thwarted.

Conclusion

The two extensions to the classical spatial model we have discussed so far, allowing for abstention and incorporating nonseparable preferences defined over multiple dimensions, accept all of the basic assumptions of the classical model. Voters use the spatial position of candidates to judge those candidates; in effect, voters are choosing among platforms rather than among candidates. This type of choice is really more appropriate for votes Black (1958) called "committee" votes than for elections. To understand the distinction, consider Enelow and Hinich's (1984a) comparison.

Committee voting is generally characterized by a small number of well-informed voters who make choices from among a set of *policy alterna-*

tives. Mass elections, on the other hand, feature a large number of voters who must choose from among a set of *candidates* on the basis of limited information (Enelow and Hinich 1984a, 1, emphasis in original).

There are two important parts of this distinction: (*a*) Is the choice over policy alternatives or candidates?, and (*b*) Are the choosers (voters) well informed, or do they possess only limited information? Most of the literature on elections treats the difference as only that contained in (*a*): committee voting is on policy, and elections on candidates. But the crucial difference is (*b*), or the information possessed and used by voters in choosing among *either* candidates *or* the expected vector of policies that their platforms represent. To the extent that the classical spatial model has been built on the assumption of fully informed voters, the distinction originally made by Downs (1957) and Black (1958) has lost much of its utility. For the fully informed voter, after all, the candidate is simply a deterministic vector of policies. There is no candidate at all, in the sense that any real-world political observer understands that term.

In this chapter, we have reviewed the classical spatial model, and have briefly introduced several additions and extensions to the model. The "median voter theorem" has a justifiably important place among the theories used to describe the outcomes of mass voting behavior in the aggregate. As an observation explaining the power of the center of the voter distribution for predicting which candidate or party will win an election, the median voter theorem is crucial. Empirical research by social scientists in economics, political science, and sociology have all consistently found the median voter approach valuable as a theoretical point of departure.

However, the pure, unamended "rational" model of voting has performed rather poorly in describing voting by individuals. The attempts to explain theoretically, or predict empirically, the pattern of individual participation and abstention, and the pattern of choice among those who do participate, are much less impressive than for aggregate level phenomena. Later, in chapter 8, we will use one of the variants of spatial voting mentioned in this chapter (the probabilistic theory of voting) as a framework for representing ideological preferences and predicting voter choice. Before this can be done, however, we must introduce the theory of ideology, itself. It is to the theory of ideology that we now turn.

CHAPTER 4

Ideology, Candidate Strategy, and the Theory of Elections

In the previous two chapters, we reviewed the microeconomic approach and the classical spatial approach to the problem of political choice. The problems, or apparent flaws, we pointed out in these models are actually results, conclusions that circumscribe what can be said about politics. It is interesting, and surprising, that the extraordinarily powerful microeconomic model of choice does not represent public sector preferences. The simple median voter model, which relies on extreme separability between public and private preferences, is not very useful in investigating political phenomena. Although this approach is commonly claimed to represent public sector preferences in the literature purporting to study "public choice," it really does nothing of the sort.

In this chapter and the next, we set out a simple model that *does* represent political choices, by which we mean collective choices or choices over public goods. The model of ideology we advance improves on the existing state of knowledge on public sector preferences in two ways. The first, which we argue for in this chapter, is verisimilitude: the ideological model accurately captures the way citizens think and the way parties and political elites talk. The second is discussed in chapter 5: the spatial model of ideology simultaneously accounts for the observed empirical regularity of the reduced-dimension space in which political debate is observed (in many countries and many settings) to occur, and answers the Slutsky-Denzau-Parks nonrepresentation objections.

We now turn to a discussion of ideology in real political discourse. It is well to list at the outset the theses we seek to advance.

Disparate local disagreements over property rights and the distribution of wealth tend to become (1) more centralized and (2) based on some set of principles, or moral imperatives, that answer the dispute that first gave them birth, but extend beyond this dispute, in terms of political implications.

A political party cannot be successful without an ideology. Thus, the need for a coherent and understandable ideology is a substantial barrier to entry of new parties.

Ideologies constrain political debate. As we shall see, these constraining and restricting effects have profound implications for spatial theory. Tullock's (1981) question, "Why so much stability?" is best answered, "Ideology!"

Ideologies prevent compromise, or make it more difficult. The convex combination of two opposing ideologies is not a new ideology, but an inert and politically useless mishmash.

The Creation and Maintenance of Ideologies

Our thesis is that, of all political strategies, the creation and maintenance of an ideology is by far the most fundamental. Other strategic moves, be they choosing candidates, issues, or coalitions, and tactical decisions of the campaign, such as spending money on advertising, or taking public positions, can be understood only in their broader ideological context.

The creation (or, more neutrally, the origin) of an ideology must, therefore, be considered a metastrategy, the precursor of what we have, until now, considered political strategy. We repeat the definition of ideology given in chapter 1:[1]

Ideology. *An internally consistent set of propositions that make both proscriptive and prescriptive demands on human behavior. All ideologies have implications for (a) what is ethically good; (b) how society's resources should be distributed; and (c) where power appropriately resides.*

Ideologies are ideas. Their origin is in the justification of existing positions in private disputes, but once created, they exist separately from the creation, intentions, or control of those who first advanced the ideas. Their implications, the conclusions about behavior drawn by followers, may be in no wise part of the original intention of the person or group who had the idea. The ideas embodied in a religion or moral system may be difficult to trace back to the dispute that gave these doctrines birth. In truth, the creator of the original idea may have had no interest in any one dispute. But the ideology is successful because its followers found it useful in resolving disputes, even if they are no more than personal, internal confusions over "what do I do now?"

---

1. It is also worth repeating that our definition differs from the orthodox Marxist usage of ideologies as "false consciousness," or veils between workers and reality. To quote Von Mises (1981):

The expression "ideological" is used here not in the Marxist sense or in that in which it is understood by the sociologists of knowledge, but in its scientific meaning. (chap. 6, note 12)

For a more detailed review of the definitions of ideology, and their merits, see Seliger (1976).

After the successful creation of an ideology, survival requires the two types of consistency discussed earlier: logical and temporal. An ideology cannot imply that something is both right and wrong. Neither can it leave its followers with no course of action, ruling out as "wrong" all available alternatives. It is important to keep separate the temporal and logical consistency of the ideology, on one hand, and the consistency of behavior of its proponents on the other. Followers of an ideology may act in contradiction to its principles, and still quite fervently believe themselves to be followers. Proponents of an ideology are, thus, people persuaded of its correctness, its moral force, or even just its coincidence with their own private, nonideological goals.[2] Political arguments will virtually always be made in terms of ideologies with contradictory implications for how the dispute should, in a normative sense, be resolved, not in terms of the self-interest of the disputants.

Ideologies are not restricted to justifying change or income redistribution, as would appear from the examples above. Ideologies serve also to justify the status quo, to preserve the existing distribution of income and rights to property. The effects of such ideologies may be complex; an ideology of laissez-faire or "government should do nothing" simply codifies the status quo.[3] While this result may not be the intention of the creator(s) of the ideological position, all who would benefit from the fixing of the status quo will seize on the ideology, because of its effects. It may often occur that an ideology is popularized or adopted by a party or coalition, not because they are persuaded by the ideas advanced, but because of the interests advantaged. Once the ideology is seized upon and popularized, however, it takes on a life of its own, and politicians, clerics, or monarchs can contradict its precepts only at a significant cost to themselves. The reason for this is that a regime that depends for its legitimacy on an ideology is prevented from openly transgressing the ideology, lest it imperil that legitimacy.

The Tendency to Centralize

The creation and popularization of an ideology is not simply a strategic matter of choosing a set of ideas with the desired implications and then reaping the benefits. Instead, it is an enormously expensive and complex process. No single person, no matter how intelligent or charismatic, could hope to move an idea from nascence to established ideology without the involvement of a group of individuals of intense commitment. It may be difficult or impossible

---

2. For a discussion of the distinctions among ideology and interest, see Congleton (1991).

3. A *real* laissez-faire ideology would do more, for it would have to insist that government be abolished. As Robert Higgs (1987) points out, this kind of ideology is actually inconsistent with viability for a political party. What we see, instead, might better be called "laissez-faire at the margin," or a rationalization of doing nothing *more*, and accepting the status quo distribution of income, regulatory rents, and government-produced benefits.

to choose such a group in an instrumental or foresighted way. More likely is slow expansion, with an evolution and growth of the ideology that, in turn, persuades more people to join, if the ideology is successful, and stagnation and decline otherwise. This distinction, between instrumental or strategic choices and successes due to purely evolutionary forces, is made far too rarely in rational choice theory.[4] Analogous to the analysis of profits in Alchian's (1950) famous piece, ultimately, we know only that successful ideologies persuade enough people to make a commitment to persuade others. Their reasons may vary from personal conviction to cynical support based on self-interest, but the effect is the same.[5]

This effect can be thought of as a kind of economy of scale. Put differently, the importance of ideologies in the practice of politics rewards the large-scale organization, and creates a tendency to centralize. As we will see in the next chapter, and as Downs, himself, believed, this means ideologies are more often associated with parties than with individuals. Myriad small disputes might, individually, come to divers different resolutions, and for idiosyncratic reasons. In fact, we would expect this to happen because of variations in local conditions and the differential abilities of the disputants. But if some entrepreneur can identify a single issue that unites the apparently disparate disputes into a single cause, the situation is ripe for the propagation of a successful ideology. Such preconditions are neither sufficient nor necessary, but they provide a new ideology a fecund setting in which to flourish and grow.

A second reason exists for the tendency toward centralization. Either in the creation of the original ideology, or in the heterodox response, it is clearly advantageous to gain the cooperation of higher levels of government. Local disputes do not remain local, but are appealed by the loser to higher authority. Provided some organizing principle can be found to exist by state or national government, these disputes can be resolved in one quick stroke, and to considerable political advantage. If an ideology or organizing principle is persuasively invoked, the decision gains the imprimatur of legitimacy. Again, we see that local economic disputes contain an almost ineluctable impetus toward resolution by appeal to an ideology.

A brief example would be useful to illustrate this tendency. Consider the role of the constitutional Parliament of England of the mid–seventeenth century, particularly in the Civil War (1642–46).[6] Two aspects of our conception of ideology are clearly illustrated by the events of the war and the conflict leading up to them. First, there were two sides, divided by economics, but

---

4. We will return to this point, made by Frank (1988), in the final chapter.

5. Saying the effect is the same is too strong. As Gauthier (1986) argues, morality and conviction is a public good that can be devalued by unconstrained self-interest.

6. For a much deeper and more thorough consideration of these events, see North and Weingast (1989).

separately united over ideas. The Puritans were united by a complex set of religious and political beliefs; the Royalists were united by nothing so much as their desire to oust the Puritans. This single split came to cleave along several important dimensions:

> First, there was a geographical division . . . most of the east and south-east of England was Parliamentarian, and most of the north and west of England (and almost the whole of Wales) Royalist. That is, by and large the areas of the country which at this date were the more populous, the economically more advanced were for the Parliament; the economically more backward, the less populous were for the King.
>
> Secondly, there was a religious division which partly corresponded with this geographical one. . . . Most strong Puritans were Parliamentarians; very few active ones supported the King. Nor can many strong Anglicans, who had no Puritan leanings, be found on Parliament's side. . . . There were also significant social and economic divisions. Up to a point it was a war of town against country: London, most of the larger market and cloth-manufacturing towns and almost all the seaports . . . were for the Parliament. The larger part of the rural areas . . . were for the King. . . . Up to a point this corresponded to a class division. . . . Another division suggested recently, is that between the "ins" and "outs," or Court and Country. . . . According to this view, the Civil War was a conflict between people who were office-holders, had some connection with royal court or shared in the benefits of the previous regime, and those who were excluded from these advantages. (Aylmer 1963, 126–28)

The war was fought by adherents of two opposing ideologies, over issues that were, in many ways, identical to the interests of the combatants. Indeed, the ideologies existed because of disputes over economics. Large-scale war broke out, however, *only when the ideologies transformed these disputes into a battle of good versus evil*. Men were persuaded by the language of duty, and by emotion. Economics can send men to battle, but only ideology can give a spring to their step and give them any hope of winning.[7]

Second, the ideas in conflict united apparently disparate interests into organic units:

> There is a sense in which the war consisted of a large number of local and even personal conflicts coming together on a national scale. It involved

---

7. For a discussion of the importance of ideological conviction and notions of morality in persuading rational actors, see Congleton (1991) and Congleton and Vanberg (1992).

the settling of many private and family feuds. . . . It is difficult to single out one factor among so many, to explain why people took sides as they did. But at least within the upper social groups (the gentry in particular), differences of political, or constitutional outlook were perhaps decisive. . . . [Many] members of the upper classes who thought of the King as the upholder of the traditional system in church and state, rallied to him out of instinctive loyalty, while those who thought more rationally about it and recognised the need for further changes, tended to be Parliamentarians. With some this may have been a matter of temperament, with others of material interest or what they believed to be their interest; but it was also at least in men's conscious minds a matter of outlook and beliefs. (Aylmer 1963, 129)

Another example, one that contains elements of both aspects of ideological development, comes from Duverger (1951).

In April 1789 the provincial representatives to the Estates General began to arrive at Versailles where they felt rather bewildered. Quite naturally the representatives of the same region tended to meet together so as to escape from the feeling of isolation which assailed them, and at the same time to make preparations for the defence of their local interests. The initiative was taken by the Breton deputies, who hired a room in a cafe and organized regular meetings among themselves. They then perceived that they shared certain ideas not only on regional matters, but also on the fundamental problems of national policy. So they tried to enroll the deputies from other provinces who shared their views, and in this way the 'Breton club' became an ideological group. When the Assembly was transferred from Versailles to Paris the meetings of the club were at first interrupted and a new meeting place had to be found. This time, no room in a cafe being available, the leading spirits hired the refectory of a convent, and it was under the name of this convent that they were to become famous in history. Almost everybody has forgotten the 'Breton club,' but who does not know of the Jacobins? An analogous process, transforming a local group into the nucleus of an ideological faction, was later to give rise to the Girondin club. (Duverger 1951, xxiv)

Both of the influences we seek to emphasize, the usefulness of translating disputes over economics into ideological causes, and the tendency to centralize and proselytize, are clearly visible in these passages. But we have not yet offered any theoretical reason that ideology should play such an important role, even if we have tried to make clear, as an empirical matter, that it does. We now turn to the usefulness of ideology.

The Usefulness of Ideology

Consider the standard spatial model of voting, discussed briefly in the first chapter. The assumption is that candidates locate in the feasible policy space to maximize their chances of victory. In game theoretic terms, if candidates choose strategies based on an objective of winning elections, and the distribution of voters is symmetric around the median, the equilibrium strategy for the two candidates is to choose the median. As an equilibrium condition, and a means to identify one powerful force in political competition (namely, the tendency to move toward the middle), the classical spatial model has proved invaluable.

Still, the discipline may have gone too far in applying the metaphor of game theoretic competition to the political process, which has, in truth, a very different set of incentives. More accurately, a political campaign is better depicted as a sequence of two separate, though related, games. (1) Where do candidates locate? (2) Once these locations are taken, how are campaign resources best allocated to win the election by persuading voters that the candidate is where he claims? This is an outline of the approach taken in the remainder of this book, but for now, we wish to emphasize only the metaphor used to understand political competition.

The standard game theoretic treatment of spatial competition discussed above asserts that candidates know the distribution of voter preferences along a single, or several, policy dimensions. The game is for them to take turns "moving" (much as the hot dog vendors in the earlier chapter moved their carts). When neither has any further desire to move, equilibrium is reached and the election (whose outcome is already certain) is held.

This approach is powerful, because it applies the machinery of equilibrium theory to the problem. But its power is also partly a chimera, because it strips away what observers of politics would consider the heart of the campaign: persuading voters that you will do what you claim, and that you can be trusted. The "location" of the candidate in the policy space presents a dilemma for both the theorist and the candidate, himself. On the one hand, the candidate would prefer to take no specific positions but tell a different story to each group. Because there is no immediate exchange, as there was for the hot dog vendor, voters cannot see the precise link between what is promised and what is later done in office. If they can discern it clearly, there is no mechanism in the classical spatial model to make them believe it.

Consequently, a reputation for a variety of amorphous, but desirable, qualities (honesty, probity, consistency, trustworthiness, guts) is a competitive advantage for the candidate. Voters are unsure with what issues the candidate, if elected, will be faced. One possible solution would be for the candidate to be forced by some contractual arrangement to vote in particular ways or be impeached. In this extreme "delegate" type of representation, the legislator is no more than an information conduit, a carrier of letters from constituents to the clerk of the legislature, who records votes on all issues. The problems with this approach are that (1) it is slow and cumbersome, requiring that new issues be put before the voters so the "delegate" can simply be told how to vote; and (2) someone must still monitor the legislator to find out if he has transgressed the contract.[8]

It is better, by far, to use reputation as the performance bond.[9] The stronger the position a legislator takes in his campaign, the more he reduces the uncertainty of what he says he will do, once in office, the more voters know what the ideological underpinnings of his behavior are. Now, monitoring is easy: choose a single vote, at random, and check the legislator's decision against what you understand (from the campaign) his ideology to be. If there is no conflict, stop; if there is conflict, check more thoroughly. This kind of monitoring, analogous to McCubbins and Schwartz's (1984) "fire alarm" oversight, ensures that extensive (and from the voters' perspective, expensive) checks take place only when there is some evidence of malfeasance.[10]

A fascinating discussion of a similar phenomenon is found in Kreps (1990). He addresses the question of "corporate culture," and the apparent paradox that, though such a concept is quite outside the orthodox worldview of neoclassical economic theory, the culture of corporations is something taken very seriously by corporations themselves. His explanation is extraordinarily insightful, and worth reproducing here at length.

Kreps's theory derives from the observation that transactions within firms or other kinds of organizations (by which he can be interpreted to mean a broad category of human interaction) are characterized by three crucial attributes: (1) hierarchical relationships, (2) ongoing or repeat dealings, and (3) fundamental, irreducible uncertainty, implying unforeseen contingencies.[11]

> Many transactions will potentially be too costly to undertake if the participants cannot rely on efficient and equitable adaptation to those unfore-

---

8. Actually, the problem is far worse than this. Relatively little of the important work of the legislator is done in mechanical votes to register constituents' preferences. Negotiations, committee hearings, and the writing and amending of legislation all would require a monitor who is herself a legislator. Otherwise, she (1) could not see, and (2) could not understand, the actions she is supposedly charged with monitoring.

9. This point has been emphasized by Ferejohn (1986), Lott (1986, 1987a, 1987b), Dougan and Munger (1989), and Lott and Reed (1989).

10. As is always the case when monitoring is costly, this approach does not ensure zero inconsistencies, or "shirking."

11. Kreps notes that reducing uncertainty may just be costly, rather than impossible, with no real damage to his conclusions.

seen contingencies. Note that such reliance will necessarily involve blind faith; if we cannot foresee a contingency, we cannot know in advance that we can efficiently and equitably meet it. (Kreps 1990, 92)

The implication of hierarchical relationships may be even more potent when applied to government than to the firm or corporation.

Some transactions will be hierarchical in that one party will have much more authority in saying what adaptation will take place. . . . When I am employed by a firm, I accept within broad limits the firm's right, as expressed by my superior, to specify how my time will be spent as contingencies arise. Or, to take another example, when students attend a university, they accept the university's right, through administrators, to spell out the terms of the commodity students have bought.

Employees or students will grant such authority to a firm or a university, they must believe that it will be used fairly. What is the source of this faith? It is that the firm and university are characterized by their reputations. The way an organization adapts to an unforeseen contingency can add to or detract from that reputation, with consequences for the amount of faith future employees or students will have. . . . The organization, or, more precisely, those in the organization who have decision-making authority, will have an interest in preserving or even promoting a good reputation. . . . (Kreps 1990, 92–93)

With these three essential elements, Kreps goes on to offer an explanation of "corporate culture" that emphasizes the importance of long-run reputation over more immediate concerns, even when this looks irrational from the perspective of the neoclassical rational model.

In order for a reputation to have an effect, both sides involved in a transaction must *ex ante* have some idea of the meaning of appropriate or equitable fulfilment of the contract. Potential future trading partners must be able to observe fulfilment (or lack of) by the hierarchically superior party. These things are necessary; otherwise, the hierarchically superior party's reputation turns on nothing. (Kreps 1990, 93)

So long as the fulfillment of even implicit promises can be monitored, we are in the bailiwick of the neoclassical principal-agent model. But now we must turn to situations where the premise of unforeseeable contingencies is invoked. Here is where Kreps makes the key point, at least for our purposes.

When we speak of adaptation to unforeseen contingencies, however, we cannot specify *ex ante* how those contingencies will be met. We can at best give *some sort of principle or rule that has wide (preferably universal) applicability and that is simple enough to be interpreted by all concerned. . . . The organization will be characterized by the principle it selects.* . . . In order to protect its reputation for applying the principle in all cases, it will apply the principle even in areas where it serves no direct organization objective if doing so helps preserve or clarify the principle. (Kreps 1990, 93, emphasis added)

Finally, Kreps observes that both the quality of the principle (in terms of the results it creates in the organization) and the level of commitment the organization shows to the principle are crucial. The two, together, determine the prosperity,[12] or failure, of the organization in economic competition.

Because decision-making in a firm is diffuse, those who make decisions in the firm's name will be judged by their diligence in applying and embracing the principle. In this light I interpret corporate culture as partly the principle itself (or more realistically, the interrelated principles that the organization employs) and partly the means by which the principle is communicated to hierarchical inferiors. . . . Because it will be designed through time to meet unforeseen contingencies as they arise, it will be the product of evolution inside the organization and will be influenced by the organization's history. (Kreps 1990, 93–94)

There are several important differences between "corporate culture," the phenomenon that Kreps is investigating, and the political ideologies that are our subject. The most important differences are (1) the nature of competition in a political system, (2) the importance of the universality of the organizing principle, and (3) the nature of the hierarchical relation between government and voters. The essential point Kreps makes—the importance of an organizational reputation in solving problems of unforeseeable contingencies—is exactly analogous to the ideological reputations of parties, however.

Competition in political systems is quite different from economic competition, because, for the employee or stockholder, it is possible to judge *ex post*

---

12. There, is of course, a long history of using "culture" to explain different levels of prosperity and growth in economic systems. One of the most coherent early statements focused on the comparison between Catholic and Protestant European nations was Weber (1950). This theory was widely criticized, but has recently been resurrected. Inglehart (1990) notes that the theory was largely confirmed over the period 1870–1938. Harrison points out that much of the growth of the Catholic countries after World War II has occurred because "they—above all, Spain and Italy—had been so far behind non-Catholic countries. . . . " (Harrison 1992, 7)

the quality of the firm's response, even to unforeseen contingencies. It is not possible, as Kreps points out, to compare the outcome to any *ex ante* commitment, but it is possible to judge profits, output, employment, and other measurable results of the firm's decisions. Most firms have some well-defined product. If the firm is a conglomerate, then its success in a particular industry (say, textiles or apparel) is relatively independent of its success in others (such as producing microprocessors).

The optimal extent of the firm's diversification into other industries, given this measurable standard of profitability, will be determined by the scope of the applicability of the "cultural" organizing principle. If the principle is equally applicable to textiles and microprocessors, the firm may profitably produce both. If not, the firm that tries to produce both will go bankrupt. *The point is that the firm will optimally expand across industries, according to the universality of the cultural organizing principle; the firm is under no organizational or competitive imperative for such diversification.*

This is not true of the ideology of the political party. Political competition requires that ideologies are applicable to all activities. Better, an ideology that is universally applicable has a much bigger advantage over its competitors than a corporate culture with equally broad applicability, because the competitive imperative in politics is to control all of the government, or none.

Finally, the hierarchical relation in politics is unique. Kreps's description of the hierarchy is quite accurate, but we already have an apt description of this problem in the work of an earlier scholar: Thomas Hobbes, in *Leviathan* (1651). Hobbes does not describe democratic political competition; instead, he outlines the theoretical basis for the existence of monarchy. His contribution is his recognition of the abjectness of the hierarchical relation of the governed to the government. There is a paucity of alternatives, except in temporal sequence, to the current government. The only alternatives, even in a democratic system, are immediate revolution or to toss the malefactors out in the next election. The path of revolt holds little promise in Hobbes's world:

> The condition of man . . . is a condition of war of everyone against everyone. . . . [In a state of nature] no arts; no letters; no society; and which is worst of all, continual fear and danger of violent death; and the life of man, solitary, poor, nasty, brutish, and short. (Hobbes 1651, part 1, chaps. 4 and 13)

The only recourse, then, is to rely on the threat of replacement of the current government by an alternative whose commitment to its organizing ideology is largely unknown. Two firms compete by simultaneously producing output and displaying commitment to their cultural organizing principles, in their daily activities. By definition, a party out of power has no daily activities in government by which it could show commitment to an ideology. Power in the market is shared (though contested), but power in government is exclusive.[13]

When we combine these points, we see we are dealing with a very different phenomenon, in political ideologies. Competition of ideologies for the control of government means competition for universal control, which requires universal applicability of the ideology. The hierarchical relation of government to voter places more powers in the hands of the hierarchical superior than the analogous relation in the market. Finally, the party (or better, ideology) that is out of power faces a problem of commitment, since any claims it makes about commitment could quite plausibly be dismissed as cheap talk.

If anything, this makes the value of a coherent ideology, with a history of consistent application in a variety of settings, even more important. The value of ideology as a performance bond confers on a candidate associated with a known commitment to a clear ideology a substantial competitive advantage, other things being equal. No party could be successful, either in seeking to elect its candidates or to advance a particular position, without some coherent and appealing ideology. We must be careful, however, lest it sound as if an ideology is something one simply acquires or creates, and is therefore fungible. An ideology is an extraordinarily complex mechanism for transmitting information and persuading others about what is "good" in politics and social intercourse. Potential candidates for ideologies are almost impossibly sparse, because the creation and popularization of a new ideology are difficult tasks, requiring time, money, considerable organizational skills, and a compelling and exciting set of ideas.

---

13. The concept of culture is also useful in analyzing competition among nations, or in comparing their relative performance in serving citizens and achieving economic growth. Three important recent examples include Grondona (1992; quoted in Harrison 1992), Harrison (1992) and Inglehart (1990). In considering the relative economic performance of nations over the last twenty-five years, Harrison avers:

Economic policies that assure stability and continuity and nurture entrepreneurship correlate better with growth performance than do climate, resource endowment, or geography. But why have so many countries failed to pursue such policies with the necessary persistence to reap their benefits? Why [for example], faced with the oil shocks of the 1970s, did Argentina and Brazil try to borrow their way out of trouble and end up mired in debt and galloping inflation, while Taiwan and Korea adopted austerity programs that led to rapid recovery? . . .

In my view, it is impossible to answer these questions without examining the impact of culture on human progress—the values and attitudes of a nation, society or ethnic group, and the institutions that both reflect and reinforce those values and attitudes. (Harrison 1992, 6)

Constraints on Behavior

Much of the reason ideology is useful is that it transmits information to, and excites enthusiasm in, the listener or reader.[14] These attributes, alone, would suffice to make ideology a powerful competitive advantage in political discourse and in electoral politics. But there is an additional attribute of ideology, alluded to but not completely developed earlier, that makes it crucial for candidates and parties. This is its capacity to constrain "movement," to restrict the capacity of political actors to modify their positions to increase their vote share. Campaigns are designed to accomplish two things. First, they establish a candidate's, or a party's, position in the policy space. Second, and no less important, they persuade citizens that, once in office, the candidate or party will support or enact policies close to those they promised. Elections reflect the aggregation of individual voters' assessment of the candidate's or party's success in *both* of these endeavors.

For two reasons, the latter function of campaigns (establishing credibility and commitment) is the more important. First, debate centers on the ideological dimensions, not the policy space. Most voters know little of a candidate's actual policy stands, and establishing a position in the reduced-dimensional ideological space is more easily accomplished. The problem then quickly becomes convincing voters both that the candidate genuinely believes this position and will pursue it, and that it is the right thing to do. Second, voters are concerned separately with the candidate's character, integrity, ability to lead, and vision.[15] The policy issues on which an elected official must decide are very difficult for voters to predict. Consequently, voters must depend on his ideological position, and his apparent commitment to it, as guides for judgment or comparison. Such future events are unknown, and unknowable; in Knight's classic distinction, such forecasts represent uncertainty, rather than risk. This is exactly Kreps's insight; if anything, it applies in the political context with even greater force. As Goertzel notes:

> Ideological thinking focuses on issues where the objective truth simply is not known. Ideologies are more about future potentialities than current realities. They are often so vague and ambiguous that it is difficult to know what they mean, let alone whether they are true. Ideological beliefs are often concerned more with feelings and values than with verifiable facts. (Goertzel 1992, 51)

---

14. For a review of recent work relating to information and democratic choice, see Ferejohn and Kuklinski (1990).

15. See, for example, Enelow and Hinich (1982).

Political science has focused primarily on the first function of campaigns, establishing a position. In formal or game theoretic treatments of campaigns, this focus has been virtually exclusive. Consider for a moment the phrase *spatial theory*. In political science, this phrase has come to mean a predictive model designed to predict where candidates will "locate" in a policy space, given the distribution of voter preferences. The game is to establish the "best" position in the space, defined as the vector of policies that maximize the candidate's expected vote share, given the expected response of the opponent. When the expected best response of the opponent implies, as a best response, the position the candidate chose in the first place, an equilibrium is established and we can all go home.

Compare this analysis with an actual election. Incumbents run on, and challengers run against, the record the incumbent has established. Even in open seat elections, there are party cues, endorsements by political elites, or prior experience by the candidates to give voters some means of guessing what the candidates claim they will do. The question is, why would anyone believe them? That is what campaigns are primarily about, and the inattention of formal theory to the campaign is why we have yet to develop a very useful equilibrium theory of politics.

We check to see if the positions taken are an equilibrium. If they are, the analysis is complete, just when the campaign is beginning. If not, we have the candidates, or at least one of them, "move." If, as we have argued, the primary goal of campaigns is to persuade voters the candidate or party will *not* move, this analytical approach seems paradoxical. Elections are not conducted in a static or timeless setting. Instead, voters evaluate candidates based on their reputations for probity, commitment, and consistency. Movement devalues these reputations.

One of ideology's chief functions is to establish the principles that organize political discourse. But the importance of ideology prevents movement, and creates stability, for a very different reason. The party or candidate in power is typically restricted to the set of issues that legitimize their power. Opponents attack the incumbents on these issues, and along the dimensions established by this struggle for legitimacy. The policy space may be enormous, and of very high dimensionality. The ideological space in which the political debate of the campaign takes place, on the other hand, is of low dimensionality, and "positions" in this space (i.e., distinct ideologies) are extremely sparse. In short, in campaigns, politicians can't move without hurting their chances, couldn't move far because the space is small and simple, and can't move anyway because there aren't many places to go. If true, this conclusion is important from two distinct theoretical perspectives. First, it answers Gordon Tullock's famous question, "why so much stability?" Second, it forces a reexamination of the equilibrium theorems we have received from game theoretic models of politics. We consider each of these perspectives in turn.

Why So Much Stability?

Tullock (1981) challenged scholars in public choice and political science to reconcile a contradiction. On the one hand, all the best models of voting predict the absence of equilibrium because of the demonstrable nonexistence of a Condorcet winner, or single alternative that defeats all others in pairwise comparisons. These models (e.g., McKelvey 1979; Schofield 1980) place few restrictions on preference profiles or feasible policies, and tend, strikingly, to imply an endless wandering among all feasible policies (McKelvey and Ordeshook 1976) or among some proper subset (McKelvey 1986; Schofield 1985, 1992b; Cox 1987, 1990), such as the "top-cycle set" or "yolk."

On the other hand, instability in real politics is the exception, rather than the rule. We have earlier discussed Riker's "heresthetics," and the process of realignment or shifting of the support coalitions of the parties. Such events are noteworthy mostly for their rarity, however. The typical progress of political choices is stable and almost changeless. This is not to say voters may not want to change, or that political leaders might not be eager to provide it. Something about the nature of the political process itself dictates this stability.

Of the answers that have been offered to Tullock's question, including logrolling (Tullock 1981) or legislative institutions (Shepsle and Weingast 1981), none seem to address the question in any direct way. Their focus is on legislative voting, when, in fact, referenda voting exhibits the same general stability. To be successful, an answer must account for something in the very nature of political discourse. Our answer, of course, is that the importance of ideology dictates this stability. Moving from one position to another means neither position is credible. Changing position in the policy space requires changing position along the ideological dimension—saying, in effect, "I no longer believe what I once asserted and tried hard to persuade you was moral and good."

The Classical Spatial Metaphor

Let us now turn to a consideration of the nature of classical spatial models of the political process. Generally, these games are conducted under an assumption of Nash-Cournot behavior (though occasionally Stackleburg leadership is assumed). This means each politician makes his best (i.e., vote-share maximizing) response to the position of the other, assuming the opponent's position to be fixed. This approach to modeling is extremely convenient, and can be used to motivate experiments in which participants choose policy positions to maximize their payoffs. Such an approach is most interesting from a scientific perspective, but is of little direct, descriptive use in studying the process of political interaction. The assumption is that a candidate who chooses a position is somehow forced to deliver that position, or at least that voters believe he will, in spite of constant evidence to the contrary. We have claimed that constant movement makes *all* claims incredible, particularly if the candidate is committed only to winning, with no policy preferences of his own.

This is not to say these equilibrium results from game theory are incorrect or useless. They are clearly correct on their own terms, because they are *proved* correct in a rigorous fashion. Their utility requires only a bit of imagination and a willingness to accept "as if" reasoning. The most valuable results of the classical spatial/game theoretic approach are the restrictions they place on possible outcomes. These restrictions are just as applicable, and just as useful, in real politics as they are in the stylized world of game theory. It matters little how an outcome in the top-cycle set is chosen, but we know that any outcome outside this set cannot be sustained, and it is unsustainable for precisely the reasons game theorists claim. Game theory allows us to place an additional restriction on the set of ideological positions we expect to observe. But it is important to distinguish the value of the results from the misleading strategic premise of unfettered movement by candidates.

Ultimately, a gap exists between what we know about information in politics and what we can predict as outcomes of democratic processes. One approach is to model voters' use of information on all issues. Recent work by Austen-Smith (1990), Banks (1990), Banks and Sobel (1987), and Chappell (1988) places rather strict limitations on how voters might rationally process information they receive from candidates with incentives to misrepresent their likely behavior in office.[16] These highly sophisticated models challenge the ability of the classical spatial model to represent political competition in any useful fashion. Banks (1990) states this challenge most clearly:

> [The] strong assumption implicit in the Hotelling-Downs model is that the positions the candidates announce prior to an election will be the positions they subsequently enact once in office. Since voters typically have preferences defined over policy outcomes and not over electoral announcements per se, but their only information at the time of voting consists of these announcements, the equivalence of announced position and policy outcome appears to be one of analytical tractability at the expense of realism. (Banks 1990, 311)

---

16. This literature is derived from results in information theory in economics, including Kreps and Wilson (1982), Milgrom and Roberts (1982), and Crawford and Sobel (1982), but the

This work is important, for it highlights the shortcomings in previous work in spatial models. The Banks (1990) piece is easily the best work yet produced on the subject. Unfortunately, it substitutes a new, impossibly complex, set of informational requirements for the old, impossibly unrealistic, model of the campaign. Voters are assumed to know exactly what they want on each of a large number of policy dimensions, and to know exactly what candidates claim they aim to do. The only problem voters face is whether or not to believe the messages candidates send out.

By contrast, ideology offers two advantages the games of asymmetric information lack. The first, noted by Downs, is that ideology serves as a means of reducing the costs of gathering information. What Downs did not recognize is the attenuated incentive to gather information, even on one's own most desired policies; voters simply do not know which policies are being considered, much less which position on these policies they most prefer. Ideology offers a means for parties and candidates to communicate, and for voters to decide, even when information is asymmetric.

The more important point, of course, is that information is not (just) asymmetric; it is grossly, irreducibly, incomplete. As Kreps noted, in his discussion of corporate culture, simplifying principles with wide applicability have evolved to mitigate the contracting problem that inheres when both parties to a hierarchically structured contract recognize the importance of unforeseeable contingencies. If anything, this problem is worse in politics: the hierarchy puts even more power in the hands of the superior, the inferior has fewer alternatives, and the alternatives that do exist face a far greater problem of commitment.

Ideology, Compromise, and Irrationality

The theory of ideology and its importance in political discourse we have developed in this chapter improves our ability to understand behavior that would otherwise seem to be irrational. The two specific phenomena we discuss here are compromise and continuance. The two are related, and each turns out to be consistent with the theory we have put forth, and can be seen, in that context, to be a rational action. In fact, to do otherwise would be irrational.

Politics is, in one sense, the science of compromise, but at the same time, we often see conflicts that clearly make every participant worse off, yet the Pareto-superior compromise is never even seriously suggested. The con-

---

application to political choices in the face of asymmetric information has, in some ways, proved even more important.

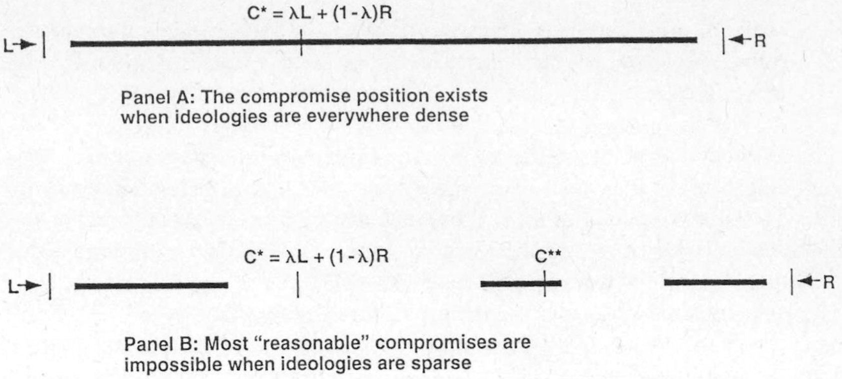

$$C^* = \lambda L + (1-\lambda)R$$

L→ | ———————————————————————————— |←R

Panel A: The compromise position exists
when ideologies are everywhere dense

$$C^* = \lambda L + (1-\lambda)R \qquad C^{**}$$

L→ | ———————— | ————+————   ———— |←R

Panel B: Most "reasonable" compromises are
impossible when ideologies are sparse

Fig. 7. Why won't people be reasonable?

flict in Lebanon among various factions throughout the 1980s is, on its face, a case of collective irrationality; why don't they just compromise? Compromise has several definitions, a comparison among which is instructive:

> (1) to come to agreement by mutual concession; (2) to make a shameful or disreputable concession; (3) to expose to discredit or mischief. (*Websters Collegiate Dictionary*, 1980)

In the terms of classical spatial theory, the first definition is easy to depict as a convex combination of two positions. This compromise is demonstrated in figure 7, where $\lambda L + (1 - \lambda)R = C^*$, with $0 \le \lambda \le 1$ and C^* being the compromise position between L (the left) and R (the right).

There seems to be no clear way of discussing the second or third definitions, until and unless one begins thinking in terms of our theory. It then immediately becomes clear that C^* equally illustrates these definitions, showing that no one may be happy with "compromise," because no one knows what it means. Suppose $\lambda = .4$; then the new system may be 40 percent Marxist and 60 percent laissez-faire capitalist. There is no such thing; no ideology exists to legitimate such a bastard offspring. In the Lebanon example, a compromise might reflect a 50 percent Druse and 50 percent Christian ideology. But the new ideology does not mean that this combination of previous ideas is, itself, a coherent and persuasive ideology, as we have defined it. Rather, it is an unstable and purely political artifice, with no one's support. This difficulty with compromise has been widely remarked, perhaps best by Duverger (1951, 215):

> The dream of the centre is to achieve a synthesis of contradictory aspirations; but synthesis is a power only of the mind. Action involves choice and politics involve action . . . for the centre is nothing more than the

artificial grouping of the right wing of the left and the left wing of the right. The fate of the centre is to be torn asunder, buffeted, and annihilated. . . .

In general, it is impossible to average ideologies to create new ones. This is not entirely obvious until one considers the mechanism by which we claim ideologies are created. But if the dominant ideology legitimates the status and the heterodox ideology opposes it, compromise must reflect a destruction of principle, as well as a renegotiation of the allocation of goods and services. The sparseness of ideologies that imply certain positions are "good" or "best" means that the menu of choice is not continuous, but has gaps. Of course, some compromises do exist. For example, C^{**} in figure 7 falls in the area of existing ideologies. But if a compromise, or convex combination of existing ideologies, falls in a gap in the historical and cultural understanding of politically tenable positions, it will be stillborn.

The impossibility of compromise often leads to a process of continuance of apparently irrational behavior. The commitment of an individual, a party, or a regime to a particular ideology may prevent movements that even the agent(s) involved would agree would improve their position. There are two reasons for this, both of which have been alluded to earlier. First, a movement from one position to another quite likely means voters and supporters believe neither, whereas continuance (particularly in adverse, apparently irrational circumstances) maintains, or even enhances, credibility.[17] Second, ideologies are not donned or doffed, like a mantle, for strategic purposes, though such a use would suffice to explain their utility. Instead, devotees of ideologies have a personal commitment, a sense of connection, intellectually and emotionally, that prevents or resists change, even when it would be to the agent's clear strategic advantage.

For both reasons, we expect political actors, as well as religious and other elite leaders, to persist in a pattern of behavior that casual observation would indicate is patently irrational. In fact, their foregone choice is illusory. Whether because they cannot move without discredit, or because they cannot move without discomfort, they are pursuing the only feasible course of action.

This verbal overview of some of the reasons why ideology is important has served to introduce the concept to those who have not thought of ideology in this way. We turn now to a more formal presentation of the theory of ideology as a means of portraying party competition, keeping sight of our ultimate goal, the representation of citizens' preferences.

---

17. Dougan and Munger (1989) note this aspect of commitment as a means of reconciling what appears to be irrational behavior.

CHAPTER 5

Parties and Ideology

We use the word "parties" to describe the factions which formed round a condottiere in renaissance Italy, the clubs where the members of the Revolutionary assemblies met, and the committees which prepared the elections under the property franchise of the constitutional monarchies as well as the vast popular organizations which give shape to public opinion in modern democracies. . . . There is some justification for this identity of name, for there is a certain underlying relationship—the role of all these institutions is to win political power and exercise it. Obviously, however, they are not the same thing.
—Maurice Duverger, *Political Parties: Their Organization and Activity in the Modern State*, 1951, 4; emphasis added

It would be the height of hubris to pretend to develop a theory of party development and competition in one chapter. Duverger (1951) devoted an entire volume to the question. Literally hundreds of works have attempted to define and categorize parties, coalitions, and their relation to issues and voters since, some more prominent being Key (1955); Campbell, Converse, Stokes, and Miller (1960); Burnham (1970); MacRae (1970); Duverger (1972); Sartori (1976); Fiorina (1977); Kau and Rubin (1981, 1984); Kalt and Zupan (1984, 1990); Poole and Daniels (1985); Poole and Rosenthal (1985); Nelson and Silberberg (1987); and Laver and Schofield (1990).[1] What we will do here is briefly outline the process of origination of parties and the coalitions of factions they represent, and then explain the link between parties and ideologies, for the purpose of this book.

Defining "party" is little easier than defining ideology, a lengthy discussion of which we have already offered. There are at least three sets of definitions of political parties.

The first is a mass organization that responds to the manipulative, charis-

---

1. A special issue of *Public Choice* (Grier 1993) was devoted to empirical studies of ideology. The reader in search of more extensive references may want to look at those sources.

matic leadership of a few powerful rulers. The consequence of the activities of these "parties," or factions, is ruinous:

"Party-spirit, which at best is but the madness of many for the gain of a few" (Alexander Pope in letter to E. Blount, August 27, 1714).

"By a faction, understand a number of citizens, whether amounting to a majority or minority of the whole, who are united and actuated by some common impulse of passion, or of interest, adverse to the rights of other citizens, or to the permanent and aggregate interests of the community. . . . [Though there are many causes] the most common and durable source of actions has been the various and unequal distribution of property" (James Madison, *The Federalist*, no. 10, 1787).

The second type of definition of a party is an organization with both mass- and elite-level participation by members who hold a common doctrine dear:

"Party is a body of men united, for promoting by their joint endeavours the national interest, upon some particular principle in which they are all agreed" (Edmund Burke, *Reflections on the Revolution in France*, 1790, p. 11).

"Party is organized opinion" (Benjamin Disraeli, speech in British House of Commons, November 9, 1878).

"A party is group of men professing the same political doctrine" (Benjamin Constant in a letter, 1886).

"Candidates view winning as a means to policy. . . . In order to predict which government policies will be implemented, it is not only necessary to know the voters' preferences, but the candidates' preferences as well" (Donald Wittman 1977, 182).

The third definition of a party is an organization that seeks to obtain and maintain political control over the institutions of government; the mechanism for exercising this control is the choice of public policies the party will advocate.

"Parties formulate policies in order to win elections, rather than win elections in order to formulate policies" (Anthony Downs 1957, 41).

"Political parties are basic institutions for the translation of mass preferences into public policy" (V. O. Key 1964, 22).

"The only kind of organization that can translate into fact the idea of majority rule is the political party" (E. E. Schattschneider 1960, 2).

The particular view of the third of these perspectives outlined by Downs is by far the most common in the formal literature on elections. Yet, as we pointed out earlier, there is a contradiction between assuming an ideology communicates something to voters and assuming that the only goal of parties is winning. This mistake is a primary reason that Downs's theory is incomplete and has been misinterpreted. We will not assume that there is an absolute correspondence between a party and a fixed and well-defined ideology, where all members of the party "profess the same political doctrine." But neither will we allow that parties choose ideologies without regard to the beliefs of their partisans.

The conception of parties that will be pursued here can be outlined as follows. When parties are first established, and (if successful) are growing, they must appeal to the beliefs and interests of prospective members through an ideology. Once the party is established, the link to a specific ideology may grow more tenuous, and the party becomes a brokering agent among factions in the legislature.[2]

This view is hardly novel, having existed since David Hume's 1760 "Essay on Parties." Hume's argument can be summarized by dividing the development of political organizations into two parts. The first emphasizes program or platform, the set of specific policies the party proposes, or the set of moral principles the party claims will guide its policy choices. The second stage emphasizes the organization of the party itself. Once the individual members have been joined by the platform, the platform becomes less important. Duverger (1951) points out this description is often accurate, but need not be the only path of development: "The statement does not apply to certain contemporary political parties in which doctrine has taken on a religious character that gives the parties a totalitarian hold over the life of their members" (Duverger 1951, xv).

---

2. An extreme perspective on the "brokering" function of parties is the view of George Stigler, who held that parties and other political intermediaries have little *independent* effect:

> The Chicago students of regulation have usually assumed, explicitly as often as tacitly, that the players who count in regulation are the producers and consumers. Political intermediaries—parties, legislators, administrators—are not believed to be devoid of influence, but in the main they act as agents for the primary players in the construction and administration of public policy. (Stigler 1988, xv).

Parties can therefore be left out of the overall analysis, except as details of the process by which policy is made. There is a precedent for this claim; the source, somewhat surprisingly (at least to those familiar with the work of the Chicago School), is The Communist Manifesto, by Marx and Engels:

> The executive of the modern state is but a committee for managing the affairs of the whole bourgeosie. . . . The ruling ideas of each age have never been the ideas of [the government]. (1848, 3)

Clearly, the disagreement here is what happens after the party is established. For some parties, ideology has a maintained effect (as it has on followers of Marx, Lenin, or Mao, who either become "theological" or reject the ideology completely). For others (such as the Republicans and Democrats in the United States, or, to a lesser extent, the Conservative party in Great Britain), once the party has many adherents who accept its basic competence to select leaders, the platform begins to look more pragmatic and becomes oriented toward preservation of the organization. In other words, the established party may begin to look more Downsian.

Our discussion of the relation between party and ideology accepts this distinction, but it is important to note that the character of the party (theological or pragmatic) has a great deal to do with the original ideology. Marxist-Leninist ideology, which is "revolutionary" and is constantly reinventing itself, actually has most of the essential characteristics of a theology: doctrine is strictly derived from a few books (in most cases, selections from Marx, Engels, Lenin, and Mao), dissenters are punished as heretics, and followers are promised future reward for present sacrifice. The Democratic party in the United States, on the other hand, is "evolutionary," and wants government to "help people" in whatever way is currently expedient.[3] Established, organized parties may have only amorphous ideologies, particularly as regards the tangential issues on which they must, nonetheless, take positions.[4] Nonetheless, virtually all parties depended on ideologies at their birth, and during their early life. It may be that the Marxian "continuing revolution" prevents even many established Communist parties from departing from a doctrinaire interpretation and application of their guiding ideology.

In the remainder of this chapter, we will first define what we will mean by *party*. Next, we will examine the origin and development of parties. Finally, we will consider the relation between three concepts: ideology, party, and interest group, or "faction."

Definition

On the whole the development of parties seems bound up with that of democracy, that is to say with the extension of popular suffrage and parliamentary prerogatives. The more political assemblies see their functions and independence grow, the more their members feel the need to group themselves according to what they have in common, so as to act in concert. The more the right to vote is extended and multiplied, the more necessary it becomes to organize the electors by means

---

3. P. J. O'Rourke (1989, xx) points out: "Santa Claus is a Democrat, God is a Republican."

4. This observation is hardly original, having been discussed by several authors in the early study of the life cycle of organizations. In particular, see Heberle (1951) and Weber (1947).

of committees capable of making the candidates known and canalizing the votes in their direction. The rise of parties is thus bound up with the rise of parliamentary groups and electoral committees. . . . The general mechanism of this genesis is simple. First there is the creation of parliamentary groups, then the appearance of electoral committees, and finally the establishment of a permanent connection between these two elements.

—Duverger 1959, xxiii–xxiv

This passage contains all the essential elements of a definition of a party. Obviously, there are myriad other definitions; in fairness to Duverger, he is careful to note exceptions and alternatives.[5] By quoting selectively, we have narrowed the definition to exclude court parties or factions in single-party regimes, such as the old Soviet Union. Because we are interested in citizen choice in a democracy, the definition of party will be restricted to require democratic institutions and processes in a way our definition of ideology was not.

The definition of party that will be used here is this:

Party. *A group of citizens who (a) hold in common substantial elements of a political doctrine identified, both by party members and by outsiders, with the name of the party; (b) choose candidates, either from within the group or by considering outsiders, for political office with the object of carrying out this doctrine; and (c) organize the members of their delegation to the parliament or legislature of the political unit where the party is active.*

As this definition makes clear, there is an association between party and ideology.[6] The party in government depends on this association in citizens' minds to allow it to communicate; citizens depend on this association to allow them to make voting and contribution decisions without devoting their life to research.[7] But this link is not causal, and there is no necessary temporal

---

5. Duverger points out, "In practice there are various departures from this strict theoretical scheme. There have usually been parliamentary groups before electoral committees. Indeed there were political assemblies before there were elections. Parliamentary groups can be formed in an autocratic chamber just as well as in an elected chamber. In fact the struggle of 'factions' is generally to be seen in all hereditary or co-opted assemblies, whether it be the Senate of classical Rome or the Diet of Poland." (Duverger 1951, 45)

6. Empirical work on measuring this distinction faces a difficult task. Similarity in voting patterns has been taken to indicate either shared ideology or partisanship. MacRae (1970) tried hard to distinguish the two notions, and Poole (1981), Poole and Rosenthal (1984), and Poole and Daniels (1985) have derived sophisticated means of identifying the differences.

7. There is consistent empirical support for the association of party and ideology based on the mapping to economic issues: "On average, voters who identify themselves as strong Demo-

sequence of establishment: the party may have come into existence with only the simplest of doctrinal commitments, and then its ideology evolved into a more complete set of ideas. As Duverger (1951) notes regarding parties in government:

> A priori it would seem that community of political doctrine has consti-tuted the essential impulse in the formation of parliamentary groups. Yet facts do not always conform to this hypothesis. Often geographical prox-imity or the desire to defend one's profession seem to have given the first impulse. Doctrine only comes afterwards. Thus, in certain countries the first parliamentary groups were local groups which eventually became ideological groups. (Duverger 1951, xxiv)

Barnes goes even further, claiming that parties are "the communications network that functionally specializes in the aggregation of political communi-cations (i.e., communications relating to the authoritative allocation of values) for a polity" (Barnes 1967, 241). If we accept "authoritative allocation of values" as a shorthand for "ideology," then parties are the organizations that elaborate ideologies and express their implications to the public.

As regards selection of candidates, it is not at all clear who selects whom. Parties may choose, and groom, an obvious prospect in much the same way a baseball farm system works. The candidates face increasingly difficult tests, of both electoral competition and conformity with the party ideology, in local and then intermediate-level elections before they can com-pete for the parliament or legislature, the governorship or presidency.

On the other hand, politically ambitious, talented young people may choose a party based on what they expect the implications of that choice to be for their electoral fortunes.

> Sometimes it is less a case of the party choosing a candidate than of the candidate choosing the party. Under the Third Republic it used to be said of such and such a candidate that he had 'received the investiture' of such and such a party. The terminology is interesting: it suggests that the initiative comes from the candidate rather than from the party, that the candidate has solicited the party, which has then granted its support. (Duverger 1951, 355–56)

For our purposes, this distinction is not of immediate importance, though of course it is of great practical significance. Differences in the power of the

---

crats also identify themselves as liberals, whereas strong Republicans identify themselves as conservatives. Further, these two scales are based on economic issues" (Enelow and Hinich 1984a, 202).

party to use electoral laws to determine who runs and in what district, awards of power in the legislature or in government ministries, and so on, largely determine the power relation between candidate and party.[8] What is important for now is that this relation is a crucial part of the definition of the concept of party itself.

The final part of the definition is the role of parties in organizing the national legislative assembly, regardless of the form the representation in that assembly takes.[9] Parties provide answers to many of the organizational and implicit contracting problems faced by legislatures (Weingast and Marshall 1988; Cox and McCubbins 1993; Aldrich 1994). Although the party organization in the legislature may change in response to changes in the political system, as Aldrich (1994) shows, the form of organization that the legislature has at any given point is understandable only in the context of the parties that contest for political power.

The definition of party offered in this section is designed to facilitate exposition and distinctions involved in making our main point on the importance of ideology. It is not original (though it is somewhat more inclusive than is usual), nor is it perfect. Clearly, other definitions are possible.[10] Our definition spans multiple levels of party activity, including citizens, candidates for electoral office and the professional organization that nurtures them, and incumbent officials, who organize the legislature or parliament through party affiliation.

Before we can conclude the discussion of what parties are, it is useful to emphasize what parties are not. The most important thing that parties are not is factions; the distinction turns out to be important later when we seek to

---

8. For a discussion of the evolution of the exercise of the power of parties in the U.S. House, see Cox and McCubbins (1993).

9. Duverger gives the following description of the origin of parliamentary form and procedure that have had a broad impact on both sides of the Atlantic:

Over a long period, English ministers made sure of substantial majorities by buying the votes, if not the consciences, of Members of Parliament. . . . In 1714 the post of Political Secretary of the Treasury was set up to take charge of these financial operations; the secretary in question soon became known as the 'Patronage Secretary.' . . . Responsible for distributing the government's largesse to the members of the majority party, the Patronage Secretary kept a close watch on their votes and their speeches. He thus became . . . 'the Whip,' just as in hunting the 'whips' gather hounds into a pack. Strict discipline was in this way gradually instituted in the majority party. It was in the nature of things that the minority should adopt in self-defence a similar discipline—although it was based on different methods. Later, when parliamentary morality had been gradually improved, the structure of the groups in Parliament, including their strong organization and the authority of the whip, outlived the causes which had given it birth. (Duverger, 1951, xxvi)

10. For example, there is the popular empirical definition used by many political scientists: party members in mass publics are citizens who identify themselves as members (Ladd and Hadley 1973a; 1973b).

incorporate interest groups into the analysis. The best discussion of the similarities, and differences, between party and faction can be found in Sartori (1976). Sartori outlines his definition of the concept of party as follows:

1. Parties are not factions.
2. A party is part of a whole.
3. Parties are channels of expression. (Sartori 1976, 25)

Much of chapter 1 of Sartori's book is devoted to a discussion of the distinction between party and faction. He gives an excellent account of the historical evolution of the use and meaning of *faction*, beginning with the derivation of each word from its Latin root.

> Faction, which is by far the older and more established term, derives from the Latin verb *facere* (to do, to act), and *factio* soon comes to indicate, for authors writing in Latin, a political group bent on a disruptive and harmful *facere*. . . . the primary meaning conveyed by the Latin root is an idea of hubris, of excessive, ruthless, and thereby harmful behavior. . . .

> "Party" as well derives from Latin, from the verb partire, which means to divide. However, it does not enter in any significant way the vocabulary of politics until the seventeenth century—which implies that it does not enter the political discourse directly from Latin. . . . "Party" basically conveyed . . . the idea of part; and part is not, in and by itself, a derogatory term: It is an analytical construct. . . . The term enters the French *partager*, which means sharing, as it enters the English "partaking" (let alone partnership and participation). . . . When "part" becomes "party", we thus have a term subject to two opposite semantic pulls: the derivation from *partire*, to divide, on the one hand, and the association with taking part, and thereby sharing, on the other. The latter association is, in fact, stronger than the former derivation. (Sartori 1976, 3–4)

To paraphrase Sartori's argument on why parties and factions are distinct, parties are a necessity of a pluralistic political system; factions are not necessary, but simply exist. Factions are manifestations of disagreement and conflict based on self-interest; parties are means by which factions are unified and given voice.

> The difference is, then, that parties are instrumental to collective benefits, to an end that is not merely the private benefits of the contestants. Parties link people to a government, while factions do not. . . . In short,

parties are functional agencies—they serve purposes and fulfill roles—
while factions do not. (Sartori 1976, 25)

Sartori also identifies parties as "part of a whole" and "channels of
expression." He goes to great lengths to expand on Duverger's notion of
parties as parts of a pluralistic, democratic system. Sartori's emphasis on
"party systems" demonstrates a concern with the relation among parties in a
polity. Parties may consciously be shaped by their position as part of the
whole. Admittedly, Rousseau's notion of the "general will" is an amorphous
master for a party system to serve. Still, the competition among groups of
parties, representing collections and coalitions of factions and citizens'
groups, is the only means available in a democracy for preventing the ex-
cesses of pure faction.

For our purposes, the most important function of all for parties may be
"channels of expression." The platform of a particular party, and the understanding that citizens have of that party's likely actions if it takes office,
represent the success (or failure) of the party in representing citizens, and
groups of factions, by expressing their desires effectively and persuasively.
Parties have both a representative and an expressive function, in Sartori's
conception. But the representative function is difficult to uphold, particularly
in the absence of ideologies. In fact, if there were no need for ideologies,
there would be no need for parties at all as representative instruments. Representation could take place simply by individuals, or through direct democratic
decision making.

But ideologies are required, as a means of giving form and coherence to
the desires of citizens and factions alike, in the face of pervasive uncertainty,
lack of information, and difficulty of commitment. Consequently, Sartori
identifies (correctly, we believe) the primary function of parties to be expressive.

Above all, then, parties are expressive instruments performing an expressive function. The suggestion is conveyed, thereby, that parties can best
be conceived as means of communication—and perhaps under cyber-
netic auspices. . . . [But if] parties were nothing more—as instruments
of expression—than "transmitting information," then it would follow
that their time is bygone. Parties could well be replaced by opinion polls,
surveys, and—as technology already permits—by the citizens themselves sitting at their computer termininals and typing in, for machine-
processed auscultation, their political preferences and thoughts. However, parties provide for something that no poll or machine can supply:
They transmit demands backed by pressure. . . . The objection remains
that my reconstruction highlights only half the picture. Parties do not

only express; they also channel. In Neumann's wording, parties "organize the chaotic public will." They aggregate, select, deviate, and distort. . . . And the objection can be pushed further by asserting that more than expressing and reflecting public opinion parties shape, and indeed manipulate, opinion. . . . It may well be that people have no opinions of their own or that their opinions are largely formed by opinion makers. (Sartori 1976, 28–29; quote is from Sigmund Neumann 1956, 397)

In this chapter, we try to draw together a large number of disparate strands of thought, but most of what we want to say is aptly summarized in the quotation from Neumann: parties organize the chaotic public will. In the absence of parties, factions operate for their own self-interest, divorced from any coherent philosophy, or any practical political or ethical constraints. Dysfunctional democracy is rule by faction, or by the mob. This is not to say that dysfunctional democracy will not have parties. What it does mean is that parties that simply express the interests of faction or the inchoate rage of the mob are not, themselves, fully functioning parties. Sartori points out that "factionalism is the ever-present temptation of a party arrangement and its ever-possible degeneration" (Sartori 1976, 25).

In order to expand on both the definition of party and its place in a functioning and effective government, we now turn aside for a moment, to consider the origin of parties.

Origin

The classic account of the origin and development of parties is Duverger (1951). He lists three factors as means by which groups of individuals come together to form a party. The first is local or regional identification, as in the example cited earlier of the Jacobins and Girondins. Local groups that meet and find they share problems, and ideas about solutions, develop an ideology and a party to put this ideology into effect. The second is an already shared proto-ideology, a set of ideas that are beginning to coalesce into a true ideology. Duverger gives the example of numerous "parties" in the French Constituent Assembly of 1848 whose names derived from their meeting place:

There should be no confusion between such local groups and those whose name is derived from their meeting-place. . . . There were the groups of the Palais National, the Institut . . . the Rue de Poitiers . . . , the Rue de Castiglione and the Rue des Pyramides. . . . We have a very different phenomenon from that of the Breton club or the Girondin club. The deputies meet in the same place because they have ideas in common; instead of becoming aware of their community of ideas after meeting as a result of their common origins. This is an ideological group and not a local group, but the fact that the name is derived from the meeting-place shows that the doctrines are still too vague to be used to define the party. (Duverger 1951, xxv)

The third factor Duverger lists is the personal interest of the legislative or parliamentary members of the party.

Certain groups are more or less obviously parliamentary unions for common defence. The desire for re-election has naturally played a great part: it never completely disappears from parliamentary groups, even when they have reached maturity. Obviously, voting techniques which require a collective effort, for example voting by list and proportional representation, strengthen this tendency. . . . Hope of a ministerial post is also an important factor leading to the coagulation of parliamentary energies: several Centre groups in French Assemblies are nothing but coalitions of candidates for office (*ministrables*). (Duverger 1951, xxvi)

Regardless of the original impetus for the creation of a party (local identification, coincidence of proto-ideology, or entrepreneurial parliamentary organization), the actual establishment of what we formally identify as a party is more complex. Duverger claimed that in order for a party to exist, there must be an organized parliamentary (or legislative) group, and electoral committees with a mass orientation. Only when there is an explicit and routinized linkage between the activities of these sets of groups can it be said that a "party" exists.

Ideology, Party, and "Faction"

It is, by now, clear that ideologies can exist without parties (as in the example of the divine right of kings), and that parties can exist (in principle) without real ideologies. For example, in the 1992 Parliamentary elections in Great Britain, a party calling itself the "Monster Raving Loonies" advanced candidates for a number of seats. The aim of this party is anarchy (apparently; it is hard to find a spokesman who will take responsibility for the organization, or lack of one). Not surprisingly, the party had no program for accomplishing this (perhaps out of concern for doctrinal orthodoxy). Still, for the most part, and crucially, for our definition of party, there is some link between a party and a substantial conformity of opinion of its members about the correctness of its organizing ideology.

A crucial distinction, common in the political science literature but not yet addressed here, is the relation between parties and factions, or what are now more usually called "pressure groups." As is made clear by Key (1964), Duverger (1972), and a host of others since, the key distinctions are (1) the means by which parties and factions go about their business, (2) the base from which each draws its membership and resources, and (3) the goals of the respective organization.

Both parties and pressure groups want to influence government activity, but parties seek to influence government by actually operating its mechanisms and by controlling its actions directly. Pressure groups do not run candidates identified with the group, though the role of the group in choosing candidates who run under a party label may be significant. Neither do pressure groups have any direct role in organizing the legislature, though the organization of the legislature may facilitate service to pressure groups for the advantage of incumbent legislators or members of Parliament.

The source of membership and support for a party is mixed. Much of the membership is the mass public, though elite membership by owners of valuable resources, and money in particular, is crucial to a party's success. The motivation of members to commit their votes, time, and financial resources ranges from genuine commitment to the ideals of the party and its policies (even if not in the member's apparent self-interest) to the purest form of self-aggrandizement and rent seeking. The membership of pressure groups is drawn from those with a specific interest in the goal of the group. Pressure groups range from the purely economic (such as the National Association of Manufacturers, in the United States, or the *Union do Defense des Artisans et Commercants*, in France) to the purely ideological, such as groups who seek to outlaw (or guarantee) abortion rights.

Finally, parties present platforms that have an underlying, or even explicit, ideological source. The platform must have answers for the important policy questions facing the nation. Pressure groups focus on only a few, or even a single, issue. There need be no overarching set of ethical norms or ideas; pressure groups want what they want because they want it. Party ideologies represent a recounting of the shared ideas of a coalition of interests, but pressure groups focus on an interest or idea that may have no relation to any other policy.

MacRae (1970) recognized the complexity of differentiating between "issues" and "factions." In fact, his work was designed to measure and explain the relation between patterns of voting on issues and patterns of membership in parties.

To explain the division on a roll call, or to generalize about a number of similar divisions, we may look to the issues at stake or to the interrelations of the legislators grouped on each side. . . .

These two considerations, of issues and factions, are related. The effect of a bill may impinge directly on groups represented in the legislature—parties, factions, or their constituent interests. Conversely, *the very existence of parties or factions may depend on their having common ideological principles that relate the substance of bills to the group's existence and cohesion.* (MacRae 1970, 6; emphasis added)

Clearly, the definition of a pressure group is difficult and amorphous, and the relation between pressure groups, parties, and ideologies is complex. In later chapters, we will examine the role of interest groups in the political process; for now, it is worth quoting Duverger (1972) on the difficulty in distinguishing party and interest:

> If the concept of the political party is relatively precise, the definition of a pressure group is not. One can draw up an accurate list of political parties in any given country, but not of its pressure groups. All parties are in effect organizations specializing in political warfare, their political role being their primary or exclusive function. On the other hand, pressure groups fall into two categories: for some, the sole or primary purpose is to directly influence political power; others have an indirect and occasional influence on power, but their basic purpose and activity is essentially nonpolitical. Every association and every group can thus assume the character of a pressure group in some particular area to defend the interests it represents vis-à-vis the state. . . . (Duverger 1972, 2)

This short chapter has served to introduce the concept of the political party as we intend to use the term, and to distinguish it from two related concepts: ideology and pressure groups. In the following chapter, we will consider some empirical work on the measurement of ideology, and on the relation between parties and ideological positions.

CHAPTER 6

Theory and Evidence on Spatial Models of Ideology

So far, we have done two things in this book. First, we have identified some problems with the classical formal model of politics. There is an important positive interpretation to the flaws discussed above, of course. The "problems" represent the conceptual building blocks for a new and more complete theory of politics. Second, we have defined and distinguished two important concepts: ideology and party. In this chapter, we begin to bring together the concept of ideology and the fundamental formal model of political choices using ideology. The theory is based on the "predictive dimension" approach originated by Hinich and Pollard (1981), and later amplified by Enelow and Hinich (1984a, 1989c). This theory solves the problems that have stymied substantive interpretation of the classical spatial model, and satisfies the theoretical and empirical criteria for a successful model of representation established in chapter 2.

A formal theory of political choice based on ideology rests on a rejection of the traditional forms of representation, and looks, instead, to the mechanics by which citizens make decisions. One assumption that the theory emphatically *does not* reject is purposive behavior. Political information is costly, and the incentives to acquire information are attenuated by the properties of collective choice and public goods. In such an environment, citizens rationally choose particular cues in comparing policy alternatives. The theory of ideology is applicable primarily to elections (where mass groups vote for bundles of policies, typically candidates), rather than to committee voting (where a small, well-informed group votes on specific issues). Ideology is the basis for choice in large, mass electorates; party is the basis for choice in legislatures.

Because our emphasis is primarily on the theory of political choice by citizens, party is a "channel," or organizer of opinion, based on ideology, to use Sartori's conception. We will occasionally consider the role of parties, but the first, and most important, goal is to make explicit the functioning of ideologies, using parties as intermediaries. Ideology allows us to depict the decision process of citizens. The word *depict* is used here advisedly: beyond *representing preferences*, in the technical sense of economics, we give what

95

we believe to be an accurate picture of the *decision process* of citizens making collective decisions. Preferences explicitly underlie this process, as we will show, but our depiction of the decision process requires far less information than the orthodox approach. We assume citizen choice is made rationally. The context of the decision process includes uncertainty, costly information, and public goods. Rationality dictates a simpler approach than is assumed by the classical model, based on what is known about decision making. The next two sections present first the conceptual, and then the theoretical, justifications for using ideology as the key to understanding mass-level political choice.

Introduction

Promises by political candidates are notoriously unreliable, as guides for predicting the future. The candidate may simply be lying and have no intention of doing what he claims. Even if his expression of intent is sincere, no single actor in our complex political system can guarantee anything. Finally, the world is uncertain: what citizens want may change, or a new issue may arise that no one anticipated in the campaign. For all of these reasons, citizens can be expected to apply certain simplifying cues or organizing principles in making decisions. Only rarely are voters presented with a direct policy choice (such as a referendum on one issue).

Instead, citizens choose among candidates who represent packages, or bundles, of expected policies. These bundles derive from everything the voters know, or believe they know, about the candidates' reputation and appearance. They aid voters in making some prediction of the candidates' expected stands (policy), and how effectively they expect he will lead and deliver on his abstract promises of a better or fairer society (character or other nonpolicy characteristics).

If such bundles of projections of policies to be followed after the candidate takes office were randomly gathered from the actual policy space, this bundling would provide citizens with little information. They would somehow have to discover the policy positions of candidates on each dimension, and then choose the candidate closest to their own most-preferred set of policies. In fact, this is the way classical spatial theory envisioned the choice process. However, as Downs himself noted,

> In the real world, uncertainty and lack of information prevent even the most intelligent and well-informed voter from behaving in precisely the fashion we have described. Since he cannot be certain what his present utility income from government is, or what it would be if an opposition party were in power, he can only make estimates of both. . . . To decide what impact each government act has upon his income, he appraises it as

good or bad in the light of his own view of "the good society." (Downs 1957, 46)

How is such a view of the "good society" related to parties? The answer commonly given is that voters choose based on party identification, and this explanation is more or less powerful as voters are "strong" or "weak" identifiers. That is, a strong identifier always votes for his party, where there is a choice. The opposite extreme is a pure issue voter, whose affiliation with parties is purely accidental. Of course, we have argued earlier that the link between issues and satisfaction, in voters' minds, is based on ideology. Thus, strong identifiers accept the ideological position a party advances without further thought. An issue voter is not satisfied, or not persuaded, by any of the ideologies that viable parties are acting to channel.

As Sartori points out:

Issue voting and partisan identification are best conceived as the opposite ends of a continuum. If so, it is useful to have an in-between concept in which issues and identifications can blend, albeit in very different ways and proportions. Moreover, under the assumption that voters are identified, their way of linking to a given party is obvious; but how do the issue voters link to parties and select among the parties? On both counts we need at least another concept: *party image*. . . . Parties communicate to mass electorates via party images and . . . much of their electoral strategy is concerned with building up the appropriate image for the public from which they expect votes. . . . (Sartori, 1976, 329)

Matthews and Prothro (1966) point out that party "image" is very different from party identification. That is, voters may strongly identify with a party, in the sense that they always vote for its candidates, but their perception of the ideology that the party embraces may be quite inaccurate. More subtly, the emphases of the party and the focus of interest of the voter may differ sharply. The image of the party in one voter's mind may be the same, or very different, from the image other voters have (see, e.g., Searing, Schwartz, and Lind 1973; Conover and Feldman 1982).

Obviously, this leads to the question of whether it is (1) true, or (2) important, that individuals have widely shared perceptions or images of parties. From the perspective of explaining individual behavior, it may be sufficient to investigate the individual's perceptions, much as economists consider the individual's utility function. Kinder (1982) argued that the emphasis on ideology was misplaced and misleading, and that the key is individual perception. Conover and Feldman (1984, 1986) and Feldman and Conover (1983) take this approach to its logical conclusion, focusing on individual "schema" as the appropriate tool for understanding how citizens mentally organize their political environment. It is quite possible, Conover and Feldman claim, that "people can have very organized, but atomized, ways of viewing the political world" (Conover and Feldman 1982, 100).

Other work, as varied as Enelow and Hinich (1982) and Conover and Feldman (1989), has shown that, while party is an important "cue" for voter choice among candidates, there are other important political, and personal, aspects of the choice. These other factors complicate the old notion of "identification" as an exogenous explanatory variable. We are not prepared to debate the issue of individual versus shared schema, because our goal is not the prediction of individual behavior, but rather an explanation of the effectiveness of parties in creating images based on ideologies. For our purposes, the most interesting perspective is Sartori's:

> An image is—in my understanding—a vague policy package condensed in, and rendered by, one word or slogan. "Good for the workers" or, even better, "workers' party" is an image (*not an issue*). How does one select, then, a given party? If the answer is—as I suggest—via a party image, then *the question turns on how the image (not the identification) interplays with the issues.* Therefore, from the issue end of the process the question is: *How do issue preferences enter the image and eventually alter the identification?* . . . Issue identification, and image are thus the major concepts employed for understanding why voters vote as they do? *How do these concepts relate to the Downsian model of spatial competition?* (Sartori 1976, 328–30; emphasis added)

Sartori has identified the important aspects of ideology, as it links issues in the minds of voters to the images that those voters have of the parties. His question about how these notions relate to Downs's model are answered in the remainder of this chapter.

The spatial theory of ideology provides a mechanism for making explicit the reasons for the systematic bundling of alternatives. It formalizes Downs's intuition that "ideology" is an internally consistent set of principles that inform this "good society." The value of an ideology, for a candidate or party, is to provide a cue about how the candidate solves complicated problems. Ideology is the organizing principle for how the candidate thinks, implying internally consistent predictions or forecasts about the explicit bundle of policies he will choose.

It is quite true that, as Downs believed, an ideology is partly a means of economizing on the cost of gathering information for voters. A position on an ideological dimension (e.g., "liberal Democrat") yields predictions of positions on a variety of issues (pro-choice, against aid to the Nicaraguan Contras, for increased aid to the homeless, etc.). Not all of these predictions may be correct, but the ideology provides a shorthand for expressing complex information. Clearly, if the ideological position of a candidate does not fulfill this function, leading to many incorrect predictions, voters must revert to judging candidates by their policy positions, issue by issue. Such an ideological position is, then, of little value.

Ideologies yield predictions that, on average, satisfy citizens making uncertain political choices. Otherwise, we would not see candidates for office, and the parties that back them, investing such enormous amounts of energy and financial resources into ideological reputations. This investment in ideology as an asset, or brand name, suggests that ideological reputations can be thought of as cues. The cues serve as signals to voters about how certain types of outcomes are related to the choices that they and others make. Such cues must work at two levels: First, the signals must be simple enough, and clear enough, to make voters understand what is being said. Second, the signals themselves must be credible, and therefore believed, by voters.

The empirical literature in political psychology has repeatedly shown that voters do use simple cues (Brady and Sniderman 1985; Conover and Feldman 1984, 1986, 1989; and Sniderman, Brady, and Tetlock 1991). There is some question in this literature concerning (a) whether these cues are related to the policies voters are supposed to care about, and (b) whether there is any consistency across voters in the cues that are taken to be meaningful. Obviously, the first point is difficult to measure without exact information on voters' true preferences. If, regarding the second point, there is no consistency across voters, there would be no coherence, or even value, in macro-level ideological messages or reputations. Our assumption, consistent with the empirical work discussed in the following chapter, is that ideological messages may be diffuse, and that this diffuseness may change over time. On average, however, voters do have at least similar understandings of the content, and meaning, of cues.

The second major point, on the credibility of the signals, has to do with equilibrium. That is, a cue or message will have value as a signal only if, on average, it means what voters think it means. This literature (reviewed thoroughly in Banks 1991)[1] is quite technical, and the results, themselves, are not thoroughly worked out. Ultimately, the equilibrium approach will demonstrate the conditions under which particular kinds of ideological messages are

---

1. The most important recent papers include Banks (1990), Banks and Sobel (1987), Calvert (1985), Grofman and Norrander (1990), and Lupia (1992). Much of the foundation of this work is derived from the seminal model of Crawford and Sobel (1982).

effective, and have values as signals, in the technical sense. At a minimum, this work has shown that the classical spatial conception of announcing policy positions is a poor model of real-world politics.

We have argued that ideology is a means of creating coherent and meaningful cues to aid voter choice, and that the form of these cues is consistent with the assumption of purposive behavior by both voters and candidates. It is important to emphasize, however, that ideologies are more than just coherent cues; there is more to the value of ideology than its utility in forecasting policy. A truly successful ideology must persuade—must *influence*—voters' perception of the good society. As a practical matter, the models presented below focus on ideology as the means of linking a "predictive" space (whose units and form we discuss in the next section) to the policy space. This makes no sense unless we also consider ideology's intellectual and emotional persuasive capacity. There is little information, or political advantage, in associating a position on an ideological dimension (say, conservative Republican) with a slate of policy positions (more aid to the Contras, banning abortion, deregulating financial markets, etc.) *if that correspondence had to be memorized.*

But it doesn't! It can be inferred from a simple ideology. For example, if we know conservative Republicans believe "the government governs best that governs least," we can reasonably infer that such officials will oppose intrusions or aggressions by socialist or communist foreign governments, support reduced government intervention, and so on. There are problems with this inferential correspondence, of course (conservative opposition to abortion, pornography, or civil liberties increases, not reduces, government intervention), because ideologies are rarely fully specified by a single aphorism. Further, aspects of an ideology may contradict one another (though such an ideology is inherently weaker than one where this is not true).

Finally, as asserted above, an ideology allows citizens to forecast a candidate's position on novel issues, or to predict actions in the abstract when the possible issues are unknown, part of a dimly perceived and irreducibly uncertain future. Voters with access to information about ideology have at least some idea of how the candidate approaches new problems. Much as Kreps (1990) argues that corporate culture provides an "organizing principle" to solve the combined problems of hierarchy and uncertainty, ideology provides voters with some means of comparing candidates and parties. A candidate cannot, after all, make credible promises on how he will react to unforeseen exigencies of politics in the future. A strongly stated ideology conveys to voters (at least to those who share that view of the good society) that the candidate will react much as they themselves would.[2] Were the ideology-

---

2. This is exactly the sense of Edmund Burke's "Trustee." In an unpublished poem, Duncan MacRae writes:

policy correspondence but a memorized cost-saving device, it would be impossible to forecast positions on new issues. To believe a candidate is a liberal Democrat would mean no more than a projection of a slate of issues known by prior association. Such a correspondence has only an expressive, or linguistic, economy, rather than a true informational advantage.[3]

An actual ideology implies, by contrast, a complete worldview that allows predictions about future actions, based on the pattern of response implied by experience with the ideology in the past.[4] Suppose, for example, that an inexpensive overnight innovation in the technology of space travel gave private firms the capacity to mine gold and silver ore on the moon. Imagine further that such mining causes significant pollution of the moon's surface, making it useless for human habitation because of the associated hazardous waste products. We might infer a correspondence between a particular ideology and a position on the moon-mining issue from comparing positions on other, similar issues (Alaskan north slope oil drilling, clear-cut lumbering in national parks, etc.). But even without such a comparison, inferences can be made from the perceived ideological positions of the parties or candidates, based on their abstract support for government intervention in the economy.

To summarize, citizens use the ideological positions of candidates in two ways. The first is as a cue, a predictor of the positions of the candidate once he takes office, based on the particular correspondence or mapping between ideology and policy. The second is more abstract, and more important: citizens judge candidates by the agreement or disagreement between their own

---

Said the Honorable Edmund Burke:
"An MP is more than a clerk.
If I seem a neglector
Of some Bristol elector,
It cannot be said that I shirk!"

3. For example, in a football huddle, the quarterback calls plays in a shorthand language, such as "Dive, 34, strong right." These words tell the "3" back to take a handoff through the "4" hole, tell the linemen to block in a pattern that will open the "4" hole, and tell the wide recievers on which side they should line up. All this requires memorization by the whole team of the list of plays. But the correspondence is simply linguistic, and cannot be carried beyond the particular play being called. An ideology is a more complex correspondence because it tells the listener *both* what a party will do in specific, known instances (given the listener's memorized experience with the party's statements and the actions that have followed) as well as what the party *might* do in an unexpected and undiscussed circumstance.

4. Patrick Henry, in a speech before a Virginia Convention in Richmond, March 23, 1775, said:

I have but one lamp by which my feet are guided, and that is the lamp of experience. I know no way of judging of the future but by the past. . . . The duty which we owe to our Creator, and the manner of discharging it, can be directed only by reason and conviction. . . .

view of the "good society" and that embodied in the candidates' attempts at making clear their ideological positions. The reason the second role of ideology is the more important is that it encompasses the first. An ideology could connote a simple linguistic shorthand, such as "'conservative Democrat' is observed to correlate with the vector $\omega_{conservative\ Democrat} = [\omega_1, \ldots, \omega_m]$." But an ideology can also *imply* certain positions. Citizens can do more than think: "candidates who have adopted the label conservative Democrats have tended to act as follows, though I don't know why." Instead, they believe: "conservative Democrats act as follows because being a conservative Democrat implies that they must act that way or contradict their worldview." This apparent implication may be proven wrong by the candidate's subsequent actions, but ideology is the organizing principle (technically, the "space") in which elections are won or lost.

Our view of ideology as an internally consistent set of organizing principles that imply a particular correspondence with good policy gives citizens a clear informational advantage in choosing among candidates. The question that remains unanswered is how might a candidate credibly commit himself to a particular ideology? We are less concerned with candidates' than with citizens' beliefs. The critical thing is that citizens believe the candidate has some reason to heed the ideological principles he endorses. In the next two sections, we will examine, first, the meaning of the ideological dimension and then the question of acquiring and maintaining an ideology.

The Spatial Theory of Ideology

The fundamental challenge to the development of a scientifically valid theory of electoral competition in a democratic society is to link the perceptions and preferences of voters on political factors that they care about with the actions of candidates before, during, and after an election. Democracy is supposed to allow the electorate to affect the outcomes of the political process by choosing the candidate or party most voters want. Yet, voters may not understand, or care about, any one set of issues. Further, voters who do care may perceive no connection between expressing their preferences and the final political outcomes, no matter what majorities may do. In such a system, there is no justification in democratic theory for the legitimacy of the political actions of the winning candidates.

As we have discussed at length earlier, the first attempt at a comprehensive statement of the linkage between voter perceptions and preferences, and electoral outcomes in a majority rule system was made by Downs (1957). Downs postulated a single ideological dimension on which parties chose positions. His theory of an ideological dimension rested on the observation that voters are poorly informed about issues in an election, and that parties have to develop a credible reputation among such partially informed voters. Downs claims to deduce, but in truth only postulates, that parties invest resources to develop an ideological position that voters understand and use to make political choices. He also makes the important intuitive leap to the conclusion that the feasible ideological positions can be portrayed as points on a left-right ideological dimension. He gives no empirical support for such an assertion, nor does he provide any plausible model for the linkage between political issues and the ideological positions parties adopt on the dimension.

The new theory of political ideological competition we build is *not* limited to one dimension. There may be several ideological dimensions; the number is an empirical question, one that is subject to statistical measurement. The basic theoretical assumption is that the positions of candidates and parties in the ideological space are unobservable, in terms of sensible units. Ideological dimensions function as *latent* factors of political competition, where the connection between issues and dimensions is given by a linear model.

Downs's emphasis on an explicit, rather than a latent, dimension has caused unnecessary confusion, and has led some important scholars to reject the notion of a spatial theory of ideology. An important example is Sartori (1976). Others (Stokes 1963; Converse 1966) have confronted the "Downsian" model of party competition with empirical evidence based on voter perceptions of issues, and *rejected the theory because its implications for issue voting have been falsified*. It is now established, we hope, that "issue voting" is not the Downsian model, at all.[5] In fact, Downs recognized the problem, as was pointed out in chapter 4, and these criticisms are better directed at the "Downsian" model than at Downs himself.

As noted above, Sartori (1976) takes the Downsian project very seriously, though he ultimately rejects it. Sartori recognizes the problem Downs faced; in discussing Downs's spatial theory that relies on ideology, Sartori says:

> One immediately senses, here, the difficulties that Downs creates for himself in order to be consistent with his premises. Ideologies are difficult to enter, and especially to rationalize, on grounds of economic rationality. . . . Downs actually lays the emphasis [in this rationalization] on 'uncertainty,' which is his major intervening variable; and the general thrust of his argument is that with regard to parties ideologies accrue to their distinctiveness, whereas with regard to voters ideologies

---

5. Sartori calls this the "third reading" of Downs, which "neglects the premises . . . does not seek a more formalized model, and tests the spatial model of party competition against evidence or voting behavior" (1976, 324).

are 'short cuts' that save them the cost of becoming informed. (Sartori 1976, 325)

Sartori is close, but not quite correct. As we noted in chapter 1, Downs does not succeed in linking policy and ideology, because he confuses two contradictory forces on parties. The first is the desire to win, and the consequent need to locate in the middle of the distribution of voter preferences. This function of ideologies is clearly analogous to the theory of "cues." The second aspect is the ability to commit, credibly, to a course of action. Sartori's "distinctiveness" is right, as far as it goes, but at least as important is persuasive and credible commitment.

Downs ties voter policy forecasts to an explicit left-right economic dimension. He never clearly defines the units of the dimension in this space, or what the exact linkages to policy look like. Worse, Downs asserts that there is only a single dimension, though the number of dimensions of relevance to an ideology is not derivable from theory. To serve Downs's goal of simplifying reality and economizing information costs, the number of dimensions should be small (one? two? three?), and the "units" of the dimension should have to do with issues of interest to voters, not just economic policy.

This is the fundamental problem facing the formal political theorist. The units of the space, and its dimensionality, *are not theoretically derivable*. The dimensions are, at best, empirically recoverable, using regression analysis or factor analysis. Sartori's criticisms of Downs, or better, of the Downsian model, are cogent. In fact, they are fatal. Sartori recognized long ago the problems of an explicitly defined, unidimensional space in which parties, or teams of "vote maximizers," choose locations. We claim that it is possible to construct a spatial theory of ideology, and of political competition, that does not suffer these flaws. This theory retains the presumption of purposive behavior, but executes this presumption in a way that does less damage either to logic or to reality.

The Downsian conception of ideology is the classical left-right economic dimension: the extent of intervention by government in the economy advocated by a party (candidate). In principle, possible positions are uniformly distributed along this explicit dimension, ranging in figure 8 from 100 percent government ownership and control of the means of production (the left, or socialist, position), through market socialism and welfare capitalism, to 0 percent (pure private control, the extreme right, or conservative libertarian, position). In fact, however, positions on the dimension must be restricted. Rather than being free to choose any position, the candidate must choose the position that accords with his ideology. If one asserts, in public utterances, the belief that markets are cruel to the little guy, and that government intervention is the only mechanism for controlling the market and achieving a just society,

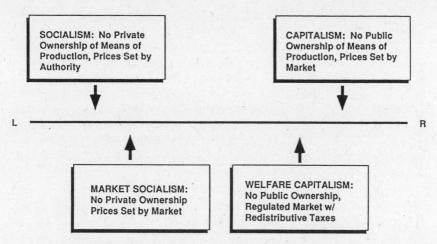

Fig. 8. Classical left-right economic dimension, or the extent of government control

a position on the extreme right of Downs's dimension will not do. A "position" is, itself, the sum of all previous public utterances, so that the full mobility of a candidate in a policy space, assumed by spatial theory, is not a useful description of political reality. Further, not all positions are possible, because of the paucity of coherent ideologies.

We must reject Downs's notion of the dimension along which ideological warfare is conducted for another reason as well. Although it has the advantage of being widely used and intuitively clear in meaning, it imposes unnecessary and unrealistic structure and information requirements on citizen decision making. The ideological dimension is *latent*, not explicit. In other words, its relation to policy can be recovered empirically, and even given units, but these units will be arbitrary and idiosyncratic. The meaning, given the dimension, is the result of sophisticated strategic choices by political combatants seeking to influence the public's perceptions. As Sartori avers, "The labels liberal and conservative, progressive and reactionary, left and right, typically exemplify the images for which parties maneuver and outmaneuver each other" (Sartori 1976, 329).

Yet, candidates are severely restricted in their mobility along (or around) this predictive space, because only *credible* ideological commitments have political meaning and, hence, electoral value. This approach represents a radical departure from classical spatial theory. It is more complex and far harder to understand, but it more accurately represents the chaotic uncertainty and severely attenuated information with which real political decisions are made. The value of using the predictive dimension approach ultimately hinges on its capacity to generate predictions different from the simpler classical approach, and its greater descriptive realism.

What does it mean to claim that the predictive dimension is "latent?" In formal statistical terms, latency means that the dimension and its units are not imposed by the analyst, but are recovered from, or dictated by, the data themselves. The statistical procedure of factor analysis straightforwardly recovers the dimension(s) that inform citizen decision making (Enelow and Hinich 1984a, 1984b, 1987, 1989a, 1989b; Enelow 1986; Enelow, Hinich, and Mendell 1986; and Enelow, Mendell, and Ramesh 1989). This procedure will be discussed in chapter 7. For now, it suffices to say that the latency of the predictive dimension is a result of allowing a statistical procedure to determine what the dimension is. The important thing is that we begin the definition, up to the technological limitations of the science of statistical inference, by measuring precisely what citizens themselves exhibit interest in.[6]

Strategy, Natural Selection, and Constrained Legitimacy

This approach allows a much more dynamic and structurally unfettered view of politics as an unpredictable and highly strategic process of adjustment and response. It is, in some ways, analogous to Riker's "heresthetics" (Riker 1958a, 1958b, 1963), a kind of strategically driven natural selection in the set of issues that inform political debate. In describing the political strategies of the then out-of-power Whigs (later Republicans), leading up to the U.S. Civil War, Riker illustrates this dynamic process.

> The particular event studied here involves losers introducing new issues in the hopes of creating cycles and disequilibrium, from which they may emerge as winners. Here the losers were ultimately successful: they did produce disequilibrium, and they did reshape American politics. . . . I want to emphasize, however, that this particular outcome was not entirely due to the wit and persistence of the losers. The outcome of efforts at manipulation is also conditioned by the external circumstances in which the manipulation occurs, the underlying values, the constitutional structure, and the state of technology and the economy. Numerous efforts are made at manipulation. Not all succeed. The choice of which ones do succeed is partially determined by these external circumstances. This is the significance of the process of natural selection. (Riker 1982, 213)

6. There is considerable literature on the relation between issues and the "space" of political discourse. For earlier attempts at measurement, see Converse (1964, 1966), MacRae (1970), Poole (1981), and Rabinowitz (1974, 1978).

We assert a more general kind of natural selection, where one ideology competes with and seeks to replace another. Riker's version has one issue (or set of issues) rising to public attention because of the constant attempts of citizens outside the winning coalition to reverse that state of affairs by splitting those groups currently comprising the winning coalition.[7] This effort may fail, and the issue return to its previous unremarked anonymity, or (more rarely and unpredictably) catch on and become the cause of a political realignment. Ideologies, like issues, arise for a variety of reasons, and are shaped by the prevailing political and economic climate. "Success," defined as prominence and longevity, will be decided by the extent to which one or another party seizes on the ideology. Ideologies serve the crucial function of legitimizing and giving moral force to arrangements of political and economic property rights whose true origin may lie in tradition, historical accident, murder, theft, or enlightened benevolence. Once accepted, and once an ideology becomes a part of a party's identity, in the minds of the voters, it takes on a life of its own. Parties depend on their perceived commitment to an internally consistent set of organizing principles for their political lives. But this ideology also severely circumscribes the party's ability to maneuver for competitive advantage. Worse, the ideology itself may become emotionally empty and logically inapplicable to the policy problems of the day. A party in power that substantially and consistently contradicts the policy implications of its ideology is forced to either form a dictatorship (and, in the extreme, fall to revolution) or lose in a democratic context.

We are hardly the first to remark on this aspect of ideology as a force that simultaneously legitimizes and constrains a ruler. This idea is advanced at length by Plato, Machiavelli, Adam Smith, and Karl Marx.[8] North (1981) notes the important role of ideology in organizing economic and political life, and presents a concise characterization of our sense of ideology.

It is important to stress three aspects of ideology.
1. Ideology is an economizing device by which individuals come to

---

7. The criticism of Riker's theory may be a bit overstated, because the logic of the transformation from one ideological "system" to another is precisely consistent with the example he gives. The point is that a new "issue," if it is to succeed in producing a realignment, must actually represent a new dimension in the *ideological space*. In this sense it is more than a new issue; it is an issue that the existing ideological cleavage cannot handle or explain.

8. On the importance of preserving the present order, regardless of its flaws, the most Machiavellian statement is, not surprisingly, that of Machiavelli:

Many have imagined republics and principalities which have never been seen or known to exist in reality; for how we live is so far removed from how we ought to live, that he who abandons what is done for what ought to be done, will rather bring about his own ruin than his preservation. (*The Prince*, 1532, 15)

terms with their environment and are provided with a "world-view" so that the decision-making process is simplified.

2. Ideology is inextricably interwoven with moral and ethical judgments about the fairness of the world the individual perceives. This situation clearly implies a notion of possible alternatives—competing rationalizations or ideologies. A normative judgment of the "proper" distribution of income is an important part of an ideology.

3. Individuals alter their ideological perspectives when their experiences are inconsistent with their ideology. In effect, they attempt to develop a new set of rationalizations that are a better "fit" with their experiences. . . . Inconsistencies between experience and ideology must accumulate before individuals alter their ideology. (North 1981, 49)

North uses ideology to describe individual preferences, but his description accords well with our notion of ideologies in the abstract. If asked to classify his ideological position, a citizen's willingness to take the label "liberal," "conservative," or such depends on his perception of the logical (not just empirical) correspondence between that ideology and his own preferences. North uses ideology to describe what he calls "noneconomic" preferences, but we find this distinction too restrictive and of little use. Better to remain agnostic on the question of whether citizens themselves possess purely ideological preferences, since ideology is so often used as a justification.[9] Surely the uses of an ideology as a shorthand and as a mechanism of persuasion show its importance in political discourse. If, in addition, it appeals to purely ideological (i.e., noneconomic, in North's sense) preferences in citizens, so much the better.

In a different context, Schofield (1985) emphasizes the importance of communication or, better, community, in solving problems of collective action. Schofield seeks to integrate several lines of research and to explore the implications of this work for the possibilities of collective action.[10]

The fundamental theoretical problem underlying the question of cooperation is the manner by which individuals attain knowledge of each other's preferences and likely behavior. Moreover, the problem is one of common knowledge, since each individual, i, is required not only to have information about others' preferences, but also to know that the others

---

9. It is common, in the economics literature on voting, to distinguish "self-interested" and "ideological" voting. This distinction has no merit here, because ideology is a primary cause, not a residual explanation.

10. Since Schofield's piece is in fact a review of the literature, we will not try to review this work here. The clearest antecedents to these conclusions are Hardin (1971, 1982), Margolis (1982), Olson (1965), Schofield (1975), and Taylor (1976, 1982).

have knowledge about i's own preferences and strategies. (Schofield 1985, 218)

The question is how this common knowledge is achieved. A simple paraphrasing of his thesis might be that community requires credible communication. Communication is clearly not sufficient for the existence of community, however, though it is quite likely necessary. If the focus of inquiry is expanded to include the origin of community, rather than just its existence, communication about the beliefs and norms that are to be shared is of paramount importance. Given this definition of community, we can conclude that the common knowledge requirement for cooperation may be satisfied in small groups. Taylor's thesis is that societies, as a consequence, will break into small groups, the size of which will be (optimally) determined by the largest "community" that can be achieved and maintained.

Schofield is less willing to conclude that only through community can cooperation be achieved. If it is *only* through community that the common knowledge basis of cooperation can be achieved, then the state, which seeks to replace community and voluntary action with hierarchy and coercion, is the enemy of community, altruism, and cooperation. The concentration of force that, by definition, the state represents both (1) reduces the need for trust among individuals who share common knowledge and (2) reduces the possibility of achieving trust and collective goals.

In short, Taylor's argument is that community is necessary and sufficient for cooperation. Schofield answers that it is sufficient, but that more work needs to be done before we can conclude that it is necessary. How can we be certain that there is no other means of achieving the level of common knowledge required for some kind of cooperation? And just what is that level?

Schofield concludes with a provocative and important observation:

> In the restricted context of a community, Taylor's argument makes good sense: social norms will be well understood and will provide the basis for common knowledge, and this knowledge will be maintained by mechanisms designed to make acts intelligible. In more general social situations, however, individuals will be less able to make reasonable guesses about other individuals' beliefs. (Schofield 1985, 219)

There may be disagreements within communities; the definition does not require unanimity. What is required is trust and shared understanding. Revolutions and realignments destroy the existing community, and require the development of new trust, new bases for shared understandings.

Returning to the analogy to Riker's heresthetics, a successful ideology, simultaneously legitimizing and constraining the majority coalition, will generally be expected to create an opposing ideology. The process works as follows. A revolution or political realignment destroys the previous balance of coalitions and makes the old ideological correspondences in citizens' minds obsolete. The new majority coalition seeks to promulgate a new ideology, or adapt an old one, to justify and perpetuate its possession of power. Those outside the majority coalition seek an alternative, more persuasive ideology that will bring the majority coalition down. As Duverger points out:

> Throughout history, all the great factional conflicts have been dualist. . . . Whenever public opinion is squarely faced with great fundamental problems it tends to crystallize round two opposed poles. The natural movement of societies tends towards the two-party system. . . . (Duverger 1951, 216)

Riker's focus on issues is ultimately correct, but misses the intermediate step: before a new issue can split the ruling coalition, citizens must be persuaded by an alternate ideology that the ideological claims for the legitimacy of the status quo are groundless. Over time, the two (or more) competing worldviews grow in complexity and become established as competing political and scholarly orthodoxies. Ultimately, the debate will be along the "best" position on a well-defined dimension, where best can be defined as an elaborate social and moral optimum.

It is worth emphasizing that this superstructure of orthodox ideology and heterodox, or counter, ideology may grow out of the simple difference between whether one is a member of the ruling coalition or not: are you an "In" or an "Out?"[11] Once established, however, the two ideologies take on separate lives of their own, influencing policy and informing the dimension(s) of political competition. We will not further address the question of how an ideological dimension is created, but turn now to a description of how particular candidates become credibly associated with positions along the dimension.

Positions Along the Predictive Dimension: Born To, or Thrust Upon?

If a particular candidate's avowed ideology is to provide some electoral advantage, it must be credible. Ultimately, it should not matter whether the candidate genuinely believes the ideological position he avers, if (1) he does it in a way indistinguishable from truth, and (2) he is consistent. Electoral

---

11. North describes a "counter ideology" as follows:

If the dominant ideology is designed to get people to conceive of justice as coextensive with the existing rules and, accordingly, to obey them out of a sense of morality, the objective of a successful counter ideology is to convince people not only that the observed injustices are

fortunes depend on the maintenance of an ideological reputation. Once that reputation is established, it binds him just as securely as if it were a strongly held conviction and he could act no other way, out of principle.[12]

Many politicians do, of course, have genuine beliefs about what good public policy is, separate from what constituents want or what the legislator believes they want. Edmund Burke (1880) clearly believed that this "trustee" form of representation, where the politician pursues the good implied by his political beliefs, was not just the right, but the duty, of the elected official. Our point is that voters prefer such an approach: a logically and temporally consistent ideology is an overwhelming electoral asset for a politician. One might believe (with Dougan and Munger 1989) that legislators adopt an ideology of expedience and become tied to it of necessity, or (with Edmund Burke, and research by Wittman 1973, 1983; and Lott 1986, 1987a, 1987b, 1989) that ideology is the very reason individuals choose to become politicians in the first place. In either case, ideology is the key to understanding and organizing political discourse. We need to understand, and represent, ideology before we can proceed to a complete spatial model of legislator, interest group, and voter interaction.

Ideology, "Issues" in Policy, and the Linkages between Them

In this section, we develop the theory of ideology, as it relates to policy. Before we can usefully begin, however, we must make clear what we mean by "issues" in the policy space. The difficulty is that "issues" has a cluster of meanings, many of which are outside of the definition we intend. Our definition of issues in the policy space is as follows:

> Issues. *Social problems large numbers of citizens care about that (1) politicians talk about (a) in public, (b) to contributors, or (c) among themselves, OR (2) the press talks about, either because some interest wants it discussed or because citizens care about it.*

---

an inherent part of the existing system but also that a just system can come about only by active participation of individuals to alter the system. Successful counter ideologies must not only provide a convincing image of the link between the specific injustices perceived by various groups and the larger system which the intellectual entrepreneurs desire altered, but also offer a Utopia free of these injustices and provide a guide to action. . . . (North 1981, 54)

12. Dougan and Munger (1989) note the irrelevance of the *actual* belief of the candidate, since the competitive forces of electoral competition prevent the liar from admitting the lie. This distinction is much less applicable for followers of the candidate and adherents of the ideology, of course. The free rider problem in mass movements can be overcome only through *genuine* belief by the masses.

Several things follow immediately from this definition. First, if many citizens care about some social problem, but neither the press nor politicians discuss it, it is not an "issue." This rules out much of the use of the word *issue* in political science, where it is almost axiomatic that campaigns are not "on the issues." We are not interested in what scholars think citizens *should* care about, and politicians *should* talk about.

Second, issues are not social problems that Congress votes on.[13] By the time the legislature votes on a bill, the set of alternatives is highly constrained. The form of the bill is the product of a strategic amendment process, where the use of language is dictated by compromise. Some issues will have bills associated with them, but bills may have subjects other than issues, and issues may be highly salient without an associated bill. Third, the number and intensity of issues in the policy space is highly variable, and is likely to differ from campaign to campaign.

The obvious question is this: How does a problem become an issue? The answer is that someone starts to pay attention to it. Obviously, those who oppose the creation of an issue are those who favor the status quo; those who want to make an issue of a problem seek to overturn the status quo. There are two contests between those who want a problem to become an issue and those who do not. The first contest is whether the problem gains enough salience to become an issue. We constantly see editorials, and political party platforms, identifying social problems in a way that invites public response. Unless there is some response or interest, no action by the defenders of the status quo is required.

If the problem becomes an issue, we move to the second contest: the contest over language. The two sides in the dispute (now an issue) seek to use their language to describe the problem. Success in using the "right" language often guarantees the "right" solution, from the perspective of the disputants. For example, imagine that the social problem is that prisons are overcrowded, so that there are more prisoners than beds in correctional facilities. This situation is not necessarily an issue, and, in fact, exactly this situation has

---

13. Not that this is not a fair definition, for some purposes. MacRae (1970) defines "issues" in roll call voting studies in legislatures as follows:

> We define an issue as a characteristic that distinguishes certain role calls from others in terms of their substance or content. Thus if we say that certain roll calls involve foreign policy and others domestic policy, we have separated them according to two issue categories. Such categories may be more or less specific: within domestic policy we might speak, for example, of agricultural and tax policy. . . . As the definition implies, it is the substance of the bill or motion at hand that must provide the basis of the classification. (11–12)

He notes that behind this definition are "extensive processes of opinion and attitude formation . . . " (11–12). For the general public, and for our purposes, these "processes of opinion and attitude formation" are obviously more important.

existed in many places in the United States for years. A precipitating event, such as a court order dictating the release of felons for whom there is no room, may transform the problem into an issue when it is reported in the press or seized on by candidates from the party out of power.

The party in power, which would have preferred that the problem not become an issue, has already lost the first contest. But they can now fight the second contest by characterizing the problem in terms they prefer. Let us call this group the "Republicans," and assume that they have an ideology whose form we will leave unspecified. The statement of the issue they choose is: "Yes, prisons are overcrowded, and the reasons are two: (1) Prisons are too small; (2) Law enforcement is too lax, so that too many people commit crimes. The solution is to double spending on prisons and police enforcement." The party out of power (call them the "Democrats") might characterize the issue quite differently: "Yes, prisons are overcrowded, and the reasons are two: (1) Too much money is being spent on punishment, rather than rehabilitation; (2) There is too much spent on law enforcement, rather than poverty programs. The solution is to cut spending on prisons and enforcement, and increase spending on job-training and welfare programs."

The problem this example creates in identifying the "issue" is obvious. Are we to call the issue here prison overcrowding, or poverty? Is it a law enforcement problem, or a social services problem? The answer is that it depends on who wins the battle to have the issue perceived in a light favorable to their most preferred solution. In a world where ideology presents the menu of choice, the "issues" are decided by the ideologies of the competing factions.

The "Republican" ideology might be simple: "Government's primary task is to maintain law and order." The "Democratic" ideology, by contrast, might be "government should help people who cannot help themselves." Although the correspondence between the simple ideological principles and the policy choices on the issue of prisons is clear, it is not clear which came first. In fact, the correspondence between ideologies and issues is complex, and is created and maintained simultaneously. The model we outline in the next section is designed to take account of this complexity in the most parsimonious fashion possible.

We claim that citizens make choices, based on their own preferences. These preferences are expressed in ways that tend to group together, so that the choices can be described by a space (ideology) of much lower dimensionality than the policy space of "issues." The reason is that political entrepreneurs act to persuade citizens whose preferences tend toward the ideology the entrepreneur seeks to advance. The essence of this political competition, and the basis of group action, is the competition to establish, in citizens' minds, linkages between the things people care about and participation in the group activity, as Olson suggested. Schofield's insight about the importance of community is a key point, because it means that trust and group action can be achieved if a form of common knowledge can be created among people of like ideological beliefs.

The contest then becomes a fight over the use of symbols and language that determine how citizens understand, and therefore choose among, policies. This contest is difficult, because there are shared understandings of symbols and language that are cultural and historical, and consequently do not allow for change or manipulation. This is particularly true because of the skepticism with which citizens have learned to view political promises. A use of a powerful symbol that is perceived to be manipulative reduces the linkage the candidate tries to create. Two well-known examples in the 1988 U.S. presidential campaign were Bush's visit to a flag factory (intended to show patriotism), and Dukakis's ride in a tank (intended to show God-knows-what). Both attempts at symbolic linkages to policy issues largely failed, and simply made voters more cynical about the credibility of the candidates.

The linkage of ideology to issues is the largest arena for political competition, contested by whole parties, rather than single candidates. Linkages relate ideological positions to things people care about. Linkages are not under the control of candidates, except for very slight changes. Linkages in voters' minds are idiosyncratic, and result from both experience and intellectual association. Each voter has heard political promises in the past, and has experience with what those promises mean, depending on which party or candidate makes the promise. Further, each voter has an intellectual understanding of the meaning of the symbolic representation that the candidate is attempting to make.[14] Checks on the linkage a citizen perceives between policy and ideology take two forms: (1) Does experience tell him that a promise is not going to be kept? (2) Do intellect and reason tell him that a promise is impossible to keep?

In sum, linkages are based in both experience and intellect, in retrospective evaluation and the thought of the citizen about the appropriate moral and ethical stance on issues. Linkages are the summary of a political culture, or a party system, in the classical phrase of Key, Burnham, and Sartori. Changes in the linkage between an ideology and issues represent a fundamental realignment of the political system. We will assume, in what follows, that politicians in any given election take these linkages as parametric, or given, and beyond their control to manipulate.

---

14. As we noted earlier, in the limit, individual "schema" may share almost nothing, as Conover and Feldman (1984) suggest. In this case, our conception of ideology simply would not exist.

A Spatial Model

Hinich and Pollard (1981), and Enelow and Hinich (1984a, 1987, 1989a) have developed a theoretical representation of the linkage between ideology and issues that is useful for our purposes. We adapt it in this section as the fundamental means of representing preferences, in the technical sense of chapter 2. Let us emphasize at the outset two factors important for this representation: (1) We make no claim that voters choose "as if" they use the predictive dimension. Rather, we make the stronger (and more easily tested) claim that this is *precisely* the way citizens choose. The predictive dimension approach allows us to *predict* voter choice, because it represents their preferences, but it also *explains* political discourse, because we directly build in the organizing principles that inform and direct the policy process. (2) The relevant dimension is not generally the "classical" Downsian left-right economic dimension.[15] It is, instead, the latent split or set of issues that divide groups at any particular time. This dimension can originate from one or several causes, ranging from strategic choice by a sophisticated political actor (analogous to Riker's heresthetics) to tradition or complex historical accident. In a statistical sense, this requires that the predictive dimension(s) be recovered through factor analysis, as we will discuss in the next chapter. For purposes of theory, however, we need only describe the mapping of candidate/ideological positions along the predictive dimension into the policy space.

Let us begin our exposition for an electorate whose candidates and parties can be represented along a *single* ideological dimension, which we denote Π. We denote the policy space by Ω, which will be assumed to have n dimensions. We will adopt the convention that points in the ideological space are denoted by lower case π's, and points in Ω are lower case ω's. These points will be subscripted by the lower case Greek letters ψ or θ if we are discussing a two-candidate race, between candidates we will call Psi and Theta, for notational consistency. In general, we will use the subscript p to index each of L candidates in an L-candidate election, so that $p = 1, 2, \ldots,$ or L.

For example, π_θ and π_ψ denote the ideological positions in Π of candidates Theta and Psi, respectively. In general, π_p is the ideological position of the pth candidate in an electoral race with L candidates (or parties). The status quo of the executive in power or the ruling coalition is denoted π_o.[16] The

---

15. The assumption of unidimensionality is obviously restrictive, and will be dropped after the initial exposition of the model is complete.

16. In chapter 6 we will discuss the relation between candidates and parties in the theory, and in chapter 9 we will make clear the formal relation between party platforms and citizen perceptions of candidate positions.

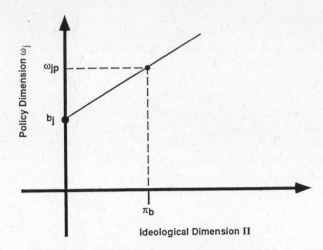

Fig. 9. The mapping from ideology to policy

origin of Π is arbitrary, so we can make the origin the status quo ideology, to simplify notation, with no loss of generality. This means that $\pi_o = 0$ is the origin of the line Π.[17]

Let us now focus on a single voter, who we call voter i, and a particular policy dimension, which we index by j. We denote voter i's perception of candidate p's position on issue j by ω_{ijp}. The following linear equation linking ω_{ijp} to π_p was first introduced by Hinich and Pollard (1981):

$$\omega_{ijp} = b_{ij} + v_{ij}\,\pi_p \tag{6.1}$$

This linear relationship between policy and ideology is depicted in figure 9, with the subscript i removed to simplify notation. The model has two parameters for each voter i, the intercept, b_{ij}, and slope, v_{ij}. The intercept parameter, b_{ij}, represents voter i's perception of the status quo policy on the jth issue. The slope parameter, v_{ij}, is voter i's perception of the way ideological distances from the status quo translate into changes in policy. We will go into more detail about the slope, or linkage term, shortly.

Let us emphasize the intellectual perspective we are taking at this first simple stage of what will be a richer model of the linkage between ideology and policy. All voters share the same perception about the ideological position of each candidate, and each voter has his own belief about the slope parameter

---

17. It is important to recognize that the dimension π is latent, and that the units are therefore arbitrary. In an actual empirical application where the status quo is important, this would require that the ideological dimension be centered so that $\pi = 0$ really does correspond to the status quo.

for the linear linkage between ideology and policy. The idiosyncratic nature of the slope parameter allows for the possibility that individual belief systems, or "schema," are well organized, but atomized, so that few perceptions are shared in the electorate about linkage between established ideological positions and policy implications.[18] Differences among voters about the location of π_p might be due to differences in perceptions of v_j or in differences of perceptions about the status quo position on issue j.

Another important theoretical proposition implied by the seemingly innocuous subscripting in equation 6.1 is that the b and v terms are not indexed by p. The indexing used in equation 6.1 actually represents a fundamental assumption about our theory of the way citizens perceive political choices. In words, what is implied can be summarized as follows: Two candidates with identical ideological positions are expected to adopt identical policy positions on issue j, but different voters may have different beliefs about what that those positions are.[19] Another implication is that candidates with widely different ideological positions will be evaluated by the same linear mapping function, whose intercept and slope are idiosyncratic to the voter.[20]

What we have argued in the first six chapters is that the origin, growth, and maintenance of ideology creates in voters' minds the perception that a particular relationship exists between ideological statements and policies. This relationship between ideas, platforms, and expected policies is summarized by the linear equation 6.1, which will later be expanded and generalized to enrich this simple model of perceptions.

We are not arguing that all statements by a party or candidate are going to be believed. The status quo (b) and the linkage (v) terms for each voter are a result of that voter's experiences and socialization. The individual's perception of the relation between ideology and policy is created slowly, by the voter's extended observations about what political rhetoric means for policy reality. Some people are highly informed about politics and others are not, but even the most informed has only a very partial grasp of the complexities of the actions of governments. For that reason, we allow the perceived relations to differ across voters. *Nonetheless, there must be some coherence in these perceptions across voters, if our theory of ideology is to have predictive power*

---

18. See Conover and Feldman (1984); Feldman and Conover (1983). Even if perceptions are shared, of course, this could arise from "projection" rather than genuine agreement (Conover and Feldman 1982).

19. This assumption thus contradicts the assumption of purely atomized "schema." What is required is that voters use similar cues to arrive at their judgment of what ideological positions are.

20. When we introduce uncertainty in chapter 6, this will still be true in the sense that the point estimates of policy will be the same across candidates. But the variance of these efforts will differ, and citizens with quadratic utilities will use both the mean and the variance of the estimates of the policy position in evaluating the candidates.

and be able to explain how the political activities of large groups of people are organized. While we allow for different perceptions about the slopes of the linkages and the status quo policies, these differences must not be too large. If they are large, then our concept of a macropolitical ideological space will be have been falsified.

To clarify the meaning of the linkage parameter, consider the following example. Imagine that the single ideological dimension is economic liberalism, with the far left representing state ownership of the means of production, as in figure 8. As we move rightward, levels of regulation decrease. The far right represents "pure" laissez-faire capitalism. For an issue (call it 1) such as regulation of advertising, the linkage parameter $v_1 \neq 0$. The far left would require only state-sponsored information messages, and would outlaw private advertising. The center would impose some sort of antifraud regulation, and the far right would brook no restrictions on advertising whatsoever. This relation is illustrated in figure 10, panel A, where $v_1 < 0$. Note that a negative linkage term implies that moving to the right *reduces* the amount of regulation.

Consider another issue, call it 2, which is the level of toleration of political or social dissent. It is possible that $v_2 = 0$, which means that voters perceive no linkage between ideological positions on the left/right economic scale and tolerance of dissent. This may mean that tolerance is a new issue in the polity, so that there really is no linkage. The existing ideological framework may have implications for this issue, but no party has tried (successfully) to exploit the linkage before. Alternatively, it may mean that political parties have taken such diffuse and contradictory positions that there is no coherent overall relationship. Consequently, the zero linkage term may represent *either* ignorance or uncertainty by voters.[21] A zero linkage is depicted in figure 10, panel B. If, on the other hand, the left is perceived to be intolerant of dissent, while the right is consistently libertarian, then $v_2 > 0$.

It is worth emphasizing that the linkage parameters represent a *linear* transformation from ideological dimensions to issue dimensions. Because the

---

21. It is worth noting that $v_i \approx 0$, for all i, is the prediction of the strong form of "schema" theory, where individual belief systems are well-developed, but atomistic. Again, see Conover and Feldman (1984, 1989). If, on the other hand, some of the v_i's are zero, but not all, this is quite consistent with a theory of ideology. Heberle (1951) distinguishes ideas that make up, or "constitute," the ideology of a social movement, from the issues that the movement may address but has no real position on.

> Some of these [ideas] may be regarded as specific and essential to the movement; these are the really integrating ideas. Others may be of mere accidental significance for this particular movement. The former may be called the *constitutive* ideas, since they form the spiritual-intellectual foundation of group cohesion or solidarity. (13)

Since ideologies must support parties, and parties must take some position on all issues, there may be some issues for which the party's ideology has no implications.

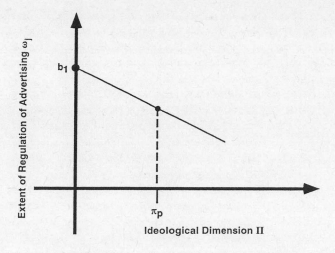

Panel A: A negative mapping ($v_1 < 0$)

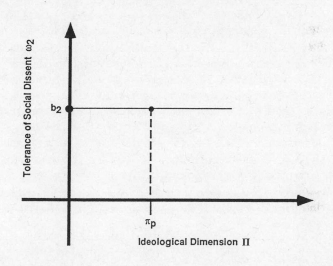

Panel B: A zero mapping ($v_2 = 0$)

Fig. 10. Mappings from ideology to policy: Regulation of advertising and tolerance of social dissent

linkage terms are not indexed by candidates, this relationship is assumed to be constant across candidates or parties. The ideological dimension(s) that exist at a point in time are, thus, a product of what Sartori called the "party system," rather than a result of a particular ideology. It is the opposition of ideas contesting for rule that give the dimension(s) its shape. The only information most voters get from campaigns are broad normative ideological messages with symbolic representations. Each voter intuitively arrives at a prediction of a set of issue positions for the main candidates, based on their ideological stances. For the sake of the simple model exposited here, these perceptions of ideological stances are not indexed by i, so that the simple model assumes that voters agree on where the candidates stand ideologically. In chapter 8, we will expand the definition of "positions" on the ideological dimension to include distributions, rather than points. This will allow us to account both for candidates who are not known to many voters and for eccentric candidates, whose past is known but inconsistent. For the present, however, all voters see each candidate p as a point π_p on Π.

Turning back to figure 10, we can see that Π is overlaid on Ω. In figure 11, we give an example of the relation of the unidimensional ideological space to a policy space Ω; it is assumed that there are two policy choices, so that Ω is two-dimensional. Any point π_p on Ω corresponds to a unique policy pair $\omega_p = (\omega_{1p}, \omega_{2p})$. The position of ω_p depends on the status quo (b) and linkage (v) parameters, so that:

$$\omega_{1p} = b_1 + v_1 \pi_p \text{ for issue 1}$$

$$\omega_{2p} = b_2 + v_2 \pi_p \text{ for issue 2} \tag{6.2}$$

These two equations can be compactly written (using vector notation, where bold characters are vectors, and $'$ means "transpose") as $\omega_p - \mathbf{b} = \mathbf{v}\pi_p$. Each of these terms is a 2×1 column vector, except for the scalar ideological position. Unless otherwise noted, all vectors hereafter are assumed to be *column* vectors, so that $\mathbf{b} = (b_1, b_2)'$. From now on, we shall also write equations so that all policy positions are on the left-hand side, which means that policy positions of parties are expressed as changes from the status quo (i.e., $\omega_p - \mathbf{b}$).

The number of ideological dimensions is an empirical issue, as we have said before. Many observers of electoral competition in democracies label candidates along some sort of left/right scale, following the lead of Downs (1957). This unidimensional economic representation of the political world may be a result of the influence of Marx, or it may simply seem to accord with the view of the researcher, in most cases. Unfortunately, the attachment of any precise meaning to recovered dimensions (such as those generated by multidimensional scaling or factor analysis algorithms) is probably a misleading

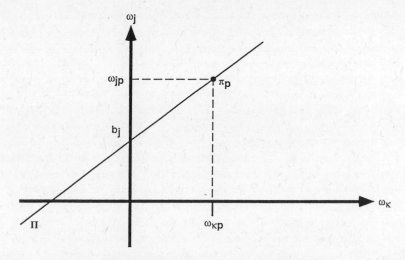

Fig. 11. The ideological space overlaid on the policy space

simplification of a complex reality. The dimensions themselves are latent, and their units and directions describe the empirical structure of the positions taken by candidates and parties. The number of dimensions usually depends on some purely statistical criteria (in the case of factor analysis, the size of the eigenvalues indicating statistical significance of the "next" factor). The number of dimensions, from a theoretical perspective, is arbitrary; in the next chapter, we argue that there is compelling empirical evidence that the number of dimensions is, at most, three, and rarely more than two.

There is an important scientific difference between our approach and classical spatial theory, though this difference may be immediately apparent to the casual reader. Using subjective judgment or intuition to depict political choices as points on a line or plane whose units are known and fixed does simplify examples and explanation, because we can compare positions on defense, school spending, and the intensity of regulation. Our argument is that these examples are misleading, because real political decision making takes place in the ideological dimensions. We are able to validate these dimensions using rigorous statistical methods, and based on a large body of empirical research (reviewed in chap. 7). The important thing is that the candidates' positions on the recovered dimensions are the actual positions, *as voters themselves perceive them*, rather than the position attributed to the candidates by the researcher.

At least as important, if there is a breakdown in the party system that has governed both by rule and by rhetoric, our method reflects this immediately. If there is no fundamental coherence across idiosyncratic schema in the electorate, either as a result of a realignment or because there is no such thing as ideology, as a macropolitical phenomenon, our method will show this also. The evidence for this kind of dysfunctional political system is *not* that the number of recoverable dimensions goes to zero, however. Instead, the *mapping* parameters, v_{ij}, either (1) go to zero for all voters, since the voters have no intuition about the implications of ideological statements for policy, or (2) vary widely, since voters have strong, but wildly variable, expectations about policy implications. Classical spatial theory, relying on policy positions of candidates, cannot detect either of these phenomena because of the intellectual limitations underlying the metaphor of its application.[22]

Let us now expand the model for a point π drawn from a multidimensional ideological space Π. Suppose that Π has ℓ dimensions where $\ell \geq 2$, and the policy space Ω has n dimensions. To generalize expression 6.2, let $\boldsymbol{\omega}_{ip} = (\omega_{i1p}, \ldots, \omega_{inp})'$ denote an $n \times 1$ column vector of voter i's perceptions of candidate p's policy positions in Ω, and let $\mathbf{b}_i = (b_{i1}, \ldots, b_{in})'$ denote an $n \times 1$ column vector of i's perceptions of the status quo. Let $\mathbf{v}_{ik} = (v_{i1k}, \ldots, v_{ink})'$ denote an $n \times 1$ column vector of mapping parameters for voter i, and let π_{kp} denote candidate p's ideological position on each ideological dimension $k = 1, \ldots, \ell$; then the generalization of equation 6.2 is as follows.

$$\boldsymbol{\omega}_{ip} - \mathbf{b}_i = \mathbf{v}_{i1}\pi_{1p} + \mathbf{v}_{i2}\pi_{2p} + \ldots + \mathbf{v}_{i\ell}\pi_{\ell p} \tag{6.3}$$

Using matrix algebra, expression 6.3 can be rewritten as: $\boldsymbol{\omega}_{ip} = \mathbf{b}_i + \mathbf{v}_i\boldsymbol{\pi}_p$, where:

$$\pi_p = \begin{bmatrix} \pi_{1p} \\ \pi_{2p} \\ \cdot \\ \cdot \\ \cdot \\ \pi_{\ell p} \end{bmatrix} \quad v_i = \begin{bmatrix} v_{i11} & v_{i12} & \cdot & \cdot & \cdot & v_{i1\ell} \\ v_{i21} & v_{i22} & \cdot & \cdot & \cdot & v_{i2\ell} \\ \cdot & & \cdot & & & \cdot \\ \cdot & & & \cdot & & \cdot \\ \cdot & & & & \cdot & \cdot \\ v_{in1} & v_{in2} & \cdot & \cdot & \cdot & v_{in\ell} \end{bmatrix} \tag{6.4}$$

The matrix $\mathbf{v}_i$ can be written as a vector of column vectors as follows:

$$\mathbf{v}_i = (\mathbf{v}_{i1}, \mathbf{v}_{i2}, \ldots, \mathbf{v}_{i\ell}).$$

This simplified overview of the spatial theory of ideology has served to introduce, rather than fully develop, its implications when there is fundamental uncertainty in the electorate about candidate positions and mappings. We

---

22. As Enelow and Hinich (1984a, section 4.9) demonstrate, a large variation in perceptions implies a shrinking of extremes in the ideological space toward the center. For example,

develop the theoretical and strategic implications at some length in the following chapters. The last remaining introductory step is to integrate the spatial model with a utility function that determines voter preferences for policy alternatives, which then translate into preferences among candidates, using the ideological linkage model. The utility model is adapted from the classical quadratic spatial utility model introduced by Davis and Hinich (1966, 1967) and expanded in Enelow and Hinich (1984a).

Let $U_i(\boldsymbol{\omega})$ denote voter i's utility for a vector of policy positions $\boldsymbol{\omega} = (\omega_1, \omega_2, \ldots, \omega_n)'$. Given a choice between policy vectors $\boldsymbol{\omega}_\theta$ and $\boldsymbol{\omega}_\psi$, i prefers $\boldsymbol{\omega}_\theta$ over $\boldsymbol{\omega}_\psi$ if and only if $U_i(\boldsymbol{\omega}_\theta) > U_i(\boldsymbol{\omega}_\psi)$, using classical utility-based preference theory. Suppose that candidate Theta advocates position $\boldsymbol{\omega}_\theta$, and candidate Psi advocates $\boldsymbol{\omega}_\psi$. We will again make use of the Downsian concept of voter i's "net candidate differential," or NCD_i, as we expand our theory to handle voter uncertainty about candidates. The definition of NCD_i is:

$$NCD_i = U_i(\boldsymbol{\omega}_\theta) - U_i(\boldsymbol{\omega}_\psi) \tag{6.5}$$

Thus, i prefers Theta to Psi if and only if $NCD_i > 0$.

Let $\mathbf{x}_i = (x_{i1}, x_{i2}, \ldots, x_{in})'$ denote voter i's ideal (or most preferred) positions on the n policy dimensions. Davis and Hinich's quadratic utility model for an arbitrary policy $\boldsymbol{\omega}$ is:

$$U_i(\boldsymbol{\omega}) = c_i - (\boldsymbol{\omega} - \mathbf{x}_i)'\mathbf{A}_i(\boldsymbol{\omega} - \mathbf{x}_i) \tag{6.6}$$

where $\mathbf{A}_i = [a_{ijk}]$ is an $n \times n$ positive definite matrix. The constant c_i can be set to any arbitrary value for a given individual, since the preference ordering is invariant to change. The matrix $\mathbf{A}_i$ is positive definite if and only if $\boldsymbol{\omega}'\mathbf{A}\boldsymbol{\omega} > 0$ for any vector $\boldsymbol{\omega}$ that is not a zero vector. If $n = 2$, then the points (ω_1, ω_2) in the plane satisfying $c = (\boldsymbol{\omega} - \mathbf{x}_i)'\mathbf{A}_i(\boldsymbol{\omega} - \mathbf{x}_i)$, for arbitrary c, form an ellipse. But since utility is also defined up to a positive scalar multiple, the matrix $\mathbf{A}_i$ can be multiplied by an arbitrary scalar without changing the preferences being represented. More simply, each of the elements of $\mathbf{A}_i$ can be multiplied by a number $a > 0$, and the preference ordering remains unchanged.

Applying equation 6.6 to equation 6.5, and expanding by the quadratic, it follows that i prefers $\boldsymbol{\omega}_\theta$ to $\boldsymbol{\omega}_\psi$ if and only if:

$$(\boldsymbol{\omega}_\psi'\mathbf{A}_i\boldsymbol{\omega}_\psi) - (\boldsymbol{\omega}_\theta'\mathbf{A}_i\boldsymbol{\omega}_\theta) - 2(\boldsymbol{\omega}_\psi - \boldsymbol{\omega}_\theta)'\mathbf{A}_i\mathbf{x}_i < 0 \tag{6.7}$$

---

many German voters were probably confused about the economic and social implications of National Socialism in the 1920s, and chose the Nazis out of affinity with their extreme nationalism. Confusion over the linkages with policies made the Nazis seem closer to the center than they were.

To simplify this inequality if Π is a line ($\ell = 1$), insert the linkage model definition of $\boldsymbol{\omega} = \mathbf{b} + \pi\mathbf{v}$ into equation 6.7. It follows from straightforward vector algebra that equation 6.7 holds, and, thus, i prefers Theta to Psi if and only if:

$$(\pi_\psi^2 - \pi_\theta^2)(\mathbf{v}_i'\mathbf{A}_i\mathbf{v}_i) - 2(\pi_\psi - \pi_\theta)[\mathbf{v}_i'\mathbf{A}_i(\mathbf{x}_i - \mathbf{b}_i)] > 0 \tag{6.8}$$

To simplify inequality 6.8, assume that $\pi_\theta < \pi_\psi$, and define the scalar z_i as follows:

$$z_i = \frac{\mathbf{v}_i'\mathbf{A}_i(\mathbf{x}_i - \mathbf{b}_i)}{\mathbf{v}_i'\mathbf{A}_i\mathbf{v}_i} \tag{6.9}$$

Then, inequality 6.8 holds, and, consequently, $NCD_i > 0$ (i prefers Theta) if and only if:

$$z_i < (\pi_\theta + \pi_\psi)/2 \tag{6.10}$$

In words, this means that we have derived the Downsian result that i prefers the candidate whose position is closer to his ideal, but we have done it in the ideological dimension, rather than in the policy dimension. The point z_i is the voter's ideal point on the ideological dimension, and is induced by the voter's preferences over policies and his perceptions of the linkage between policies and ideologies. According to this interpretation, the voter is indifferent between the two candidates if $\pi_\theta = \pi_\psi$.

This utility-based preference approach for candidates can be derived from another approach, one that is equally important. The linear nature of the linkage function, combined with the quadratic form of the utility function for policies, allows us to derive the voter's utility function, $U_i(\pi)$, defined purely over ideological positions, which we shall call the "induced utility function."[23] The induced utility function is also quadratic. The easiest way to derive it is to start with the answer and then show it yields the same preference ordering for the candidates Theta and Psi as that given by expressions 6.7 and 6.9. This indirect utility function on Π is:

$$U_i(\pi) = c - (\pi - z_i)^2 \tag{6.11}$$

Expanding the quadratic, it follows that i's net candidate differential for the derived utilities of π_θ, versus π_ψ, is:

$$U_i(\pi_\theta) - U_i(\pi_\psi) = (\pi_\psi^2 - \pi_\theta^2) - 2(\pi_\psi - \pi_\theta)z_i \tag{6.12}$$

---

23. This utility function is derived in chapter 4 of Enelow and Hinich (1984a).

This expression implies that if $\pi_\theta < \pi_\psi$, then voter i prefers Theta to Psi, in terms of $U_i(\pi)$, if and only if inequality 6.10 holds. This proves the assertion that the derived utility function $U_i(\pi)$ for ideological positions on the latent ideological dimension yields the same preference orderings for voter i among candidates as the utility function $U_i(\omega)$ did for policy positions.

Suppose that the ideological space has more than one dimension; let there be ℓ latent ideological dimensions. Define the $\ell \times \ell$ positive definite matrix $\mathbf{M}_i$ as $\mathbf{M}_i = \mathbf{v}_i'\mathbf{A}_i\mathbf{v}_i$. Applying the vector and matrix generalization of the linear linkage terms given in expression 6.3 to the quadratic utility function defined by equation 6.6, the general form for the derived utility function of vectors π is:

$$U_i(\pi) = c - (\pi - \mathbf{z}_i)'\mathbf{M}_i(\pi - \mathbf{z}_i) \qquad (6.13)$$

where $\mathbf{z}_i = \mathbf{M}_i^{inv}\mathbf{v}_i'\mathbf{A}_i(\mathbf{x}_i - \mathbf{b}_i)$ is a $\ell \times 1$ column vector of voter i's ideal points on the latent ideological dimensions.

To summarize, we have now derived the induced utility function for ideological positions, based on policy preferences and the perceived linkage of ideology to policy, for an ideological space of arbitrary dimension. If the spatial theory of ideology required only a single dimension (as Downs assumed), the theory would be of little use. The value of the theory derives from the fact that it can account for multiple dimensions of generalized conflict, and that these dimensions are fluid, responding to the political strategies of parties that contend for power. Having summarized the basic theory, it is now worthwhile to consider some of the empirical justifications for its use.

Empirical Justification for the Representation of Ideology in a Reduced Dimensional Space

Empirical evidence from economic and political science research, as well as political and mainstream psychology, provides rather striking evidence of the advantages that accrue to taking the reduced-dimensional ideological approach. We do not propose here to survey this literature exhaustively, but rather to provide illustrative examples of the plausibility and utility of a reduced-dimensional/mapping approach.

Psychological Theories: Limits of Cognition

Herbert Simon (1982, 1985), and a wide variety of other cognitive psychologists who have followed him,[24] have taken seriously the task of describing the

---

24. See, e.g., Taylor et al. (1978); Taylor and Crocker (1981); Resch (1978); Minsky (1975); Higgins and King (1981); and Fiske and Taylor (1984).

precise process by which information becomes knowledge. This approach is variously known as *bounded* or *procedural* rationality, but it has at its core some surprisingly simple observations about actual human mental processes.

> The human eye and ear are highly parallel devices, capable of extracting many pieces of information simultaneously from the environment and decoding them into their significant features. Before this information can be used by the deliberative mind, however, it must proceed through the bottleneck of attention—a serial, not parallel, process whose information capacity is exceedingly small. Psychologists usually call this bottleneck short-term memory, and measurements show reliably that it can hold only about six chunks (that is to say, six familiar items) of information. (Simon 1985, 302)

Too little use has been made in social science of the fact (and it *is* a fact) that there are physical constraints on the capacity of people to process information. This is not a problem with "rationality"; to paraphrase Mae West, rationality has nothing to do with it. Economists and political scientists have provided elaborate rationales for the use of cues, heuristics, and rules of thumb, and these theoretical contributions are surely of some value. But more can be said than that the opportunity cost of time for a utility-maximizing agent encourages the use of time-economizing conventions. Such conventions, be they heuristic cues or principles of organizing political discourse, such as our predictive dimension, are dictated by the bounds on human capacity to focus on and comprehend complex flows of information.

This reasoning has been explicitly applied to political discourse and persuasion by political psychologists since the middle of this century (Lasswell 1934; Lazarsfeld, Berelson, and Gandet 1948). The Lazarsfeld et al. work, in particular, focuses on campaigns and political oratory as primarily the art of focusing voter attention on certain salient and representational issues. In this view, political messages do not persuade, in any usual sense of the term, but rather, evoke in voters' minds an agreement with the candidate, the general outlines of which must already have existed in a latent form.

There need be no explicit spatial positioning for political oratory to be effective. In fact, precisely the opposite may be true: witness the importance of the Pledge of Allegiance, and Willie Horton, in the 1988 U.S. presidential campaign. This kind of appeal to latent, yet very real, dimensions of cognitive organization of information is precisely what we mean by the ideology.

Political Dimensions

Significant empirical work on measuring the dimensionality of political space has been done by numerous social scientists (MacRae 1958, 1965; Weisberg

1968; Weisberg and Rusk 1970; Rabinowitz 1973; Cahoon, Hinich, and Orde-shook 1978; Poole 1981; van Schur 1984; Poole and Daniels 1985; Poole and Rosenthal 1984a, 1984b, 1985, 1991; Palfrey and Poole 1987; Brady 1988; Koford 1989; Snyder 1992; Schofield 1992a, 1992b). Although this work uses a variety of methods, and attacks the question of measurement using several different theoretical perspectives, there is a surprising consistency in the results. At different times, at the federal or state level, and even at the international level, the number of dimensions that describe the vast majority of the issue positions of candidates, parties, and voters is very small. This is true even in cases such as MacRae (1958, 1965, 1970), Rabinowitz (1974), Snyder (1991), or Schofield (1992a, 1992b), where the number of policies included is quite large.

Of particular interest in this regard is the recent work of Schofield (1992a, 1992b). His findings, resulting from a series of studies of issues in Western European nations in the 1970s and 1980s, reveal a fascinating dynamic process in the dimensionality of what we would call the ideological space. Using a multidimensional scaling procedure, Schofield finds that most nations exhibit an ideological space of two dimensions, with occasional periods of stability with only one dimension.

Most interestingly, in a few instances, a single issue grew in salience until it changed the dimensionality of the ideological space by becoming, itself, a new dimension. An example is the controversy over teaching multiple languages in British schools in the 1980s. The dimensionality of the ideological space had been two, but this issue increased in salience until there were three dimensions. Within two or three years, there was a political realignment in England, manifested by a reduction in the dimensionality of the ideological space from three to two. More important, the two postrealignment positions were different from those in the previous stable system.

The meaning of the empirical regularity of a low-dimensional ideological space is this: even if citizens care about myriad issues, and even if these issues are defined and measured carefully, so that they are, in fact, analytically distinct, there is a general and relatively simple coherence in political views about these issues. The researcher is able to predict, with fair accuracy, a citizen's positions on all issues if he knows that citizen's positions on just a few.

There are at least two possible explanations for this phenomenon. The first is that apparently complex, distinct issues are, in fact, different combinations of just a few "tangible" characteristics of policies, such as protection of property, security from threats of physical violence, availability of food and clothing, and the capacity to educate and care for children. What this would suggest is a neo-Lancasterian (after Lancaster 1966) theory of political choice, where all issues are some combination of a limited set of political characteristics.

Unfortunately, the Lancasterian approach is not useful in describing political choices, because it is contradicted by the fact that the dimensions, though few in number, as a Lancasterian would predict, move around over time and are very difficult to describe with concrete and lasting labels. The fixed underlying dimension approach puts the cart before the horse: rather than the dimensions dictating preferences on more complex policy, the debate about policy forces the evolution of the dimensions. The dimensions are not physical, but are, instead, latent, recovered structural descriptions of political differences between groups of positions. We have called these groups of positions ideologies, and have claimed that the groupings result from a similarity in the basic worldview of the adherents of those ideologies.

As is apparent, the empirical regularity of a reduced-dimension space for describing political interaction is not proof that ideology is the explanation. Our argument in favor of ideology does, however, imply that the empirical measurements of the relevant space should find a severely limited set of dimensions, compared to the number of policies or issues in which citizens are interested. Finding this result is an indication that the theory is, at least, not falsified.

Confirmation of the Theory Itself

Not least are we confident of the utility of the spatial theory of ideology because of the repeated confirmation of the theory by direct empirical testing. Enelow and Hinich (1982, 1984a, 1984b, 1989a, 1989b) and Hinich and Munger (1992) have extensively examined the theory and its implications, using actual and simulated election data. This work is described in the following chapter. Regardless of the source, the results tend to strongly confirm that a reduced-dimensionality approach preserves most of the useful political information obtained from voters about preferences or particular issues. The dimensionality of the ideological space is rarely more than two, and often, the simple unidimensional space is quite adequate.

Summary

In this chapter, we have laid out the intellectual justification and the bare bones of the formal theory of the predictive dimension. Our argument has been that the use of one or more ideological dimensions represents citizen choice in a way that improves significantly on previous efforts. The predictive dimension is explicitly designed to solve the theoretical problems of citizens, rather than being adapted from the quite different (and, we have shown, inapplicable) theory of consumer choice. Further, the predictive dimension technique more accurately represents the actual process by which citizen choice is made.

The next chapter details empirical applications of the theory of ideology applied to political choices. The following two chapters develop the implications of ideology, or perceived position on the predictive dimension, for voter choice and candidate strategy, respectively. This order is important, because candidates must largely react to the set of incentives and perceptions with which they are presented by voters and electoral institutions. As we shall see, the ideology-based approach to political choice turns out to yield both substantive implications for the form political competition will take and a rich and useful game situation for formal analysis.

CHAPTER 7

Empirical Models Based on the Theory of Ideology

The classical spatial theory of elections is based on the assumption that citizens choose alternatives that are "closest," in some weighted Euclidean space of "issues." The conclusion of the previous chapters is that this approach is neither realistic nor accurate as a means of representing political choice. We have not claimed that the theory is wrong, or that it is not useful. Rather, we have claimed that a theory based on ideology, one that more realistically depicts the dynamic setting and constraints on "movement," is better, because it is more realistic and is capable of accounting for mass movements, such as parties. In this chapter, we give evidence for this claim by discussing the theory of ideology at greater length and by offering an illustrative test of the theory on simple survey data. We also discuss the use of factor analysis to estimate the factor loadings, π_p, and the scores, v_i.

A Simplified Version of the Theory

Hinich and Pollard (1981), Enelow and Hinich (1984a, 1989a, 1989b), and Hinich and Munger (1989, 1992) developed a useful theoretical representation of ideology that can be adapted to represent choices in the face of uncertainty. Two aspects of this representation merit emphasis: (1) We make no claim that voters choose "as if" they use the predictive dimension. Rather, we make the stronger (and more easily tested) claim that this is *precisely* the way that citizens choose. The ideological approach allows us to *predict* voter choice, because it represents their preferences, but it also *explains* political activity, because we directly build in the organizing principles that inform and direct the policy process. (2) The predictive dimension is not generally the classical Downsian left-right economic dimension. It is, instead, the latent split or set of issues that divide groups at any particular time. This dimension can originate from one or several causes, ranging from strategic choice by a sophisticated political actor (analogous to Riker's "heresthetics") to tradition or complex historical accident.

This formulation of ideology in a spatial model is not the only attempt to simplify the concept of issues and reduce the informational requirements facing voters. An important variant on the standard spatial model that addresses and solves many of the problems we raise is the "directional theory of

131

voting" in MacDonald and Rabinowitz (1987, 1990, 1993) and Rabinowitz and MacDonald (1989). The emphasis in this work is not on ideology, but on symbolic politics, which implies a different modeling approach:

> If we attempt to represent this type of symbolic response in a formal way, we can imagine two qualities that are evoked by the symbol. First, there is a *direction* to the response. Does the person feel favorable or unfavorable toward the symbol? Second, there is a magnitude or an *intensity* to the response. How strongly does the person feel about the issue? (Rabinowitz and MacDonald 1989, 94)

The directional model emphasizes the diffuse, rather than the coherent, response to individual issues by voters, and highlights the very low levels of information under which voters appear to make important political decisions. Still, though there are similarities in our approaches, there is a crucial difference: we assert the existence of a higher order of coherence across issues. The ideology model requires that there is a basic understanding by voters of the relation between issues and ideology. The linkages among issues, though tenuous and diffuse for any single issue, are still the basis for voter choice among candidates. The directional model would deny these linkages. In the remainder of this section, we provide a detailed description of a descriptive and predictive theory of ideology, derived from the spatial model.

As was highlighted in chapter 6, the key is to be able to describe theoretically, and then statistically estimate, the relationship between the ideological dimensions Π and issues in Ω that voters actually care about. The relationship is assumed to be linear, with slope parameters that vary across voters. To reestablish the notation from chapter 6, voter i's perception of candidate p's vector of positions on $j = 1, 2, \ldots, n$ issues is given by ω_i, $\mathbf{b}_i$ is i's perceptions of present government policies on the issues (that is, the status quo), $\mathbf{v}_i$ is the $n \times \ell$ matrix of linkage parameters idiosyncratic to the voter, and π_p is the ideological position of candidate p in an ℓ-dimensional ideological space Π.

Let us once again, for simplicity of exposition, start with $\ell = 1$, and generalize for $\ell \geq 2$. Thus we begin with the following model:

$$\omega_i = \mathbf{b}_i + \mathbf{v}_i \pi_p \qquad (7.1)$$

Our concept of positions in an ideological space requires a substantive extension of the spatial model we have presented, using the model of "linkages" between a predictive dimension and policy positions. It is too simplistic, and misses important political information, to represent the ideological position of a candidate, let alone a party, as a point on a dimension. Such a representation leaves out the fundamental uncertainty inherent in predicting the future outcomes of a social process. Even if a voter was an identical twin of a certain candidate, the twin would have some uncertainty about what the candidate would do if he were elected. Politics is inherently social, involving many people at many different levels of power and information; consequently, it is impossible to predict with certainty the outcomes from any policy initiative, even on the part of a strong executive or party leader.

Furthermore, policies are determined by a complex interaction of the executive, legislative, judicial, and bureaucratic branches of any government. The actual policies that emerge from a law, even if the legislators approved the bill unanimously, may be different from what the legislators intended. The actual results of an attempt to implement a policy, even one the executive favors strongly, may be modified or frustrated by the bureaucratic organizations charged with carrying it out. Thus, voters need not only information on ideological position, but also on the ability of leaders to translate that ideology into action. The logical inferences voters make must be combined with their experience.

We conceive of voters as using the information they have accumulated over time, as well as what is said during an election campaign, to come up with a guess of what politics will become if a candidate is elected. If the office is unimportant to a voter, then the linkage between ideologies and policies is small, even though the voter may hold strong preferences about the actual outcomes. For example, local governments provide many of the most basic public services on which citizens depend, and it is in local elections that each vote counts the most. According to the classic spatial theory, when the issues are clearest and votes count the most, citizens should participate the most. Yet, turnout for local elections, as well as participation in pubic city council or county commission meetings, is small. Turnout is much (five or ten times) higher for national elections, especially for the chief executive, even though each individual vote is trivial in this context.

This seeming paradox is easily resolved by a theory of political choice based on ideology. Local issues tend to be just that: disjoint, unrelated policies, such as how much to spend on garbage collection and where to put the new school or garbage dump. Only those people immediately affected by these decisions participate. National elections tend to be ideological, providing voters with some means of making broad judgments, and some motive to participate by exciting emotions, not just narrow self-interest.[1]

In any election, future policy outcomes are inherently uncertain. We will now extend our model to capture some of the essence of this uncertainty. At

---

1. This difference between ideology and narrowly self-interested preference is emphasized strongly by North (1981). Nonetheless, it is important to note that North does not distinguish between ideology as individual belief system and ideology as a collection of ideas with implications for policy. We restrict our definition of ideology to a mass-level phenomenon.

present, the model conceives of an ideological position as a point adopted by a politician. Citizens choose among these points based on their induced preferences for ideological positions (derived in the previous chapter). The extension to account for uncertainty requires that ideological position be modeled as a random variable, with some distribution (indexed by politician) in the ideological space. A formalization of such a model of ideological uncertainty is: $\hat{\pi}_p = \pi_p + \mathbf{e}_p(\pi)$, where $\mathbf{e}_p(\pi)$ is a random variable in Π whose expected value is zero. Thus, π_p is the expected value of $\hat{\pi}_p$, denoted $E(\hat{\pi}_p)$.

To accord with our argument that the number of viable ideologies in the space is small, and that it is costly to change an ideology, we assume that there are only a few viable distributions in the ideological space. In other words, there are only a few points, π, that people link with policy outcomes. The distribution of the random error term, $\mathbf{e}_p(\pi)$, is determined by the nature of the candidate "p" who adopts that position. The same model holds for parliamentary systems, where the parties, rather than individual candidates, are the main actors in elections.

We use the notation with the "hat" (^) since it is commonly used in statistics to connote an estimate computed from a sample of a population. In our case, the concept of sampling is more complex and abstract than is the case in the classic random selection of a few individuals from a larger group. Further, a random variable is an abstract concept to use as a representation for a person or a party; an example will help clarify what is meant. Suppose that a society is holding an election for its chief executive, and that the society's ideological cleavage can be represented by a unidimensional Π. Suppose that there are only three ideological positions on this dimension: $\pi \in \{-1, 0, 1\}$, and that the three candidates for the office locate at these three points. In other words, $\pi_\theta = -1$, $\pi_o = 0$, and $\pi_\psi = 1$. As we have said before, the zero point on the latent ideological dimension is calibrated to correspond with the status quo, so the incumbent chief executive has implemented policies linked in voters' minds with π_o. Theta is claiming to represent π_θ, and Psi espouses π_ψ.

In most cases, the status quo ideology is a centrist set of compromises and mixtures of competing ideologies that pull at the center. Although we have argued against the viability of a mixture of competing, contradictory worldviews, the centrist status quo is an exception, provided it satisfies two conditions. These conditions are (a) the government is seen by citizens to be reasonably effective in providing basic services and keeping order, and (b) this order, and this centrist compromise, has proved stable. The first condition means that most citizens have no pressing interest in changing the existing order. The second qualifies the center as a "pragmatic ideology."[2]

---

2. The notion of a "pragmatic ideology" makes clear how different our conception is from that of Sartori. To reprise the difference, ideology is, for our purposes, the set of ideas that motivate policy; for Sartori, it is the "temperature" of the party system.

In our simple three-choice model, think of $\pi = 0$ as a compromise between the two ideological positions $\pi = -1$ and $\pi = 1$. Given the uncertainty inherent in life and politics, a realistic voter should consider the possibility that Psi may end up producing policy outcomes that should be linked with a point somewhere between $\pi = 1$ and 0; say, for example, $\pi = 0.5$. There is also a possibility that Psi may produce outcomes that are indistinguishable (up to the limit of the citizen's ability to discern differences) from what the incumbent would provide. The same voter may also believe that Theta may actually implement a leftist compromise linked with point $\pi = -0.5$, or may become a "pragmatic" (i.e., purely reelection-oriented) executive once elected. What we are doing is moving to a representation of a candidate as a number of possible ideological points, so that there is not one concretely defined (that is, a *point*) position at election time. This approach generalizes point positions to become distributions of possible ideological positions (and, therefore, clouds of policy positions), and is characterized by a probability distribution.

Let us put some probabilities into our simple three-candidate race. Suppose that all voters hold the perceptions of the probabilities of victory for the three candidates shown in table 3.

What this table describes is the discrete probability distributions of candidates perceived by voters faced with uncertainty. Theta's probability of actually representing his avowed ideological position ($\pi_\theta = -1$) is 0.85, whereas the probability of his being at a rightist compromise position $\pi = -0.5$ is 0.10, and the probability of his adopting a pure reelection position ($\pi = 0.0$) is 0.05. No probability is assigned to a leftist position. Psi is the mirror image of Theta on the left, with no probability of adopting a rightist position. We have assigned some probability (0.01) to the event that the incumbent adopts either the leftist or rightist compromise; he is, after all, a pragmatist.

The expected value of Psi's (uncertain) ideological position is 0.9. The

TABLE 3. Probabilities of Ideological
Stands by Three Candidates

Prob (π)	Candidates		
	Theta	Incumbent	Psi
−1.0	0.85	0.00	0.00
−0.5	0.10	0.01	0.00
0.0	0.05	0.98	0.05
0.5	0.00	0.01	0.10
1.0	0.00	0.00	0.85
	1.00	1.00	1.00

expected value for Theta is -0.9, and the expected value of the incumbent is 0.0. Thus, using the notation of a mean plus a random variable, as introduced above, Psi's perceived position is $\hat{\pi}_\theta = 0.9 + e_\theta(\pi)$, Theta's is $\hat{\pi}_\psi = -0.9 + e_\psi(\pi)$, and the incumbent is perceived to be located at the random variable $\hat{\pi}_o = 0.0 + e_o(\pi)$. The three random variables, $e_p(\pi)$, have different probability distributions, defined over a total of five possible outcomes, but for each candidate, there are but three outcomes assigned positive probability.

Returning to the exposition of our stochastic model for uncertainty, the ideological position of candidate p is no longer a point on Π, but is a distribution of possible points determined by the probabilities assigned different realizations of $\hat{\pi}_p$. What this means is that the focus of the voter is on the random error term, $e_p(\pi)$. In any case, π_p is now the expected value of the uncertain ideology of candidate p. Notice that π_p is not necessarily identical to the (modal) point position that voters expect the candidate to take. The two are the same only if the distribution of possible departures is symmetric around p's claimed position.

The distribution of $e_p(\pi)$ is not indexed by i, for two reasons. First, in this generalization, we wish to preserve the structure of our cruder deterministic model, where the ideological choices are not individually held psychological constructions, or atomistic "schema." In the uncertainty model, the ideologies are distributions with a mean value and a common standard deviation around the mean. The second reason for not modeling the ideological distributions with an idiosyncratic component is empirical. Consider the measurement problem of determining a distribution of each voter in a sample of voters. One would have to elicit from each subject a reliable measure of each subject's probability assessment of a latent variable on a recovered ideological scale, assuming that the model is a reasonable representation of complex mental activities. This is a very difficult task, even if the subjects are politically sophisticated and are willing to try to respond to an experiment aimed at estimating these distributions.

The distributions of $\hat{\pi}_p$, and thus, their means and variances, differ *across candidates*. This variation, and efforts to affect both one's own distribution and that of one's opponents, is the fundamental force that guides an election campaign. Candidates, and their campaign workers, try to influence the shape of the distributions that the candidates represent in voters' minds. The more experience voters have with, and the more (true) information[3] voters have about, candidate p, the closer $e_p(\pi)$ is to zero. Recall that we have argued that it is very difficult for any candidate to make a credible move along

---

3. Obviously, the judgment about whether information is "true" is crucial here. This is the contribution of signalling theory: it highlights patterns of information transfer that are consistent and credible.

Π. Candidates who are little known may have some latitude to choose their initial position, but they will not be able to choose their own variance, which will be much higher than that of an established candidate. Even for extremely well-known candidates, the variance of $e_p(\pi)$ will be positive.

Replacing π_p by $\hat{\pi}_p$ in expression 7.1, voter i's belief about the policies that candidate p will pursue once elected is the random vector

$$\hat{\omega} = \mathbf{b}_i + \mathbf{v}_i(\pi_p + \mathbf{e}_p(\pi)) \tag{7.2}$$

That is, candidate p's policy on issue j is a random variable $\hat{\omega}_{ijp}$ whose expected value is $\omega_{ijp} = b_{ij} + v_{ij}\pi_p$. The variance of the random variable is $v_{ij}^2\sigma_p^2(\pi)$, where $\sigma_p^2(\pi)$ denotes the variance of $\mathbf{e}_p(\pi)$.

We have shown that the induced utility model given by expression 6.12 for a unidimensional Π, or by equation 6.14 for an ideological space of arbitrary dimension, yields the same preference ordering as the one based on the utility function based on policy, given by expression 6.6. The same result holds for voter i's expected utility using the linkage model 7.2 in equation 6.7, which is:

$$E[U_i(\omega)] = c_i - (\omega - \mathbf{x}_i)'\mathbf{A}_i(\omega - \mathbf{x}_i) - \sigma_p^2(\pi)\mathbf{M}_i \tag{7.3}$$

where $\mathbf{M}_i = \mathbf{v}_i'\mathbf{A}_i\mathbf{v}_i$ is now a scalar ($\mathbf{M}_i$ was defined in chap. 6). Using the same algebraic manipulations as before, voter i's expected induced utility for candidate p is:

$$E[U_i(\pi)] = c_i - (\pi_p - z_i)^2 - \sigma_p^2(\pi) \tag{7.4}$$

It then follows, from expressions 6.14 and 7.4, that voter i's expected net candidate differential between Theta and Psi, using the induced utility function, is as follows:

$$E[NCD_i] = E[U(\pi_\theta) - U(\pi_\psi)] = \pi_\psi^2 - \pi_\theta^2 - 2(\pi_\psi - \pi\theta)z_i$$

$$+ [\sigma_\theta^2(\pi) - \sigma_\psi^2(\pi)] \tag{7.5}$$

Assume that voter i strictly prefers Theta to Psi if and only if $E[U(\pi_\theta) - U(\pi_\psi)] > 0$. Then, it follows from equation 7.5, assuming $\pi_\theta \neq \pi_\psi$, that voter i prefers Theta to Psi if and only if

$$z_i - (\pi_\psi + \pi_\theta)/2 < [\sigma_\psi^2(\pi) - \sigma_\theta^2(\pi)]/\mid \pi_\psi - \pi_\theta \mid \tag{7.6}$$

If, instead, $\pi_\psi = \pi_\theta$, then it follows from equation 7.5 that voter i prefers

Theta if and only if the variance of Theta's position is smaller than that of Psi, because all but the last term drop out of equation 7.5. This is the most important extension of the simple distance model of choice derived in chapter 6, because this result gives some role to the campaign.[4]

To further illustrate the way that the variances change the distance choice rule, suppose that z_i is actually closer to π_ψ than to π_θ, but that $\sigma_\psi > \sigma_\theta$. Thus $z_i > (\pi_\theta + \pi_\psi)/2$, and the classical choice model would imply that the voter should choose Psi. However, equation 7.6 may hold if the variance of Psi is enough greater than the variance of Theta to offset Psi's advantage of proximity. In words, this means that voters may prefer an extreme ideologue to a lukewarm centrist. The difference between the variances, $\sigma_\psi^2(\pi) - \sigma_\theta^2(\pi)$, provides a direct utility comparison that enters the voters' decision calculus in an intuitively plausible way. More important, for each candidate, *variance is a simple inverse measure of integrity*.[5]

This difference in variances has several very important implications. First, regarding the literature on the "Strategy of Ambiguity" (coined by Shepsle 1972): in our model, ambiguity is harmful because it reflects on the character and strength of will of the candidate. As the example above shows, the voter may choose the committed ideologue over a pragmatic centrist, because the voter is unable to determine with any certainty just what the centrist will do if elected.

A recent real-world example illustrates the point. In the late summer and fall of 1992, British Prime Minister John Major made two major "policy" errors. First, in response to pressure to devalue the pound sterling, particularly against the German mark, he made impressive statements of determination to raise British interest rates and defend the pound. But within two months of these brave words, Major's government allowed the pound to drop dramatically on international currency markets. The free market, internationalist weekly *The Economist* (September 10, 1992) responded with a story beginning with the sentence "All political dramas are about character as well as about policy." *The Economist* went on to compare Major to Harold Wilson, the Prime Minister renowned (and often reviled) for his verbal cleverness, his ability to avoid taking positions, and his apparent lack of any genuine political philosophy. This was not intended to be a felicitous comparison.

In September of 1992, Major announced that British Coal, the nationalized employer of thousands of British coal miners, would lay off at least a

---

4. This aspect of the spatial model has been examined by several authors, without the focus on ideology. Previous research includes Austen-Smith (1987), Hinich and Munger (1989), and Cameron and Enelow (1990).

5. There have been several works focusing on the possibility that candidate integrity enters the utility function of voters in a multiplicative, rather than an additive, fashion. See Grofman (1986) and Enelow, Endersby, and Munger (1993).

quarter of its work force to cut costs and pave the way for privatization. Met with strong protests, including dissent from within Major's own Conservative party, this position was soon reversed, with no real decision being made on the number of miners to be let go, if any. This may have been the right decision, in tactical terms, but again, Major said one thing and soon did quite the opposite. *The Economist* had a less severe reaction than most of the rest of the British media, but still observed acerbically of Major: "He may still be the calm administrator and expert negotiator that he has already proved himself to be. But as Lord Wilson found, short-term manoeuvering is no substitute for loss of authority and direction." (*The Economist*, September 10, 1992, 41)

There have been many attempts to measure the importance of what have been variously called nonpolicy attributes, competence, character, and integrity, as means of judging candidates separate from the policies they are expected to seek to implement. Enelow and Hinich (1982b, 1984a, 1993), Grofman (1985), Enelow, Hinich, and Mendell (1986), Enelow, Endersby, and Munger (1993), and others have focused on the importance of either the candidate's ability to do what he says, or else the more abstract, additive sense that the candidate is a leader, with will and strength of character.

In previous work, however, the incorporation of the character or competence terms have been ad hoc, either tacking on an additive term or inserting a multiplicative term to account for nonpolicy attributes the candidate is presumed to possess, and that voters are assumed to value in deciding for whom to vote. It is gratifying, and potentially quite important, that the spatial theory of ideology allows us to derive a role for character from the logic of the basic model, rather than having to add it on as an afterthought.

Further, it is useful to note that it is only the difference between the variances that matter. Any reduction in variation is an improvement, but a candidate with character problems can still win if his opponent is perceived as being still more directionless and untrustworthy. A likely example of this effect is the 1992 U.S. presidential election between Bill Clinton and George Bush. Forced to confront in voters' minds his breach of the "no new taxes" pledge, Bush tried to make Clinton's character one of the central issues of the campaign. Only in this way could Bush's own character problems be neutralized. Although it didn't work, Bush clearly recognized that it is the comparison (i.e., the *difference*) between the two characters that influences voters' decisions.

Having established the basic single dimensional model, and having discussed the intuition of the various terms in equation 7.6, we are in a position to state the more general, multidimensional model. If the ideological space has ℓ latent dimensions, then voter i's belief about the policies that candidate p will pursue once elected is the random vector:

$$\hat{\omega}_{ip} = \mathbf{b}_i + \mathbf{v}_i(\boldsymbol{\pi}_p + \mathbf{e}_p(\boldsymbol{\pi})) \tag{7.7}$$

where $\mathbf{e}_p(\boldsymbol{\pi}) = (e_{p1}(\pi_1) , \ldots , e_{p\ell}(\pi_l))'$ is an $\ell \times 1$ vector of random variables for candidate p's position on all the latent ideological dimensions, given the voters' uncertainty about that position. Since $\mathbf{M}_i = \mathbf{v}_i'\mathbf{A}_i\mathbf{v}_i$ is an $\ell \times \ell$ positive definite matrix, the quadratic form $\mathbf{e}_p(\boldsymbol{\pi})\mathbf{M}_i\mathbf{e}_p(\boldsymbol{\pi})$ is a positive scalar value for any $\mathbf{v}_i$. This quadratic form is a double sum taken over j and k: $\Sigma_{i=1}^{n}\Sigma_{j=1}^{m} \mathbf{M}_{jk}\mathbf{e}_{p,i}(\boldsymbol{\pi})\mathbf{e}_{p,k}(\boldsymbol{\pi})$. The expected value of this scalar can be considered as a generalized variance of the vector $\mathbf{e}_p(\boldsymbol{\pi})$, since it is a weighted sum of the variances of the $\mathbf{e}_p(\boldsymbol{\pi})$'s and all the covariances of the pairs of the $\mathbf{e}_p(\boldsymbol{\pi})$'s. The weights are the elements of the matrix $\mathbf{M}$. We write this generalized variance as follows:

$$\sigma_p^2(\boldsymbol{\pi}) = E[(\mathbf{e}_p(\boldsymbol{\pi}))'\mathbf{M}_i(\mathbf{e}_p(\boldsymbol{\pi}))] \tag{7.8}$$

It then follows, from linear algebraic manipulations, that the ℓ-dimensional extension of the expected net candidate differential for the induced utility functions is:

$$NCD_i = [(\boldsymbol{\pi}_{\psi} - \mathbf{z}_i)'\mathbf{M}_i(\boldsymbol{\pi}_{\psi} - \mathbf{z}_i) - (\boldsymbol{\pi}_{\theta} - \mathbf{z}_i)'\mathbf{M}_i(\boldsymbol{\pi}_{\theta} - \mathbf{z}_i)]$$

$$+ [\sigma_{\psi}^2(\boldsymbol{\pi}) - \sigma_{\theta}^2(\boldsymbol{\pi})] \tag{7.9}$$

Another avenue for formally incorporating fundamental uncertainty into the model is to make the linkage values $\mathbf{v}_{ij}$ random variables. Thus, in addition to uncertainty over the correspondence between candidates' statements and their actual ideological position (captured in $\mathbf{e}_p(\boldsymbol{\pi})$), we allow for voter uncertainty about the meaning of ideology for the policies that p will follow.[6] Let us replace the vector $\mathbf{v}_i$ in expression 7.2 with $\mathbf{v} + \mathbf{e}(v)$ where $\mathbf{e}(v) = (e_1(v) , \ldots , e_n(v))'$ is a vector of zero mean random variables, and $\mathbf{v}$ is the column vector of linkage parameters. Note that $\mathbf{v}$ is not indexed by i; by the simple change in notation, we have replaced the idiosyncratic, but deterministic, perception of linkages with the uncertain, but shared, sense of party system.

This is a strong assumption; stronger, in fact, than it needs to be. If data were available on groups, we could estimate mean $\mathbf{v}_i$ for each group, and it is quite likely that these mean linkage perceptions might differ statistically. The best we can hope to do from survey data is to estimate the variances and

---

6. We do not distinguish among the many possible sources of such uncertainty, such as the competence of the candidate, the institutions through which the ideological preferences are expressed, or the process of bureaucratic implementation.

covariances of the random components, if the survey questions are carefully tailored to elicit this information reliably. Unfortunately, it is very difficult to word questions so that we can be sure that the understanding of the question is the same across voters, so that the differences in the answers could be attributed solely to differences in political perceptions. Measuring issue perceptions and attitudes by asking people to respond to questions is a formidable task for the social scientist. It is easy to fall into the trap of letting the popular press set the language and definition of "issues."

Continuing with the random linkage model given in expression 7.2, it follows from equation 7.5 that the expected NCD_i (in *induced* utilities) is given by:

$$(\pi_\psi^2 - \pi_\theta^2)(1 + \rho_i) - 2(\pi_\psi - \pi_\theta)\mathbf{z}_i + [\sigma_\psi^2(\pi)$$

$$- \sigma_\theta^2(\pi)](1 + \rho_i) \tag{7.10}$$

where

$$\rho_i = E[(\mathbf{e}(\mathbf{v}))' \, \mathbf{A}_i(\mathbf{e}(\mathbf{v}))] \,/\, (\mathbf{v}' \, \mathbf{A}_i \mathbf{v}) \tag{7.11}$$

The ρ term is a measure of the mean of the weighted variances of the $\mathbf{e}_j(\mathbf{v})$ relative to the weighted sum of weighted mean v_j. For example, if $\mathbf{A}_i = \mathbf{I}_n$ (where $\mathbf{I}_n$ is the $n \times n$ identity matrix), then:

$$\rho_i = \Sigma_{j=1}^m E[\mathbf{e}_j^2(\mathbf{v})] \,/\, \Sigma_{j=1}^m v_j^2 \tag{7.12}$$

In this case, the larger the variance $\sigma_j^2(\mathbf{v}) = E[\mathbf{e}_j^2]$ is, relative to the square of the linkage term $\mathbf{v}_j$, the larger the value of ρ_i.

Recall that we have assumed that voters choose among candidates in terms of the net candidate differential. Suppose that candidate Theta is the incumbent and thus $\pi_\theta = 0$. It then follows from equations 7.10 and 7.11 that if $\pi_\theta < \pi_\psi$, voter i prefers Theta to Psi, in terms of expected utility, if and only if the following modification of expression 6.9 holds:

$$\mathbf{z}_i/(1 + \rho_i) < \pi_\psi/2 \tag{7.13}$$

For a one-dimensional ideological space, this result implies that voter ideal points on the ideological axis shrink to the status quo (that is, the origin) as ρ_i increases, which will happen if the relative variance of the linkage values increases. All voters whose z_i lie to the left of the Theta will vote for the incumbent, and those to the right will have ideal points closer to the incumbent's ideology, as compared with the case when $\rho_i = 0$. This shrinkage to zero does not depend on the relative position of Psi to the left of the origin. In times of fundamental uncertainty about the political system, itself, our specification of the basis of political choice leads to the prediction that citizens choose the status quo. But they make this choice out of fear of the unknown, rather than out of an informed preference.

What Empirical Confirmation of the Theory Requires

We wish to develop a methodology for testing the extent to which the relationship holds across voters. We will show that standard models from the theory and application of linear statistical models can be used to measure the validity of our theory. Such results depend on the ability to obtain reliable measures from subjects that relate to the cognitive processes that citizens use to make judgments, and register choices, in politics. More simply, we wish to test two basic hypotheses.

1. The beliefs subjects hold about the positions of candidates in the ideological space are widely shared, and are more or less coherent. That is, different voters place candidates in a similar fashion in the ideological space, and the mapping (v) terms are similar across subjects. If this is true, it tends to confirm the thesis that ideologies unite personal belief systems (schema) in the population, even though individual schema will be different, if individuals or small groups are compared.

2. The beliefs subjects hold about the positions of candidates cannot be attributed solely to "projection," or the attribution of one's own ideals to a candidate the subject admires for other, perhaps unrelated, reasons. If beliefs are not projections, it tends to confirm the idea that ideologies are consistent with purposive individual behavior, and represent a useful means of simplifying complex and apparently distorted political realities.

We will use empirical data to test these theses in two complementary ways. The first is linear regression; the second is factor analysis. We will examine regression analysis first. Consider the following experiment.

Suppose that we have a sample of N individuals who are familiar with a set of L candidates and n issues. Each individual is shown $n + 1$ horizontal lines representing a left-right scale for each issue and one abstract ideological dimension. Each individual is asked to place on the scale (a) his ideal point x_i, (b) current government policy on issue j (status quo b_{ij}), and (c) each candidate on each issue (issue position ω_{ijp}). The indices are $i = 1, \ldots, N, j = 1,$

. . . , n, and $p = 1$, . . . , L. (d) Finally, each subject is then asked to place each candidate on the ideological scale.

The linear statistical model used in a least squares regression fit is

$$\omega_{ijp} - b_{ij} = v_{ij}\pi_{ip} + \epsilon_{ijp} \tag{7.14}$$

We then use ordinary least squares regression to fit the model from the data. The least squares estimates of v_{ij} provide insight into the distribution of the linkage parameters in the sample. The crucial question is whether voters share these perceptions, or if ideology means something different to each. Fortunately, there is an obvious test: a comparison of means test of these linkages across voters allows us to evaluate the null hypothesis of incoherence. Rejecting the null lends support to our view that voters share a common perception of the relation of ideology and issues.

This is a key issue in the development of a theory of ideology, and of an understanding of politics. If the understanding of the meaning of ideological statements is not shared, there is really no such thing as an ideology. As Robert Higgs (1987) points out:

> If everyone had an ideology but no two persons had the same one, social scientists could make little use of ideology as an applied analytical concept. We could deal with ideology only as economists traditionally have dealt with consumers' tastes: admit they are profoundly important yet, lacking the capacity to measure or directly observe them, assume that they are constant and therefore can be ignored in causal analysis of changes in consumer behavior. Such an approach (more precisely, nonapproach) is unacceptable in dealing with ideology. (Higgs 1987, 45)

In earlier chapters, we have discussed a tendency for party systems to group around a small number of discrete ideological positions. Duverger (1951), in particular, focused on this tendency. If two alternatives bracket the status quo on a dimension that has meaning mostly for economics, these alternatives may divide to give us two right and two left alternatives, and these may split, in turn. We end up with multiple positions on the dimension. But political systems are dynamic, and another cleavage arises, perhaps on a social, or religious, debate, and again there are fundamentally two positions, "for" and "against," on the new dimension. Each of the many ideological positions on the first dimension take one of these two perspectives; this perspective is probably predictable, given their original positions on economics.[7]

---

7. This pattern is just what Schofield (1992a, 1992b) finds in western Europe.

The empirical evidence, however, on whether Duverger's speculation was correct provides some reason for skepticism. MacDonald and Rabinowitz (1987) and Rabinowitz and MacDonald (1989) provide empirical findings supporting a "directional" dualism, but in a diffuse pattern, and with little coherence across issues. There have been a number of scathing criticisms of the strong form of Duverger's "dualism" theory, including Daalder (1955, 13), Wildavsky (1959, 310), and Sartori (1976, 131). Although we have claimed that ideologies tend to divide into two groups (pro and con, or more or less), the actual number of viable ideologies is an empirical and contextual question. The essence of our theory is that (1) the number of ideologies is small (usually two, occasionally three, and in periods of extraordinary stability, one), and (2) ideologies that do exist are reflected in widely shared personal belief systems.

There is already, in the empirical literature in cognitive psychology, significant evidence that individuals group stimuli into a few crude categories, often even when there is no objective basis for this categorization. Tenbarge (1990), in a review of this literature, notes that there are striking individual-level grounds for something close to Duverger's "dualism." According to Tenbarge, there is a consistent result in the process of cognition: differences *within* categories are underestimated, and differences *across* categories are overestimated. The experimental work on which this conclusion is based (Rosch 1978; Tajfel and Wilkes 1963; Tajfel et al. 1971; Tajfel 1981), consistently shows that individuals faced with objectively continuous stimuli make simplifying categorizations, often into two groups. Tenbarge notes:

> This process is greatly enhanced when two perceptual dimensions of some stimuli are correlated—such as size and value among coins—and is especially severe when many dimensions are correlated, and when some of the correlated dimensions have a particular value to the perceiver. The perceptual distortion caused by social categories—that is, social groups—is perhaps the most extreme case of this effect. This is a straightforward result of the many correlated, valued dimensions on which people are perceived (skin color, clothing style, speech, etc.). Differences between members of the same group are greatly underestimated while differences between groups are greatly overestimated. (Tenbarge 1990, 3)

While we could simply consider these results as characteristics of the human cognitive process (which is surely so), there is also a substantive interpretation. These perceptual distortions and reductions to stereotypes have value, *on average*, in interpreting the world. Again, this time considering Bruner (1957) and Lakoff (1987), Tenbarge points out:

A stimulus object which fits some of these stereotypes—and thus is perceived as a category member—can be inferred to possess the category's other stereotypes. In this way people can predict many characteristics of people and things about which they have only partial knowledge. . . . Errors will certainly occur. . . . But, without . . . the stereotypes . . . we would find ourselves in a world too confusing to contend with. (Tenbarge 1990, 3–4)

How do these personal stereotypes about members of one's own group (in-group) or members of other groups (out-group) relate to ideologies, which are *shared* personal belief systems based on ethical/causal theories about political events? Tenbarge concludes that ideologies are coherent and shared "bundles" of stereotypes, buttressed by an acceptance of the general principles theories the ideology is based on. A politician is assigned an ideological position (in a voter's mind) by the extent to which that politician belongs in-group or out-group. This categorization is based on stereotyped political perceptions (compassionate toward the poor, strong-willed, aggressive toward enemies, concerned with individual freedom, and so on).

Finally, what about the problem of "projection" (Conover and Feldman 1982; Conover 1984) for the "rational" model?[8] After all, the classical spatial model assumes that a voter has preferences over issues and chooses the candidate "closest" to that ideal. What if, instead, voters choose candidates they "like" (based on stereotypes, or physical characteristics, or some other reason), *and then attribute to those candidates the issue positions* they (the voters) most prefer? The same correlation between issue positions and candidate choices will be observed, but in the latter case (projecting one's own attitudes onto a candidate one likes), the correlation has no objective basis. The answer is, first, that ideologies must be correct, on average, or the stereotypes on which they are based will disappear and the linkage between ideological positions and issues will vanish. After all, the associations with ideology are formed through experience, and if experience consistently contradicts expectations, the stereotypes will cease to serve as a means of understanding political events.

This is quite possible, of course, and if enough political stereotypes are false, voters will abandon ideology as a choice mechanism and rely on diffuse individual schema. This leads us to the second part of the answer to "what about projection?" The fact that people may be wrong when they project is beside the point: *they still use ideological stereotypes in making political choices!* The fact that they made a mistake *ex post* is a problem, it is true, for the voters and for the political system. But the empirical literature showing

---

8. For a review of this literature, see Krosnick (1988).

that voters use these stereotypes, imperfect as they are, as a basis for choice actually confirms the theory we advance here.

An Illustrative Test Using Regression

As an illustrative experiment, we conducted a survey of undergraduates at the University of Texas. The data obtained were used to provide a pilot study on how the theory might be tested. We investigated ten different issues, seeking first to use the t-statistics to infer whether these relations are different from zero. Second, we can measure the average v_j across voters for those linkages that are significantly different from zero, which affords a measure of the relation between Π and policy. The aggregated results of the regression appear in table 4.

TABLE 4. Regression Results on Mappings from Ideology to Policy Positions (t-statistics in parentheses)

Issues	Model 1: No Intercept or Parties	Model 2: Intercept	Model 3: Separate Party Intercepts
Height	−0.19	−0.33	−0.22
	(−0.88)	(−1.53)	(−0.61)
Highways	0.54	0.53	0.65
	(2.89)	(2.70)	(2.37)
Incomes policy	1.13	1.21	0.86
	(10.82)	(11.96)	(6.51)
Elementary education	0.97	1.03	0.85
	(7.73)	(8.24)	(4.95)
University education	0.58	0.63	0.36
	(4.65)	(4.85)	(1.99)
Abortion	1.04	1.01	0.33
	(7.55)	(7.09)	(1.99)
Mass transit	0.63	0.69	0.28
	(4.46)	(4.92)	(1.46)
Health care	1.05	1.08	0.65
	(7.34)	(7.55)	(3.50)
Military policy in Middle East	0.79	0.89	0.67
	(7.75)	(9.40)	(5.35)
Tax policy	0.85	0.87	0.30
	(4.60)	(4.55)	(1.15)

Note: Results of a survey of 40 students at University of Texas, August 1990. The following were the equations estimated for each of the three models (only the estimates of the linkage terms v_js are reported here).

Model 1: $\omega_{ij} - b_j = \hat{v}_j X_j$
Model 2: $\omega_{ij} - b_j = \alpha_0 + \hat{v}_j X_j$
Model 3: $\omega_{ij} - b_j = \alpha_1 DEM + \alpha_2 REP + \hat{v}_j X_j$

where α_0 is the simple intercept, and α_1 and α_2 are the intercepts when they differ by party.
Source: Hinich and Munger (1992).

To create some variation in "issues," we included a number of mostly economic policy dimensions on which the voters placed themselves, the status quo, and the candidates.[9] The economic issues were the appropriate level of government spending on highways, elementary and university education, mass transit, and the progressivity of tax policy (for the actual questionnaire, see the appendix to this chapter). The other issues on the survey included some less closely linked with purely economic ideology, such as abortion, spending on health care, and support for military intervention in Kuwait (an important issue in the United States in the fall of 1990). As a check of the method, we also included an "issue" wholly orthogonal (presumably) to ideology, the height of the candidates. Finally, we asked voters to place themselves, the status quo, and each of the candidates on an abstract economic ideological dimension ranging from "no private property, all means of production owned by the state" on the left to "severely restricted government, all goods allocated by market" on the right. Because we used all voters in the sample, the t-statistics on the coefficient estimates test the null hypothesis that the coefficients differ across voters. A significant coefficient implies voters substantially agree on that issue (by rejecting the null that the average linkage is zero).

Before performing the regression analysis, we subtracted each voter's estimate of the status quo in each of the policy dimensions, and on the ideological dimension. The three models we estimated were the simple model implied by equation 7.8 (i.e., with no intercept), the same model with an intercept, and then a more complex intercept allowing for the possibility that party ID, rather than ideology, is the variable driving voter perceptions. Looking first at Model 1, we see that all of the linkages are positive (because the issue dimensions were arranged, with no loss of generality, along the same left-right conception as the ideological dimension) and highly significant, except the "ringer," height. Adding the intercept term in Model 2 changes the results astonishingly little, and in most cases improves the fit of the estimations. The strongest form of our model would imply that the intercept should be insignificant, of course, but this would require, in addition, that there are no errors in our measures of issues.

---

9. The political figures we used in the survey were Lloyd Bentson (U.S. Senator, R-Texas), William Clements (Texas Governor, R), Phillip Gramm (U.S. Senator, R-Texas), Jesse Jackson (Presidential Candidate, D), George Bush (President), Anne Richards (Texas Gub. Candidate, D), and Clayton Williams (Texas Gub. Candidate, R). In addition, a fictional candidate, "Jorge Luna," was included to determine if people were willing to admit when they did not know a candidate. Less than 10 percent of the respondents thought they had heard of Jorge Luna. Interestingly, most of those who did "know" Jorge Luna (1) were themselves conservative, and (2) expected Jorge Luna to be very liberal. This association between a Hispanic surname and liberal ideology is anecdotal evidence for the importance of simple stereotypes in making political judgments. It is also evidence, of course, for how often such judgments are off the mark.

The real test comes when we allow the intercept to differ across the two parties, for if voters choose based solely on party ID, the significance of the ideological variable will disappear. Not surprisingly, this is exactly what happens for tax policy and mass transit, each of which have significant "for or against" components well explained by the dichotomous party variable. A somewhat surprising middle case is represented by the coefficients on university education funding, abortion, and health care, each of which is substantially reduced in size, but retains its significance. The remainder of the policy issues (highways, incomes policy, elementary education, and the use of force in Kuwait) are little changed (the coefficient on highways actually *increases* in size!) by the inclusion of the party variables.[10]

Consequently, we are able to reject the null of incoherence, indicating that there is some commonality in the voters' understanding of the relation between policy and ideology. Further, this linkage goes beyond a simple directional relation associated with party identification, and appears to support our contention that voters use a conception of ideology as a reduced dimensional space with linkages to policy as a means of understanding politics.

Factor Analysis and Estimates of Ideological Linkage

In this section, we discuss a procedure for estimating ideological linkages on issues, using factor analysis. To provide a simple exposition, let us assume that there is only one "Downsian" economic left-right dimension. Let us suppose further that there is one political issue that is highly salient to all voters in a given election. The theory is designed to allow voters to care about different issues, but it is simpler to fix on a single issue for purposes of exposition.

Suppose that there are L candidates who are running for office in an election. Let π_p denote the positions of candidate p on the ideological scale ($p = 1, \ldots, L$). Let π_o denote the position of the status quo ideological position of the present government.[11] That is, as before, we place the origin of the ideological space at the status quo position of the present government. Turning to the issue, let ω_{ip} denote the position of the pth candidate on the

_____

10. It is possible, of course, to distinguish ideology and partisanship. However, at the mass level, this distinction is not likely to be important. The fact that the coefficients on the ideological variables are largely invariant to the inclusion of the party dummies implies that there is significant coherence in ideological perceptions, and that the party dummies are capturing something else.

11. Even if one candidate is an incumbent, his ideological position may be somewhat different from the present "government" position, due to the complexities of decision and implementation in public policy.

issue, *as perceived by voter i*, and let ω_{io} denote i's perception of the status quo. The linkage model is as follows for $p = 1$ and 2:

$$\omega_{ip} - \omega_{io} = v_i(\pi_p - \pi_o) \tag{7.15}$$

The term v_i translates a move on the ideological dimension to a move on the issue positions as perceived by voter i. The status quo ideology is imputed to be at ω_{io} by the ith voter.

Equation 7.1 is a linear relationship between ideological positions and issue positions for each voter. Since the ideological dimension is a *latent factor*, its origin is arbitrary. Let us set the origin to be π_o. Also, let $e_i(v)$ denote the idiosyncratic component (that is, the portion *not* shared by others) of the population mean translation parameter v_i. Then equation 7.16 can be written

$$\omega_{ip} - \omega_{io} = (v + e_i(v))\pi_p + u_{ip} \tag{7.16}$$

where u_i is an error due to lack of fit of the model. The critical assumption for the theory is as follows: the *idiosyncratic error* $e_i(v)$ determines any correlation between the policy preferences of the ith voter and the $\omega_{ip} - \omega_{io}$, the differences between the perceived positions of the candidates and the status quo. In other words, if the theory is correct, then there is no correlation between voter preferences and the terms in the model error u_{ip}. On the other hand, if the voters consistently "project" their own preferences onto candidates they like for other reasons, the preferences and positions of the candidates will be significantly correlated.

Before turning to the implementation of the empirical method using factor analysis, recall the direct empirical approach using regression if there is only one dimension. A reliable measure of candidate positions on this simple ideological axis can be obtained. Since there will be some variation of the reported positions of the candidates on the ideological scale (it is an instrument to measure an unobservable, theoretically assumed set of positions associated with π_p), let $\hat{\pi}_{ip}$ denote the score given by voter i to candidate $p(p = 1, \ldots, L)$. Assume that the idiosyncratic, candidate-specific error $e_{ip}(\pi) = \hat{\pi}_{ip} - \pi_p$ is a stochastic variate in the population of voters, and is independently distributed from the error $e_i(v)$. If we then average $\hat{\pi}_{ip}$ in the sample and let $\bar{\pi}_p$ denote the sample average, then a zero intercept least squares fit of the L values of $\omega_{ip} - \omega_{io}$ regressed against the $\bar{\pi}_p$ for each respondent would yield an unbiased estimate of v_i. The error of the fit and the value of the intercept, if we allow the intercept to be estimated, would provide a statistical reality check of the theory, as we showed earlier.

Unfortunately, there is a serious flaw in such an empirical analysis. We have no a priori reason to assume that there is only one ideological dimension. More important, there is no good reason to require that this one dimension (if it does exist) is an objective "economic" left-right cleavage with clearly definable units. The regression analysis *imposes* both these assumptions, but is capable of testing neither of them.

A number of empirical studies have used so-called feeling thermometer scores from various Nation Election Studies. Each respondent is asked to rate a number of politicians on a scale from 0 to 100, according to how "warm" or "cold" he feels toward the politician. In some cases, groups are rated on this thermometer scale. Thermometer scores are not issue scores. They measure something about how much the respondents like or dislike the politicians or groups.

There are some multidimensional scaling results of feeling thermometer scores from various Nation Election Surveys that provide some evidence for the existence of *two* dimensions (Rusk and Weisberg 1972; Rabinowitz 1973; Aldrich 1975; Cahoon 1975; Cahoon, Hinich, and Ordeshook 1978; Poole 1981; Poole and Rosenthal 1984; Enelow and Hinich 1984a, 1984b; and Poole and Rosenthal 1985). One dimension appears consistently to have to do with economic issues, such as Downs (1957) claimed and Enelow and Hinich (1984a) confirmed. But this association of the dimension with economic tenets means less than it seems: "having to do" with economic issues is hardly the same as the well-defined liberalism/conservatism dimension usually assumed to represent ideology. The particular economic issues depend on both the time and the party system in place. It is a (common) mistake *of the observer* to impose such an *ex ante* structure on the data. Such a structure is based on the observer's personal, *subjective and idiosyncratic*, understanding of political meaning.

In any case, it is not clear how to label the second dimension, even in the broadest conceptual terms. We have no data on respondent scoring of candidates on any other dimension(s) that could be used as an instrument to the second latent dimension. We thus look for an indirect, but more empirically rigorous, approach to testing the theory.

A Two-Factor Ideological Model of Perceptions

The model in Hinich and Pollard (1981) was deduced from the results obtained by applying the Cahoon-Hinich scaling method to thermometer data, and from an attempt to rationalize the other multidimensional scaling results (Cahoon 1975). For more than one dimension, this is a linear model, very similar to the model used to rationalize standard orthogonal factor analysis. Let us extend equation 7.16 to the case of two ideological dimensions.[12]

---

12. The following derivation, and empirical results, are adapted from Enelow and Hinich (1994).

Once again, for purposes of exposition, we will fix on only one issue to avoid notational clutter. Let ω_{ip} denote voter i's perception of candidate p on the issue, and ω_{io} denote the perceived position of the status quo. Let π_{p1} and π_{p2} denote the ideological positions of candidate p on the two latent dimensions. Since the origin of the ideological space is arbitrary, we place the status quo (present government position) at the origin of the two-dimensional space. Then our model, with *no uncertainty* in the π positions, is as follows:

$$\omega_{ip} - \omega_{io} = [(v_1 + e_{i1}(v))\pi_{p1}] + [(v_2 + e_{i2}(v))\pi_{p2}] + u_{ip} \qquad (7.17)$$

The parameters v_1 and v_2 translate moves from the status quo on the two *ideological* dimensions to a move of the position from the *issue* status quo. The status quo in the ideological space is $(0, 0)$, by construction; the status quo in the issue space is ω_{io}, and is simply the voter's perception (in the general case) of the vector of present government policies. The error terms e_{im} ($m = 1, 2$) are the idiosyncratic error terms for the translation parameters. The term u_{ip} is once again the model error term.

Equation 7.17 is of the form of a two–latent factor model (Anderson 1984). We are using two factors for purposes of exposition, just as we are fixing on only one issue. The model is quite general, being both multi-issue and multi–latent factor.[13] There can be many issues and more than two ideological latent dimensions; the determination of the dimensionality of the space (one, two, etc.) is empirical, not theoretical. Dimensionality is the result of applying standard maximum likelihood factor methods that depend on the sample covariance matrix of the observed variates, which in this case are the differences $d_{ip} = \omega_{ip} - \omega_{io}$. However, since previous empirical work strongly suggests that the space is either one- or two-dimensional, we will present the model in terms of two factors.

Before discussing the identification problem of the model *after* the dimensionality of the latent factor space (which we claimed defines the ideological space) is determined, let us enrich the model to accommodate fundamental uncertainty about the exact ideological positions of the candidates. Sticking with the two dimensional example, let $e_{p1}(\pi)$ and $e_{p2}(\pi)$ denote random uncertainty errors in the true positions of the pth candidate. As stated earlier in this chapter, *these errors are not perceptual*, but represent true uncertainty about the ideological positions of the candidates. In other words, the candidates are no longer modeled as points in the ideological space, but are represented as a probability density function (in this case, the joint density of the errors $e_{pm}(\pi)$). Recall that the ideological positions are not observed. In

---

13. We have written out the model with two latent factors, but exactly the same formulation works for ℓ factors. The greatest difference, as is often the case, is the difference between the scalar and two-dimensional cases.

factor analysis parlance, the positions π_{pm} are factor loadings of the candidates on the two orthogonal factors posited in the theory.

The general statistical model to be estimated is as follows:

$$d_{ip} = (\mathbf{v}_1 + \mathbf{e}_{i1}(\mathbf{v}))(\pi_{p1} + \mathbf{e}_{p1}(\pi)) + (\mathbf{v}_2 + \mathbf{e}_{i2}(\mathbf{v}))$$

$$\times \ (\pi_{p2} + \mathbf{e}_{p2}(\pi)) + \mathbf{u}_{ip} \qquad (7.18)$$

Assuming that the $i = 1, \ldots, N$ voters are a random sample from the population of voters, the errors are assumed to have a zero mean value in the population. The identification restrictions on the errors are as follows:

$\{\mathbf{e}_{i1}(\mathbf{v}), \mathbf{e}_{i2}(\mathbf{v}), \mathbf{e}_{p1}(\pi), \mathbf{e}_{p2}(\pi), \mathbf{u}_{ip}\}$ are *independently distributed* for $i = 1$, $\ldots, N$ and $p = 1, \ldots, L$. The independence between the perceptual error $\mathbf{e}_{im}(\mathbf{v})$ and the candidate uncertainty terms $\mathbf{e}_{pm}(\pi)$ $(m = 1, 2)$ are intuitively plausible, given that the $\mathbf{v}$ terms derive from perceptions of the entire party system and the candidate terms are specific to experience with one individual.[14] The independence assumption for the elements of the pairs is a useful working simplification, given our *a priori* knowledge of the validity of the model.

$\text{Var}[e_{i1}(v)] = \text{Var}[e_{i2}(v)] = 1$, where Var is the population variance of the indicated random variable.

The second assumption is necessary to identify the model since the units of the e_{im} are unknown and unobservable. If expression 7.17 holds but the variances are grossly unequal, then the recovered map of candidates will be very distorted. There is no "free lunch" when analyzing models with unobserved values. This assumption, however, is not crucial to the key test of the theory.

It then follows that the population covariance between d_{ip} and d_{iq}, denoted $\text{Cov}(d_{ip}, d_{iq})$, is as follows:

$$\text{Cov}(d_{ip}, d_{iq}) = \pi_{p1}\pi_{q1} + \pi_{p2}\pi_{q2} \qquad (7.19)$$

The population variance of d_{ip}, denoted $\text{Var}(d_{ip})$, is given by

$$\text{Var}(d_{ip}) = \pi_{p1}{}^2 + \pi_{\pi2}{}^2 + \text{Var}(p) \qquad (7.20)$$

---

14. This assumption might be much less plausible in a political system dominated by a long-term dictatorship with a well-developed cult of personality, such as China in the 1970s, or Chile or Romania in the 1980s.

where the specific variance, $\text{Var}(p)$, is:

$$\text{Var}(p) = (v_1^2 + 1)\text{Var}[e_{p1}(\pi)] + (v_2^2 + 1) + \text{Var}[e_{p2}(\pi)] +$$

$$\text{Var}(u_{ip}) \tag{7.21}$$

Let π denote the $L \times 2$ matrix whose p, m element is π_{pm}, and let v_d denote the diagonal matrix whose pth diagonal element is $\text{V}(p)$. Combining expressions 7.19 and 7.20, in matrix notation, the $L \times L$ covariance matrix of $d_i = (di_1, \ldots, d_{iL})'$, denoted $\mathbf{C}_d$, is

$$\mathbf{C}_d = \pi\pi' + \mathbf{v}_d \tag{7.22}$$

The sample covariance estimator of $\mathbf{C}_d$ can be used to obtain an estimate of π, up to an arbitrary rotation of the axes, by factor analysis.

If the errors are assumed to have a normal distribution, or if the sample is large enough so that the sample covariance is approximately normally distributed, then maximum-likelihood factor analysis can be employed to estimate the elements of the π_p, which are the location of the candidates in the ideological space. The eigenvalues of the estimate of $\mathbf{C}_d$ can be used to determine the dimensionality in any one of a number of related standard methods.

The Covariance Matrix When the Ideal Points Are Included

In this section we summarize previous research by Enelow (1986) and Enelow and Hinich (1989c, 1993) in testing the Hinich-Pollard model. We will continue to use x_i to denote the ideal point of voter i on the issue. The idiosyncratic error terms $e_{i1}(v)$ and $e_{2i}(v)$ are assumed to be the *only* error terms correlated with x_i. The true ideological positions π_m and linkage terms v_m ($m = 1$, 2) are fixed values in the population. This assumption rules out correlation between the model errors u_{ip} for $p = 1, \ldots, L$, and x_i. The first step is to derive the covariance matrix of the vector $a_i = (d_{i1}, \ldots, d_{iL}, x_i)'$, given the assumption about the correlation structure.

Let $\mathbf{C}_a$ denote the $(L + 1) \times (L + 1)$ covariance matrix of a_i. Since its first L elements are the d_{ip}, the upper left $L \times L$ submatrix of $\mathbf{C}_a$ is $\mathbf{C}_d = \pi\pi' + \mathbf{v}_d$. The matrix $\mathbf{C}_a$ can be written in terms of a product of $(L + 1) \times 2$ matrices analogous to $\pi\pi'$ plus a diagonal matrix of specific variances. To accomplish this, it is useful to define some additional notation. Let $\mathbf{r} = (r_1, r_2)'$, where $\mathbf{r}_m$ ($m = 1, 2$) denotes the *correlation* between $\mathbf{x}_i$ and $\mathbf{e}_{im}(v)$ (recall that $\text{Var}[e_{im}(v)] = 1$). Then the vector of L covariances between the d_{ip} and x_i

is $\sigma_m \pi_r$, where σ_m denotes the standard deviation of x_i. Let $\mathbf{V}_a$ denote the $(L + 1) \times (L + 1)$ diagonal matrix whose first L elements are the specific variances $\mathbf{V}(1) , \ldots , \mathbf{V}(L)$. The last element of $\mathbf{V}_a$ is $\mathbf{V}(L + 1) = \sigma_m^2(1 - r_1^2 - r_2)$.

Given these assumptions, the covariance matrix of a_i can be written:

$$C_a = \begin{bmatrix} \pi\pi' & \sigma_m \pi r \\ \sigma_m r' \pi' & \sigma_m^2 r' r \end{bmatrix} + V_a \tag{7.23}$$

Now let $\mathbf{Q}$ denote the $(L + 1) \times 2$ matrix $(\pi', \sigma_{mr})'$. Expression 7.23 can be written as:

$$\mathbf{C}_a = \mathbf{Q}\mathbf{Q}' + \mathbf{V}_a \tag{7.24}$$

The set of eigenvalues of $\mathbf{C}_a$ is the L eigenvalues of $\mathbf{C}_d$ plus σ_m. Calculating a factorization of the matrix $\mathbf{C}_a$ yields a matrix whose upper $L \times L$ matrix is just π, subject to the same rotation of the coordinate system in the factorization of $\mathbf{C}_d$ (see appendix to this chapter). This result implies that a factor analysis of the $\mathbf{a}_i$ will produce the sample estimates of the candidate locations as the factor analysis of the $\mathbf{d}_i$.

If x_i were correlated with the model errors, or if it were correlated with the uncertainty terms in the π_p's, then the candidate maps from a factor analysis of the sample augmented covariance matrix would not be the same as that computed from the sample $\mathbf{C}_d$. For example, suppose the ideal points were correlated with the u_{ip} and not with the errors in the $\mathbf{v}$'s. The $(L + 1)$st column of $\mathbf{C}_a$ would be the vector of covariances of x_i and u_{ip} and the variance of x_i. The first L eigenvalues of this matrix would not be the same as for that of $\mathbf{C}_d$.

This model is estimable, and the results can be used to provide measurements of the ideological linkages in real-world political contests. In an important test of the model hypothesized in equations 7.23 and 7.24, Enelow and Hinich (1994) factor analyze data from survey responses to the five issue scale questions contained in the preelection wave of the 1980 NES "Pre-Post" interview. The issues considered included abortion, defense spending, services from the government, unemployment/inflation, and a tax cut. Issue data were available on four candidates (Carter, Reagan, Anderson, and Kennedy), as well as three collective entities (the Republican party, the Democratic party, and "the Federal government." To create a respondent-specific intercept term for the linear function expressed in equation 7.1, the Federal government variable is subtracted from each of the other variables, leaving six "candidates." Consequently, an observation on a single variable in the Enelow and Hinich study is a respondent's perception of where a candidate (or the respondent) is located on a given issue, *relative* to the respondent's perception of the location of the Federal government.

To establish the empirical plausibility of expression 7.19, Enelow and Hinich compute sample correlations between respondent self-placements on a single-issue scale and factor scores on the same issue. As explained in Enelow (1986), the factor scores calculated for each case estimate the v_i's in the Enelow-Hinich-Pollard model. More specifically, if cases consist of the perceptions by respondents of candidate positions on a single issue, then v_1 and v_2 can be estimated by the factor scores computed for case i on factors 1 and 2.

Table 5 reports ten bivariate correlations between respondents' placements of themselves on one of the five preelection issue scales and each of the two factor scores computed for the respondent on the same issue. In theoretical terms, we are examining the correlations between x_i and v_{i1}, and x_i and v_{i2}, for a single issue (c_1 and c_2). As table 5 shows, the sample correlations between self-placements and scores on the first factor are all significantly positive. The sample correlations with the second factor scores are much weaker.

An explanation for this pattern of significance is suggested by the relative loadings of the candidates on the two recovered factors. On factor 1, Carter and Reagan load positively, with Reagan more positive than Carter. On factor 2, Reagan loads negatively and Carter positively. For a Reagan supporter to associate his issue position with Reagan's *positively*, the second factor score must be negative. Thus, a negative correlation between second factor scores and self-placement is expected for Reagan supporters, and a positive correlation is expected for Carter supporters. Table 5 also reports these correlations; the predictions of the model are largely confirmed.

Enelow and Hinich also test a major theoretical proposition of the model, namely, that a factor analysis of candidate variables yields the same factor loadings for the candidates as a factor analysis of candidate variables with a variable for the voters' ideal points also included. In addition, if the theory is correct, the measures of the *voter ideal points will lie in the same factor space as the candidate variables*. This is a very strong theoretical implication, and might easily be false, either because of measurement problems in the data, or because this strong form of the theory is simply false.

Table 6 reports the results of the Enelow-Hinich analysis. There are two factor analyses, one of the candidate variables and one of the candidate plus voter variables. Observations in the analysis vary across both respondents and issues; the correlation matrix of all variables for the sample is also reported in the table.

The results are striking. As predicted, the candidate loadings exhibit only insignificant differences in the two (potentially very different) factor analyses.

At least as important, and perhaps surprising, *the voter variable does not add a dimension to the factor solution*; the space is the same. A comparison of the two sets of eigenvalues of the initial factor matrices makes this point more precisely.

Enelow and Hinich (1993) note that this is a very powerful, and important, result, but the reasons why are not immediately obvious. After all, why would we expect that the ideological space, or estimated loadings of the

TABLE 5. Sample Correlations between Respondent Self-Placement and Factor Score on Five Issues

	All Respondents	Carter Supporters	Reagan Supporters
F1D	0.67	0.57	0.81
	($N = 526$)	($N = 196$)	($N = 227$)
	($p = 0.00$)	($p = 0.00$)	($p = 0.00$)
F2D	0.14	0.46	-0.08
	($N = 526$)	($N = 196$)	($N = 227$)
	($p = 0.00$)	($p = 0.00$)	($p = 0.12$)
F1G	0.60	0.39	0.82
	($N = 5.45$)	($N = 198$)	($N = 221$)
	($p = 0.00$)	($p = 0.00$)	($p = 0.00$)
F2G	0.17	0.60	-0.27
	($N = 5.45$)	($N = 198$)	($N = 221$)
	($p = 0.00$)	($p = 0.00$)	($p = 0.00$)
F1I	0.67	0.40	0.87
	($N = 387$)	($N = 153$)	($N = 152$)
	($p = 0.00$)	($p = 0.00$)	($p = 0.00$)
F2I	0.04	0.45	-0.20
	($N = 387$)	($N = 153$)	($N = 152$)
	($p = 0.22$)	($p = 0.00$)	($p = 0.00$)
F1A	0.35	0.43	0.30
	($N = 306$)	($N = 113$)	($N = 122$)
	($p = 0.00$)	($p = 0.00$)	($p = 0.00$)
F2A	0.08	0.32	-0.33
	($N = 306$)	($N = 113$)	($N = 122$)
	($p = 0.08$)	($p = 0.00$)	($p = 0.00$)
F1T	0.48	0.17	0.69
	($N = 242$)	($N = 86$)	($N = 109$)
	($p = 0.00$)	($p = 0.06$)	($p = 0.00$)
F2T	0.00	0.32	0.10
	($N = 242$)	($N = 86$)	($N = 109$)
	($p = 0.48$)	($p = 0.00$)	($p = 0.14$)

Note: F1D = score on first factor for respondent-defense cases. F2D = score on second factor for respondent-defense cases. F1G, F2G, F1I, F2I, F1A, F2A, F1T, F2T defined identically for govt. services (G), inflation/unemp. (I), abortion (A), and tax cut (T).

Source: Enelow and Hinich 1993, 17.

candidate variables, would be changed by the inclusion of an additional variable? To determine if, in fact, this result is a strong finding, or an artifactual consequence of the factor method, Enelow and Hinich employ a partial resampling, randomly permuting the rows and columns of the data matrix on which the results in table 6 are based. The results of the same two factor

TABLE 6. Sample Correlation Matrix and Principal Results of Factor Analysis Based on 1980 Preelection Issue Data

			Sample Correlation Matrix				
	C	R	A	K	RE	DE	V
Carter	1.00	0.35	0.45	0.52	0.36	0.70	0.35
Reagan		1.00	0.58	0.31	0.90	0.35	0.63
Anderson			1.00	0.49	0.59	0.50	0.53
Kennedy				1.00	0.32	0.62	0.34
Rep party					1.00	0.34	0.62
Dem party						1.00	0.39
Voter							1.00

	Unrotated Loading from Candidate Factor Analysis		Unrotated Loading from Candidate and Voter Factor Analysis	
Variable	Factor 1	Factor 2	Factor 1	Factor 2
Carter	0.50	0.59	0.50	0.58
Reagan	0.93	−0.18	0.93	−0.19
Anderson	0.67	0.22	0.68	0.22
Kennedy	0.45	0.53	0.45	0.53
Rep party	0.93	−0.19	0.93	−0.19
Dem party	0.52	0.73	0.52	0.73
Voter	—	—	0.68	0.05

	Eigenvalues of Initial Factor Matrix	
Factor	Candidate Variables	Cand Plus Voter Variables
1	3.46	3.94
2	1.23	1.30
3	0.51	0.51
4	0.41	0.46
5	0.28	0.41
6	0.10	0.28
7	—	0.10

Note: Factoring is done by Rao's canonical method.
Source: Enelow and Hinich 1993, 18.

TABLE 7. Issue-at-a-Time Candidate and Candidate/Voter Factor Analysis

Variable	Issue	Unrotated Loadings from Candidate Factor Analysis		Unrotated Loadings from Candidate and Voter Factor Analysis	
		Factor 1	Factor 2	Factor 1	Factor 2
Carter	Defense	0.36	0.66	0.38	0.65
Reagan	Defense	0.89	−0.17	0.89	−0.21
Anderson	Defense	0.70	0.19	0.71	0.17
Kennedy	Defense	0.43	0.49	0.45	0.48
Rep party	Defense	0.92	−0.24	0.90	−0.26
Dem party	Defense	0.39	0.82	0.41	0.80
Voter	Defense	—	—	0.70	0.14
Carter	Govt serv	0.43	0.55	0.45	0.54
Reagan	Govt serv	0.89	−0.17	0.89	−0.20
Anderson	Govt serv	0.64	0.28	0.64	0.26
Kennedy	Govt serv	0.38	0.63	0.39	0.61
Rep party	Govt serv	0.91	−0.17	0.90	−0.19
Dem party	Govt serv	0.41	0.67	0.44	0.66
Voter	Govt serv	—	—	0.63	0.19
Carter	Inf/unemp	0.53	0.49	0.53	0.48
Reagan	Inf/unemp	0.90	−0.22	0.90	−0.24
Anderson	Inf/unemp	0.79	0.20	0.78	0.19
Kennedy	Inf/unemp	0.48	0.56	0.48	0.55
Rep party	Inf/unemp	0.90	−0.24	0.90	−0.24
Dem party	Inf/unemp	0.50	0.72	0.51	0.72
Voter	Inf/unemp	—	—	0.70	0.05
Carter	Abortion	0.72	0.22	0.71	0.24
Reagan	Abortion	0.70	−0.50	0.72	−0.50
Anderson	Abortion	0.62	0.25	0.63	0.27
Kennedy	Abortion	0.62	0.20	0.61	0.22
Rep party	Abortion	0.71	−0.50	0.72	−0.47
Dem party	Abortion	0.82	0.40	0.81	0.41
Voter	Abortion	—	—	0.37	0.07
Carter	Tax cut	0.54	0.61	0.54	0.62
Reagan	Tax cut	0.88	−0.25	0.88	−0.24
Anderson	Tax cut	0.57	0.09	0.57	0.09
Kennedy	Tax cut	0.44	0.35	0.44	0.36
Rep party	Tax cut	0.87	0.28	0.87	−0.28
Dem party	Tax cut	0.54	0.67	0.54	0.66
Voter	Tax cut	—	—	0.50	0.01

Note: The variable-issue pair Carter-Defense specifies that cases consist of respondent perceptions of Carter's position on that issue. Other variable-issue pairs are defined similarly. There is one factor analysis per variable set for a given issue, yielding five factor analyses for the candidate variables and five factor analyses for the voter plus candidate variables.

Source: Enelow and Hinich 1993, 20.

**TABLE 8. Theoretical vs. Actual Estimates
of Specific Variance of Voter Ideal Point Variable
(as proportion of total variance)**

Issue	Est. Specific Variance of Voter Variable	VAR (x_i) $(1 - c'c)$
Defense	0.50	0.56
Govt serv	0.57	0.65
Inf/unemp	0.51	0.57
Abortion	0.86	0.88
Tax cut	0.75	0.79

Note: The issue specifies that cases consist of individual perceptions of candidate and own position on the given issue. For example, Defense denotes a factor analysis of seven variables, six candidate variables and the variable "voter," where each variable consists of perceptions of where a candidate or oneself stands on the issue of defense spending. H is estimated from factor scores that derive from an analysis of only the candidate variables. For a fuller explanation, see text.
Source: Enelow and Hinich 1993, 21.

analyses, using the scrambled data, now differ significantly, showing that the loadings are not the same.[15] The structure in the data does matter, and the structure Enelow and Hinich found is strongly consistent with the model of ideology we have been advancing.

To test the robustness of the original results, Enelow and Hinich ran separate factor analyses on each of the five issues taken separately. Table 7 reports the results of five factor analyses of (C_i, x_i) and five factor analyses of C_i. Examining thirty pairwise comparisons of 1×2 loading vectors, it is possible to conclude that the results in table 6, based on averaging across issues and voters, are not due to chance variation. Adding a voter ideal point variable to the factorization has no significant effect on the loadings of the candidate variables. Furthermore, the voter variable does not add additional factors/dimensions to the space implied by the solutions.

Finally, table 8 reports the actual versus predicted estimates of the specific variance of the voter ideal point variable for the five issue-at-a-time factor analyses. As explained earlier, $\sigma_m^2(1 - c_1^2 - c_2^2) = \mathrm{Var}(x_i) - [\mathrm{Cov}(x_i, v_{i1})]^2 - [\mathrm{Cov}(x_i, v_{i2})]^2$ is a theoretical predictor of the specific variance of x_i, where v_{i1} and v_{i2} are factor scores computed from a factor analysis of the candidate variables alone. As table 8 shows, this theoretical predictor provides a close fit with the specific variance estimated from a factor analysis of the voter and candidate variables.

These results provide further evidence of the empirical validity of the

---

15. The analysis is not reproduced here, but can be found in Enelow and Hinich (1993).

model of the correlations of voter-candidate issue data implied by the theory of ideology. Postulating that voter-candidate issue correlations are measured by the mapping terms (v_j) of the linear spatial model of ideology leads to a surprising and important prediction: estimated candidate loadings obtained from factor analysis of the candidate variables are unchanged when voter ideal points are added to the analysis. This result breaks down if the voter ideal points are correlated with the model errors or with any other systematic variation in the data not captured by the v_{i1} and v_{i2} in the model.

Furthermore, the independence of the candidate loadings from voter policy preferences means that the estimated candidate map is not an artifact of voter preferences. This is reassuring, since it implies that the conception of a stable set of candidate positions on an underlying set of dimensions, together representing ideology, is consistent with the issue data.

Conclusion

This chapter has reviewed two different methods capable of measuring the phenomena implied by a theory of political choice based on ideology. The first method is regression analysis: the regression coefficients in an experimental sample provide direct measures of the size and coherence of the mapping terms relating candidate ideologies to voter perceptions of candidate policy positions. This approach is useful as an illustration, and the overall level of significance of the regression coefficients is some evidence of the coherence of the perceptions across voters. But the regression approach assumes that there is but one relevant dimension, and forces participants to act as if one dimension were also their perception.

A clearly superior, though conceptually and computationally more complex, procedure is factor analysis. Using data and estimates from previously published studies, we have given evidence that the notion of a reduced dimensional space, as a guide to voting decisions by voters, actually outperforms the "rational" model based purely on issues. Further, the results show that the consistency of the estimates is not due to "projection" by voters, but actually arises from voters' use of ideology as a guide for political choice.

APPENDIX: QUESTIONNAIRE FOR REGRESSION ANALYSIS

This questionnaire is designed to elicit responses regarding your evaluation of eight political candidates, your perception of where our current policy is, and your own ideas about the best questions, using the following codes:

Candidate Codes

B—Lloyd Bentson, Senator from Texas
C—William Clements, Governor of Texas
G—Phillip Gramm, Senator from Texas
J—Jesse Jackson, 1988 Dem. Candidate for President
L—Jorge Luna, 1990 Candidate for Governor
P—George Bush, President of the United States
R—Anne Richards, 1990 Candidate for Governor
W—Clayton Williams, 1990 Candidate for Governor

Your Evaluation

OP— Your Own Position
SQ—Your Placement of the Status Quo

Questions

1. The first question is a practice to make certain you understand the instructions. Please place the candidates on a height (OP) and what you think the average height of the population (SQ) is. PLEASE LEAVE OUT ANY CANDIDATES YOU DON'T KNOW! DON'T ASSIGN THEM JUST ANY VALUE, OR THE STATUS QUO!

0—SHORTEST   100—TALLEST

Now, the questions are for real. Please answer them as best you can, and LEAVE OUT any candidates you aren't sure of. Rank the candidates, your own preference, and the status quo for the following:

2. Commitment to building public roads

0—NEW PUBLIC HIGHWAYS   100—NO NEW ROADS;
   WHEREVER NEEDED   ONLY MAINTENANCE

3. Commitment to personal incomes policy

0—EVERYONE GUARANTEED   100—ONLY PRIVATE
   GOV'T JOB/INCOME   CHARITY FOR POOR

4. Commitment to elementary education

    0—FREE (TAX-FINANCED)   100—PURE PRIVATE
         SPECIAL CLASSES,   VOUCHER SYSTEM ONLY
         MULTILINGUAL TUTORS

5. Commitment to university education

    0—FREE (TAX-FINANCED)   100—TUITION = AVERAGE
         TUITION, ROOM   COST, COLLEGES SET
         BOARD, NO ENTRY   ENTRY REQ'S
         REQUIREMENTS

6. Commitment to pro-choice/pro-life

    0—FREE (TAX-FINANCED)   100—ABORTION ILLEGAL IN
         FEDERALLY FUNDED   ALL CIRCUMSTANCES
         ABORTION ON DEMAND

7. Commitment to mass transit

    0—FREE (TAX-FINANCED   100—PRIVATE TRANSIT
         MASS TRANSIT IN   SYSTEMS ONLY
         ALL CITIES

8. Commitment to health care

    0—FREE (TAX-FINANCED)   100—PRIVATE INSURANCE/
         CRADLE-TO-GRAVE   CHARITY HOSPITALS ONLY
         PUBLIC HEALTH SYSTEM

9. Commitment to military intervention in middle east

    0—NO MILITARY ACTION,   100—IMMEDIATE, FULL
         NO EMBARGO, LET   SCALE INVASION TO
         THEM "FIGHT IT OUT"   GUARANTEE OIL

10. Commitment to tax policy, assuming tax increase is required

    0—WEALTHY PAY HIGH   100—FLAT TAX RATE, SO
         RATE, MIDDLE RATE   ALL PAY EQUAL RATE
         LOWER, POOR MUCH
         LOWER RATE

11. Now finally, rank all the candidates, yourself, and the status quo for the whole U.S. on the following AGGREGATE left-right economic scale.

0—NO PRIVATE PROPERTY ALL MEANS OF PRODUCTION OWNED BY THE STATE

100—SEVERELY RESTRICTED GOVERNMENT, ALL GOODS ALLOCATED BY MARKET

CHAPTER 8

Representing Public Choices by Citizens

The first seven chapters of this book have developed a simple version of the theory of ideology in the representation of political choices by citizens. The theory might be summarized as follows.

Citizens have preferences over outcomes in the n-dimensional "issue" space, where issue is defined as a policy decision that (a) affects citizens' welfare, and (b) attracts the attention of either politicians or the media. These preferences are not necessarily fixed, in the classical microeconomic sense, but are relatively stable, and, in any case, are known to the citizens themselves.

Political discourse is shaped and constrained by ideologies, which we have defined as more or less coherent sets of ideas with implications for what is right, who gets what, and who rules. Consequently, the menu of citizen political choice is determined by the viable ideological positions. "Viability" is a function of both the precepts of the ideology itself, and a successful party organization to popularize it and give it effective force in shaping the government.

The linkages between the issues citizens care about and the ideological positions of candidates among whom those citizens must actually choose are the product of the accumulated experience citizens have with the political system. The linkage between ideologies and outcomes, and the implied link between an ideological position and a citizen's welfare, can be modeled spatially, with citizens choosing the candidate "closest" to their ideal points. Citizens may make errors by using these simplifying political stereotypes, but this is a descriptively accurate outline of the process of choice.

There are at least three kinds of uncertainty that influence citizens' political choices, and also their level of welfare. The first is uncertainty over the actual ideological position of a candidate; the second is uncertainty over the existing policy of government (the status quo); the third is uncertainty over the linkage between ideology and policy.

If ideology is the mechanism for making political choices, then an empirical implication of the model is that voters' idiosyncratic perceptions of ideology, the status quo, and policy linkages are coherent and similar. Given the sources of uncertainty we outlined, this implication is certainly falsifiable, and may often be false, particularly in periods of political realignment. We found that, though there is certainly noise in the relationship among ideology, status quo, and the linkage vector, there is significant coherence across voters. Further, this coherence is consistently observed in empirical work, using a variety of methods in numerous different settings and samples.

In this chapter, we expand the spatial model of ideology on which our theory of political choice is based. To model citizen choice more accurately and completely, we drop the deterministic assumptions of voter perceptions adopted previously. The deterministic choice assumption is replaced with the perspective of probabilistic voting. Because this perspective is much more complex, and requires an understanding of probability distributions that the basic model leaves out, we have put off the presentation until now. It is not necessary that the probabilistic voting approach be employed for the model to be accepted, but probabilistic voting provides a far richer theoretical setting for the analysis of political choice. The first portion of the chapter reviews the classical model and the way probabilistic voting developed. We then move on to the fully fleshed out model of political choice based on ideology.

Probabilistic Voting: Incorporating Irreducible Uncertainty

The tendency of much modern theory has been to assume full information, in many ways analogous to the approach of economic theory. Yet this approach flies in the face of much of what Downs appears to have intended when he outlined his economic theory of democracy.

> Traditional economic theory assumes unlimited amounts of free information are available to decision-makers. In contrast, we seek to discover what political decision-making is like when uncertainty exists and information is obtainable only at a cost. . . . Immediately there arises the crucial question of how to decide which data to select and which to reject. . . . Information is necessarily gathered by means of certain *principles of selection*: rules employed to determine what to make use of and what not to. Different persons use different rules, but everyone must use some rule—even random selection follows a rule. Therefore all information is by nature biased because it is a selection of data from the vast amount extant, others of which could have been selected. (Downs 1957, 207–12)

Downs adds, in a footnote to this passage:

We have deliberately used the word *biased* to denote this inherent characteristic of reporting, in spite of its emotionally pejorative associations.
When we speak of reporting as biased, we are not implying the data
therein are false, since we have assumed all data are accurate, nor that
the reporter is immoral, since bias can be avoided. We only mean to
convey that the selection and arrangement of fact in any report are
inevitably tinged by the viewpoint of the reporter. (Downs 1957, 212,
note)

This passage and accompanying footnote are among the most important,
yet least understood, of Downs's work.[1]
We can distill its wisdom to four essential parts:

No externally generalizable rule guides voters' information search; instead, each voter uses his or her unique, idiosyncratic experiences and
values to guide the voting decision.
Even if rules were general, voters would inevitably also have different
samples from the overall set of information available. Since rules do
differ, voters' opinions about candidates may differ strikingly.
If information, and persuasion about the information's veracity, were
free, opinions would be identical. Since this is not the case, *ex ante*
opinions about candidate behavior once in office may differ widely.
As researchers, we might reasonably divide the set of determinants for a
given individual's vote into those that we, the researchers, can identify
and measure in some consistent fashion and those that are idiosyncratic (hence, for us, unpredictable) and specific to each voter.

These observations, taken together, imply that Downs, himself, advocated an approach quite different from that of classical "Downsian" spatial
modeling. Later work has taken the differences in political worldviews or
belief systems as disconfirmation of the Downsian approach. Conover and
Feldman claim that:

Liberals and conservatives view the political world not from different
sides of the same coin, but . . . from the perspective of entirely different
currencies. (1981, 624)

---

1. On the rational use of "biased" information, see Calvert 1985.

Conover and Feldman conclude, in this and later work (1984, 1986, 1989), that such differences in cognition and categorization imply that the "rational" model of political choice is unrealistic and misleading. They are partly correct, but the fault is not Downs's; the fault is the "Downsian" model that made the assumption of unlimited free information that Downs himself was trying to avoid.

Grofstein tries to reconcile the notions of rationality and inflexible, divergent belief systems.

> Both a Marxist ideologue and the ordinary [capitalist], I contend, can be rational even though identical evidence equally strengthens their divergent convictions. The conceptual interpretation of ideology I propose suggests that there need be no formal distinction between the rational thought processes of those who make these very different predictions about capitalism. The reason is that *both sides may sustain their hypotheses by filtering information through very different sets of rationally supportable categories.* . . . The point is not merely that different rational agents can reach different conclusions. That goes without saying. Rather, the idea that more and more evidence necessarily brings us ever closer to the same posterior beliefs or some best system of political categories represents wishful thinking. *Formally speaking, rational inductions oriented toward the proposition that capitalism is peaceful or toward the proposition that capitalism is unstable converge in the same way, although toward different beliefs.* (Grofstein 1993, 5–8; first emphasis added, second emphasis in original)

Given the divergence in individual belief systems, the differences in actual information sets, and the differences in reactions even if information sets were identical, we take a sharp departure from classical modeling by using the probabilistic approach. Probabilistic voting was originated by Hinich, Ledyard, and Ordeshook (1972, 1973) and Hinich (1977b). Together, these two works accounted for nondeterministic (from the perspective of the researcher) behavior by citizens in deciding *whether* to vote and by voters in deciding *for whom* to vote, respectively. Numerous recent works have taken and augmented the probabilistic perspective (e.g., Coughlin and Nitzan 1981; Enelow 1986; Enelow and Hinich 1981, 1982a, 1982b, 1984b, 1989a, 1989b; Cox 1984; Austen-Smith 1987; Coughlin 1986, 1990; Ladha 1991), but these papers have been taken by most of the profession as curiosities, or, at best, highly technical and rarified extensions of the spatial. While we cannot deny the technical and nonobvious nature of the probabilistic approach, it is important to emphasize that viewing the process probabilisitically is by no means inconsistent with the assumption of purposive behavior.

Probabilistic voting is a *correction*, not an extension, of the deterministic model. It has a different epistemological basis. It is also more general, as we demonstrate below, encompassing the conclusions derivable from the classical or deterministic model. But it possesses, in addition, an appealing theoretical richness and an intuitive appeal that make it the only appropriate vehicle for any general spatial model, and so we develop it in this section and use probabilistic voting in all that follows.

Let us recapitulate the most important assumptions of classical spatial theory: (1) "Candidates" are bundles of policy positions. When a voter evaluates a candidate he considers not at all such issues as that candidate's credibility, character, or ability to lead in an unforeseeable crisis. (2) All voters are able to, and do in fact, precisely compare the platforms and compute a determinate course of action, be it strict preference (vote for the better platform), or indifference or alienation (abstain).

Each of these assumptions contradicts both reality and a careful reading of Downs's discussion. Neither of these contradictions need, of necessity, be distressing. The use of parsimonious and powerful assumptions that abstract from the complexity of reality are often very useful, and Downs's model is, after all, frustratingly vague, imprecise, and occasionally even self-contradictory. Our quarrel with the classical model must rest on more than a critique of the metaphor, or "story," used to justify the model. We also need to present a superior alternative, capable of generating nonobvious implications about political interaction and answering the objections just raised. We now demonstrate that the probabilistic model is just that superior alternative.

Consider figure 12, an explicit example of deterministic voting. Let us again assume that there are two candidates, Theta and Psi, and three voters, I, II, and III. For the sake of simplicity, we use a single policy dimension E ($E \in \Omega$), or expenditures on education. The horizontal axis measures E, and depicts E_θ and E_ψ (the candidate platforms) as well as x_I, x_{II}, and x_{III}, the three voter ideal points. Let us suppose that votes are based on the relative proximity of the two candidates' platforms to the voter's ideal point (an objectively measurable criterion for the researcher and outside observer), just as suggested by the classical model. In addition, we allow for the possibility of idiosyncratic rules of thumb, subjective perceptions of character, leadership ability, and so on. In the context of the spatial model, this means that we cannot draw the deterministic conclusion predicted by the classical model: voters vote for the closer candidate, and abstain or flip a coin to resolve ties.

Because of idiosyncratic differences in choice rules, we can only say that voters choose one candidate over another with a probability P, where $0 \leq P \leq 1$. This probability is a complicated function, one of whose arguments is spatial closeness. The additional arguments are not directly measurable (and

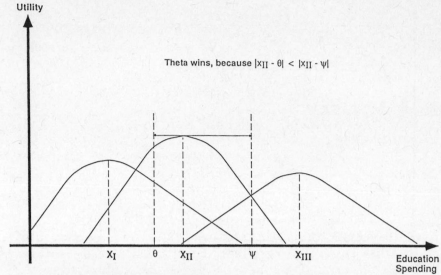

Fig. 12. **Deterministic voting example with two candidates (Theta and Psi) on education spending**

may differ across voters) in the spatial context, so we, as observers, have some uncertainty about the behavior of each voter. If the candidate who is further away is "far enough" away, the policy differences can be used to predict with certainty how the voter will react. The measure of "close enough" is the mean of the candidate platforms plus or minus an endogenously determined constant δ, on which more will be said later. For example, I votes for Theta for certain ($P_I(\theta) = 1$, $P_I(\psi) = 1 - P_I(\theta) = 0$) because Psi is so far away. Similarly, for III, Psi is the certain choice. But for II, we can make only a probabilistic prediction. The probabilistic model is depicted in figure 13. The vertical axis measures the probability of voting for Theta. In our example, $0.5 < P_{II}(\theta) < 1$: x_{II} is closer to Theta than to Psi, but the probability of II voting for Theta is less than 1. It exceeds 0.5 because $|\omega_\theta - x_{II}| < |\omega_\psi - x_{II}|$, but it isn't 1.

We have been very vague about the form of this probability distribution function (henceforth, p.d.f.). As a matter of fact, at least three different interpretations can be given $P_i(\theta) = f(x_i, \omega_\theta, \omega_\psi)$.

1. The probability is, as we have discussed it in the example above, the likelihood that a particular voter will choose Theta, *from the perspective of the observer*. The voter may well, himself, be using some deterministic, but idiosyncratic, rule. He is certain, given the information he has available, for whom he will vote, but the observer

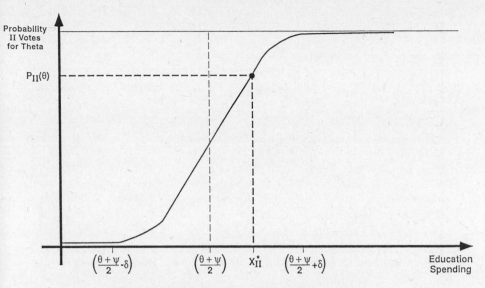

Fig. 13. Probabilistic voting on education spending

observes only the three bits of information x_i (i's ideal point), ω_θ, and ω_ψ (the candidate platforms). More than δ away from the mean platform ($\omega_\theta + \omega_\psi$)/2, these three bits of information are sufficient: $P(\theta) = 1$ or 0. But within the closed interval [(($\omega_\theta + \omega_\psi$)/2) $- \delta$, (($\omega_\theta + \omega_\psi$)/2) $+ \delta$], where $f(.)$ is symmetric, it is not enough to know the ideal point and platforms, so we must make an estimate.

2. Alternatively, x_i represents an ideal point, and we allow a large number of voters whom we identify by their ideal points. Under these circumstances, $P_i(\theta)$ is the *proportion* of the total number of voters possessing x_i as an ideal. More than δ away from the mean platform, this proportion is 1 or 0. But within this interval, some vote for Theta and some for Psi. We can predict with certainty what *overall* proportion will vote for θ, but for any individual among the group possessing x_i as an ideal, we must make an estimate.

3. Finally, voters themselves may behave this way. If voters treat a series of elections as a game, it can be demonstrated, under some circumstances, that an optimal series of votes obeys a mixed strategy equilibrium where, in any given election, the sophisticated voter chooses between Theta and Psi based on $P(\theta) = f(x_i, \omega_u, \omega_\psi)$ and $P(\psi) = 1 - P(\theta)$. For any given election, he votes either for Theta or Psi, but over time (particularly if Theta and Psi represent parties and particular, divergent, and stable ideologies), it is as if he casts (say) 0.7 votes for Theta and 0.3 for Psi *in each election.*

For any of these reasons, or some combination, we claim that the probabilistic perspective is more general, and a more accurate characterization of observed behavior. To see that probabilistic voting is more general, we need only note that for the special case $\delta = 0$, probabilistic voting is the same as classical analysis. To see that the implications of probabilistic voting may be different from, and even more useful than, classical analysis, consider the following example. In addition to illustrating the usefulness of probabilistic voting, this example allows us to further examine the concept of the quadratic utility function, introduced earlier in equation 3.8.

Let the ideal points of three voters be $x_I = 0$, $x_{II} = 1$, and $x_{III} = 20$; let candidate Theta hold platform $\omega_\theta = 0$, and let Psi hold $\omega_\psi = 3$, define δ as an arbitrary constant, and let the p.d.f. describing voter choice be symmetric. Each voter's utility function is quadratic, so $U_i(\theta) = -(\omega_\theta - x_i)^2$, and $U_i(\psi) = -(\omega_\psi - x_i)^2$. For voter i, $P_i(\theta) = f(U_i(\theta) - U_i(\psi))$, and $P_i(\psi) = 1 - P_i(\theta)$. That is, the probability that i will vote for Theta is a function of the difference in his evaluations of the two candidates. For simplicity, we assume that we are looking at a voter (no abstention), so the probability of voting for Psi is just the probability of *not* voting for Theta.

Now consider two alternative voting rules:

1. $P_i(\theta) = 1$ if $U_i(\theta) - U_i(\psi) > 0$

   $P_i(\theta) = 0.5$ if $U_i(\theta) - U_i(\psi) = 0$

   $P_i(\theta) = 0$ if $U_i(\theta) - U_i(\psi) < 0$

2. $P_i(\theta) = 1$ if $U_i(\theta) - U_i(\psi) > \delta$

   $1 > P_i(\theta) > 0.5$ if $\delta \geq (U_i(\theta) - U_i(\psi)) > 0$

   $P_i(\theta) = 0.5$ if $U_i(\theta) - U_i(\psi) = 0$

   $0.5 > P_i(\theta) > 0$ if $0 \geq (U_i(\theta) - U_i(\psi)) > -\delta$

   $P_i(\theta) = 0$ if $U_i(\theta) - U_i(\psi) < -\delta$

The only difference between the two voting rules is that rule 2 allows a smoothing of the step function assumed by rule 1. Since δ is an arbitrary constant, $\delta = 0$ means that the regions where $1 > P(\theta) > 0$ vanish, and the two rules are identical. We can now compute the expected vote for Theta, EV_θ (where $EV_\psi = 3 - EV_\theta$). The utility levels of the three voters are:

$$U_{I\theta} - U_{I\psi} = -[(0 - 1)^2 - (0 - 3)^2] = 8$$

$$U_{II\theta} - U_{II\psi} = -[(1 - 1)^2 - (1 - 3)^2] = 4$$

$$U_{III\theta} - U_{III\psi} = -[(20 - 1)^2 - (20 - 3)^2] = -72$$

Applying the two voting rules in turn, and computing EV_θ

1. $P_I[\theta] = 1$	2. $P_I[\theta] = 1$
$P_{II}[\theta] = 1$	$P_{II}[\theta] = \rho(1 > \rho > 0.5)$
$P_{III}[\theta] = 0$	$P_{III}[\theta] = 0$
$EV_\theta = 2$	$2 > EV_\theta > 1.5$

Now, suppose that Psi's position is $\omega_\psi = 2$, and we repeat the same calculations.

Rule 1 $EV_\theta = 2$
Rule 2 $EV_\theta = 1.5$

The difference in Psi's position does not influence the expected vote under rule 1, but does affect EV_θ under rule 2. The (very plausible) reason is that rule 2 allows the probability of voting for a candidate to be a function of spatial closeness *and* other factors. Clearly, the predictions of the two models are different. Rule 1 predicts that if this election were held ten times, Theta would win all ten. But rule 2 predicts five victories for each, or that any given race will end in a tie.

This is not to say that voters split their votes; there can, of course, be no ties in a three-voter, two-candidate election. Any realization of the stochastic (from the observer's perspective, or from the voters' perspective, if they are pursuing a mixed strategy) process will be of the form "Two votes for Theta, one for Psi," or vice versa. The advantage of rule 2, probabilistic voting, is that it allows us to analyze an election with far less stringent implicit assumptions about the information used by the voters or required by the research. Not least important, note that the median, voter II's ideal point, x_{II}, is no longer an equilibrium in the deterministic sense used above: we predict a *tie* if $\omega_\theta = 1$ and $\omega_\psi = 2$!

This section is hardly conclusive on the superiority of the probabilistic model, because greater generality, alone, is insufficient to justify the greater mathematical complexity that a probabilistic model entails. But we have sought to demonstrate the model's use, and we will use it extensively in later chapters. We turn now to the final extension of the classical spatial model, the predictive mapping developed by Hinich and Pollard (1981) and Enelow and Hinich (1984a).

Probabilistic Voting and Ideology

In an earlier chapter, we outlined the importance of ideological or predictive mapping as a means of representing individual citizens' choices. We are now in a position to combine the perspectives of probabilistic voting and the use of ideology.

Recall that the general form of the predictive mapping for Theta (similar to equation 6.4) is:

$$\boldsymbol{\omega}_\theta = \mathbf{b} + \mathbf{v}\boldsymbol{\pi}_\theta = \begin{bmatrix} b_1 \\ b_2 \\ \cdot \\ \cdot \\ \cdot \\ b_n \end{bmatrix} + \begin{bmatrix} v_{11} & v_{12} & \cdot & \cdot & \cdot & v_{1\ell} \\ & \cdot & & & & \\ & \cdot & & & & \cdot \\ & \cdot & & & & \\ v_{n1} & & & & & v_{n\ell} \end{bmatrix} \begin{bmatrix} \pi_{1\theta} \\ \cdot \\ \cdot \\ \cdot \\ \pi_{\ell\theta} \end{bmatrix} \tag{8.1}$$

with an analogous expression holding for Psi.

The most interesting case allows for idiosyncratic error in a voter's perception of each candidate's position in the ideological Π. For now, let us assume Π is one-dimensional, and write down a particular voter's perceptual model:

$$\hat{\omega}_\theta \quad = (\pi_\theta + e_\theta(\pi))v = (\hat{\pi}_\psi)v$$

$$\hat{\omega}_\psi \quad = (\pi_\psi + e_\psi(\pi))v = (\hat{\pi}_\psi)v$$

$$E(e_\theta(\pi)) \quad = E(e_\psi(\pi)) \quad = 0$$

$$E(e_\theta(\pi)^2) \quad = \sigma^2_\theta, \qquad E(e_\psi(\pi)^2) \quad = \sigma^2_\psi$$

The uncertainty in the perceptions of π_p, reflected by $e_p(\pi)$, is in each and every individual's frame of reference. It is a *different kind of uncertainty* from that reflected in the probabilities used to describe the vote choices from the perspective of the researcher. Thus, the expected values hold for the distribution of the perceptual error distribution.

The voter's spatial utility function and net candidate differential (*NCD*) are, respectively:

$$U_i(\theta) = U_i(\hat{\omega}_{\theta i} - x_i)$$

$$U_i(\psi) = U_i(\hat{\omega}_{\psi i} - x_i)$$

$$NCD_i = U_i(\theta) - U_i(\psi)$$

Next, assume quadratic utility and, continuing to use the notation: $[\mathbf{Y} - \mathbf{x}]^2 = (\mathbf{Y} - \mathbf{x})'(\mathbf{Y} - \mathbf{x}) = \Sigma_k(Y_k - x_k)^2$ (brackets around a vector difference imply simple Euclidean distance). Then

$$U_i(\hat{\omega}_{\theta i} - \mathbf{x}_i) = -[\hat{\omega}_{\theta i} - \mathbf{x}_i]^2$$

$$U_i(\hat{\omega}_{\psi i} - \mathbf{x}_i) = -[\hat{\omega}_{\psi i} - \mathbf{x}_i]^2$$

If Theta is elected:

$$E(U_i(-[\hat{\omega}_{\theta i} - \mathbf{x}_i]^2)) = E[(U_i((\boldsymbol{\pi}_\theta + e_\theta(\pi)\mathbf{V}) - x_i)^2] =$$

$$E(-[\boldsymbol{\pi}_\theta \mathbf{v} + e_\theta(\pi)\mathbf{v} - \mathbf{x}_i]^2) = -[\omega_{\theta i} - \mathbf{x}_i]^2 - \mathbf{v}^2\sigma_\theta^2$$

Finally:

$$E(NCD_i) = -[\boldsymbol{\omega}_{\theta i} - \mathbf{x}_i]^2 + [\boldsymbol{\omega}_{\psi i} - \mathbf{x}_i]^2 + \mathbf{v}^2(\sigma^2_\theta - \sigma^2_\psi).$$

This expectation of the net candidate differential for a single voter can be used in the probabilistic voting framework for adding up probabilities as votes. Let V denote the expected total vote for an election in the future (note that small v's are mapping parameters, and large V is the vote function). The V is an unknown random variable at the time when voting decisions are being made. We can conceive of V as an operation for adding up probabilities, where those probabilities are uncertain votes. The V operation can be specified as follows:

$$V = E_i[F(-[\boldsymbol{\omega}_{\theta i} - \mathbf{x}_i]^2 + [\boldsymbol{\omega}_{\psi i} - \mathbf{x}_i]^2 + \mathbf{v}^2(\sigma^2_{\theta i} - \sigma^2_{\psi i}))] \qquad (8.2)$$

The V function is the conceptual goal of this chapter: a mechanism for determining the outcomes of elections that satisfies the empirical and theoretical objections raised earlier, and presents a realistic depiction of the campaign and the electoral process. The *population cumulative density* function, F, allows for abstention. The perceptual variance terms allow a role for campaigns, in a way in which the deterministic spatial model is not capable. The predictive dimension embodied in this vote function allows us to significantly advance our understanding of symbolism and political rhetoric in a formal setting. In the next two chapters, we will extend the model to account for interest groups and examine candidates and campaigns in light of this theoretical perspective.

CHAPTER 9

The Role of Groups

Our goal has been to create a model of political choice that incorporates citizens' uncertainty about the likely actions of politicians. As the reader will recall, the orthodox spatial model allows for no uncertainty. The probabilistic spatial model allows for uncertainty from the perspective of the observer, but retains the essential character of the classical model in that voters act (from their own perspective) according to deterministic, though perhaps highly idiosyncratic, decision rules.

All too often in the social sciences, "uncertainty" is assumed, without any rigorous basis. In this chapter on the role of groups, we claim that the importance of interest groups that can offer resources to politicians in the political process can be explained by a specific kind of uncertainty. That uncertainty derives from the application of the theory of ideology that was developed in earlier chapters, which we can now return to explicitly. There are two types of uncertainty, from voters' perspectives: (1) knowing what politicians say they will do, and (2) knowing whether politicians will do what they say. North (1990b) has called attention to what he claims is the "transactions cost" of political exchange, or the costs of specifying and enforcing an agreement. Clearly, these two types of transactions costs correspond to the categories of uncertainty:

1. Each politician must somehow express to voters what he will do if elected. Simply saying, "If elected, I will (long list)" is not very effective, because voters do not pay attention to, or remember, statements on issues without some unifying or organizing theme. Voters who hear statements that are organized and thematically coherent (statements that we have identified as "ideologies"), have some notion of the specification of the implicit contract between the politician (or party) and themselves. Thus, ideologies reduce the transactions cost of specifying contracts. Still, ideologies are simplifying instruments that predict only imperfectly what politicians *claim* they intend to do. There remains some uncertainty in the specification of the contract between the electorate and the competing candidates among whom voters must choose.

2. Separate from the noise in the prediction of what the candidate is promising, voters are also uncertain whether promises will be carried out.

This latter type of uncertainty is strategic, not informational. Such uncertainty has been extensively analyzed in political science (Austen-Smith 1990; Banks 1990), but the analysis has been carried out separately from the informational costs listed above. Reputation, commitment, and the costs of misrepresentation are all useful notions. Still, if the problem (both temporally and substantively) is first to inform, and *then* to commit, these analyses start in the middle.

The reason for this digression at the outset of the chapter on interest groups is to remind the reader of the focus of our enterprise. Ideology is a means of expressing political choices, but this conclusion derives from the claim that ideology answers the twin questions of how to communicate and commit better than other theoretical perspectives. Earlier, we examined the relation between ideologies and parties. Clearly, by any definition, parties are "groups"; why are we now devoting a separate chapter to interest groups, as distinct from parties? After all, it might simply be the case that "groups," in the sense of self-identifying collections of individuals with similar goals, might foster ideologies to accomplish those goals. And this answer would be quite consistent with the existing work on groups (Mueller and Murrell 1986; Coughlin, Mueller, and Murrell 1990). But our answer is different: groups matter, in our model, because of money and the problem of communication. This chapter focuses first on the narrow function of providing money in elections as a role of factions in modern democracies. Toward the end of the chapter, we will expand the notion of groups to encompass the function of selection and grooming of the candidates themselves.

We have argued that ideology solves both the problems of communication and commitment. In fact, the argument is incomplete unless we can specify exactly *how* political actors speak, using ideology. In a modern election, communication requires money, and lots of it. A large campaign chest is not sufficient to guarantee victory, but neither can a successful campaign be run without it.

Information and Why Money Matters in Elections

Money would not matter in an election where voters were fully informed about policy, and needed only to be persuaded of commitment. In a full information world, campaign spending would only be expensive "cheap talk."[1] It would be possible, perhaps, to purchase votes directly (as has been alleged in many elections in the United States and elsewhere), or indirectly (by offering to hire voters if the candidate is elected). In that case, however,

---

1. "Cheap talk," in this context, implies that the claims of the speaker have no informational content about commitment to likely future action.

the campaign and its complex messages and deceptively simple arguments would be a waste of resources.

The question we ask is whether, and then to what extent, money matters in an election where the role of money is to influence opinion? Exactly how does money influence opinion, where "opinion" is an understanding of the correspondence between a party's ideology and the policies a government or party is expected to pursue? Our theory of political choice will be neither complete nor useful without answers to these questions.

We first review the literature on the importance of groups (again, as distinct from parties) in political choice, and then advance a theory that accounts for group activity in politics through financing campaigns. This is *not* a "group theory." Rather, it is a theory of choice by voters, and by candidates, where groups have influence.[2] The conception of group action adopted in this chapter is as a contributor of scarce resources, valuable to campaigns as an input to the final goal of winning votes. It will be necessary, however, to give attention to the more significant intellectual antecedents of our approach, in order to truly understand the model of contributors/investors that we employ. After briefly reviewing this literature, we will present our model, focusing on the motives of interest groups in affecting policy in the election itself. Finally, we will consider the competition among groups and the strategic aspects of contribution.

Group Theory: Pluralists, Interest Group Liberalism, and a Return to the Individual

Modern group theory dates from Bentley (1908), who presented a sophisticated (if linguistically inaccessible) model of the process of policy formation. Bentley envisioned the political process as a completely integrated competition among "groups," or collections of individuals with a common purpose.[3] The identities of the group and its "interest," or purpose, are indistinguishable, for Bentley. Consequently, individual and group interests are identical, and groups can offer votes, campaign resources, and efforts at lobbying as an organic unit. Bentley sought, in effect, to establish groups as the only appropriate analytic unit for a theory of politics.

The logic of this model is appealing, at first glance. The size of a group exactly (definitionally) represents the number of citizens in the polity who support that group's goals. Competition among groups, where government

---

2. By "group theory," we mean a focus on groups as organic entities that make up the building blocks of political equilibria, such as in Bentley (1908) or Truman (1952).

3. Bentley does not discuss parties as separate entities. This omission, or assumption, was common to all of the classical interest group literature.

acts as passive referee, is therefore decided according to the democratic ideal of majoritarianism. To put it another way, imagine a conflict between groups A and B over some policy is won by A. Victory can only result because A is larger (the preference is more widely held), works harder (reflecting a greater intensity of preference), or both. If this model were correct, representative democracy and direct democracy would be essentially identical. The reason is this: Because legislators vote to represent the largest parts of their constituencies, each votes as the majority would have voted if a plebiscite were held on the issue. The sum of the votes of the legislators represents the aggregation of the votes each voter would have cast. In fact, the outcome of "pluralism" may differ from pure representative democracy, but only if *intensity* wins out over numbers. Group competition is then quite likely an improvement.

Truman (1952) embellishes and extends Bentley's work in three important ways. First, he considers how groups form, which he attributes to a psychological predisposition for humans to act socially, rather than individually. Second, he distinguishes active, or organized, groups from those that remain latent, or unorganized. The difference is simply a question of whether some threat, or "disruption," has arisen in the government's policies. An unorganized collection of individuals faced with such a threat will band together and become a group. This point is important, because it implies that at any moment the balance among Bentley's competing forces must be extended to include "latent" groups. Moe (1981) compares latent groups to the Minutemen of the American Revolution: perhaps presently not active, but ready to organize and act in a minute if any threat is perceived. Third, Truman notes that an arbitrary individual is a member of not just one group, but of many.[4] As a result, an individual can represent any set of preferences he might possess simply by choosing the appropriate set of groups. Collectively, this extreme subdivision in multiple group memberships means that no one group's membership is very powerful.

This theory of interest group activity became known as "pluralism" for its depiction of the policy process as a complex struggle among multiple groups with a variety of goals and powers.[5] A challenge was posed by a group of scholars in the early and mid-1960s, who pointed out difficulties with pluralist theory. This work (Bauer, Pool, and Dexter 1960; Dahl 1961) was given a firmer theoretical basis by Olson (1965) and Moe (1981). The thesis of "interest group liberalism" is that not all groups are equally likely to form. Instead, successful groups are those that (1) are small enough to solve the "free rider" problem; (2) are seeking concentrated (i.e., significant per per-

---

4. This point anticipates, in a less formal fashion, Buchanan's Theory of Clubs (Buchanan 1965).

5. See, also, Shattschneider (1935, 1960), Latham (1952), and Becker (1983, 1985).

son) benefits; and (3) can offer prospective members selective incentives to join, though these incentives may bear no relation to the group's avowed collective purpose.

These qualifications break the fundamental logical linkage on which pluralist theory depended: group size and strength representing the relative weight of citizen's opinions and the intensity of these desires. If this connection is false, there is no clear relation between citizen preference and group size or the intensity of lobbying. The resources that group leaders (or what Moe [1981], calls "entrepreneurs") wield are determined primarily by their ability to offer Olson's (1965) "selective incentives" to join. Individuals become members because they want the associated magazines, club membership, activities, and so on. Support for the group's collective or political goals is irrelevant.

The policy implication of interest group liberalism is that government must intervene on behalf of the unorganized collections of individuals (who do not form even latent groups) to balance the arbitrary power of the organized groups. Because organized groups' power does not have the basis in normative democratic theory that pluralists sought to give it, government must act to counterbalance groups.

Both pluralism and interest group liberalism accept the group, rather than the individual, as the appropriate analytic unit. Both also largely ignore the institution of government and focus, instead, on the abstract struggle of competing groups. We question both aspects of these approaches, and propose a more integrated and less deterministic model. We consider individual voters, and examine policy from the perspective of a collection of legislators elected from disjoint geographic districts. This approach may be less satisfying to many readers, because we can no longer provide clear, determinate answers to Dahl's famous question, "Who Governs?" But the reason is that this clarity was misplaced, the determinism chimerical.

A representative democracy provides its elected representatives with a choice: Do your duty or be voted out. Incumbent legislators seek reelection both by taking positions and by using money to advertise those positions. The act of voting is analogous to a market transaction. It is not necessary to know other people or to organize some collective activity to go to the polling place to register a preference. Voting is an individual, decentralized act.

This observation appears obvious, but it has profound implications for the analysis of group power. First, it is not necessary that an organized group balance another organized group. Suppose an organized group wants one thing from a legislator, but voters are convinced that they want something else and are willing to turn out to the polls on election day. There is no reason to believe that the group could offer enough campaign resources to offset the loss of votes the legislator would incur from performing the task the group desires.

The balance of opposing forces may well be an organized group on one side, and the desires of unorganized citizens (expressed as votes) on the other, as Denzau and Munger (1986) and Austen-Smith (1987) point out.

Any such balance will, of course, require that voters (1) know of the policy dispute, and (2) care about the outcome. Unless both conditions are fulfilled, the legislator can do largely as he or she chooses. The last qualification is important only if the problem is asymmetric information, because then the legislator knows an opponent or the media may inform the voters. Only if voters are genuinely indifferent, not just ignorant, is the legislator truly free.

This conclusion is important for our understanding of representative democracy, because interest groups can affect policy only marginally once the representative is chosen. Even before the election, investors can influence platforms only marginally, and then only in districts where most voters are unaware of, or indifferent to, the policy in question. Much of the literature, both empirical and theoretical, on groups has focused on campaigns once the candidates are chosen, and the policy process once the elections have been decided. This literature is simply looking in the wrong place. Our approach emphasizes the initial choice of the candidates themselves, whether in a formal primary or an informal cooperative process of elite choice, and considers these choices as part of the broader theory of ideology developed earlier. Let us now turn to a consideration of the approach taken to investors/contributors once the candidates have been chosen, after which we will briefly discuss the more general role of groups in *choosing* the candidates.

A Simple Formal Model of Investors in the Policy Process

Many authors have propounded useful formal models of interest/investor groups in the policy process, and we seek to advance an amalgam of this work that preserves something of the best of each. Some of these formal models include Barro (1973); Ben-Zion and Eytan (1974); Bental and Ben-Zion (1975); Peltzman (1976); Hinich (1977); Aranson and Hinich (1979); McCormick and Tollison (1981); Austen-Smith (1981, 1987); Becker (1983, 1985); Denzau and Munger (1986); Dougan and Kenyon (1988); Magee, Brock, and Young (1989); Hinich and Munger (1989); Baron (1989a, 1989b); Snyder (1990); and Cameron and Enelow (1992).[6]

Barro (1973) established a tradition of analysis of political control in what would now be regarded a principal-agent model. The problem he addresses is how to design electoral institutions to insure the coincidence of the incentives of elected representatives with the desires of citizens. Investors in

---

6. A more comprehensive review can be found in Mitchell and Munger (1991).

his model seek overpayments from government to the factors of production of public goods in exchange for political resources. Ben-Zion and Eytan (1974) and Bental and Ben-Zion (1975) consider whether two potential sources of divergence between strict representation of citizen desires and representative's actions influence the policy process. The two sources of differences are interest group influence and the legislator's own policy preferences. Bental and Ben-Zion conclude that these forces *do* affect policy.

Ben-Zion and his coauthors conclude that interest groups are served only to the extent that voters are uninformed or indifferent. This point is echoed (though more formally) for regulatory policy by Peltzman (1976), and for a legislator's allocation of time by Denzau and Munger (1986). The proposition is rigorously proved, using probabilistic voting in a spatial model, by Austen-Smith (1987). We accept this proposition as manifestly true, and incorporate its insights into our model: interest groups affect the policy process only marginally, once the candidates in an election are chosen, or once an incumbent has occupied a seat. But we go further, because an additional reason for the near impossibility of changing a candidate's position is the theory of ideology advanced earlier.

The model of investor contributions we adopt originated with Hinich (1977a) and Aranson and Hinich (1979), with several important extensions. In words, we assume that investors consider political contributions to be but one of a variety of investment opportunities. Investors are entrepreneurs, who seek to maximize their profits (if they represent firms) or wages and benefits (if they represent unions or other labor organizations). In either case, the entrepreneurs maximize the total net expected return from all investments by allocating expenditures among political and purely business transactions. Rates of return on these two types of investment are not generally separable: political contributions may affect the rate of return in business transactions. If the opportunity cost rate of return to private investment exceeds the marginal expected net profits accruing to political contributions, the firm or union will not engage in political activity, for economic reasons.

The investor may be politically active, even if there is but a negligible economic gain on his investments. Investors pursue their own satisfaction, and profits are but one argument of their utility functions. In general, we expect that investors will be willing to trade off profit gains against ideological utility gains to have the "right" candidate in office. Of course, there may be no conflict, given the preference profiles of investors, since "interest" and "justice" so often coincide. But it is important that the model allow for such a trade-off.

The first step in outlining the model is to specify the profit function, R_h, of the kth investor, which is (1) contingent on the outcome of the election; (2) net of any campaign contributions $C_h = C_{\theta h} + C_{\psi h}$; and (3) affected by the opportunity cost rate of return, either on money borrowed to invest in politics, or on budget available for political investment that is, instead, withheld and invested in projects with higher expected net returns.

We do not specify an explicit form for the profit function.[7] The general expression (assuming, for simplicity, that Theta wins, with a similar expression for Psi) is:

$$R_{\theta h} = R(\pi_\theta, \beta_{\theta h}(C_{\theta h}), B'_h) \tag{9.1}$$

The expected ideological position, π_θ, affects all of the usual inputs in an economic profit function (input prices; output prices; regulatory policy designed to restrict output; safety, health, and environmental regulation; and explicit sales, investment, and income taxation policies). The second argument, $\beta_{\theta h}$, is the quantity of private benefits (similar to the source of what Baron [1989] calls "service-induced" contributions) that the investor expects to receive in exchange for contributions $C_{\theta h}$. The final term B'_h is the remainder, or deficit, in whatever budget is allocated to political activity by the investor. The definition of B'_h is:

$$B'_h = I_h - C_{\theta h} - C_{\psi h} \tag{9.2}$$

where I_h is the total amount budgeted in advance for political activity, and $C_{\theta h}$ and $C_{\psi h}$ are the contributions to the two candidates.[8] The distinction between I_h and B'_h is important: I_h is the amount budgeted, and B'_h is the amount of debt or surplus after the actual spending decision is made. If $B'_h > 0$, the entire budget was not spent ($C_{\theta h} + C_{\psi h} < I_h$), and the opportunity cost rate of return

---

7. An obvious possibility for the profit function is that specified in Grier, Munger, and Roberts (1992):
$$\Re = P(E)f(K, L) - r(E)K - w(E)L - \gamma E$$
where:

$\Re$ is net revenues, or profits
P is price
E is campaign expenditures
$f(.)$ is the production function
K is capital input
L is labor input
r is interest, price of capital
w is wages, price of labor
γ is cost of raising funds ($\gamma > 1$)

As Grier, Munger, and Roberts (1992) demonstrate, the first order conditions of the maximization problem implied by this profit function show essentially nothing.

8. There is some question as to whether a fixed budget is a realistic depiction. In an annual budget, it is quite plausible that the amount the firm allocates to the housing, support, and

was high enough to imply that the remainder be invested, rather than contributed. If $B'_h < 0$, then the rate of return to political investment exceeded the opportunity rate of return *and* exceeded the cost of borrowing, so that the whole budget, I_h, was spent, and more was borrowed besides.

The investor's utility function, ϕ, can be written:

$$\phi_h = \phi_h(\theta, R_h(\pi_\theta)) \text{ if candidate Theta wins} \tag{9.3}$$

$$\phi_h = \phi_h(\psi, R_h(\pi_\psi)) \text{ if candidate Psi wins} \tag{9.4}$$

where π_θ and π_ψ are the candidate positions in the ideological space and R_h is the investor's total net profits from all activities, whether he engages in political activity or not.

The general utility maximization of the kth investor can now be stated as an expected value expression:

$$u_h = P_\theta[\phi_h(\pi_\theta, R_h(_\theta))] + P_\psi[\phi_h(\pi_\psi, R_h(\psi))] \tag{9.5}$$

where P_θ and P_ψ are the probabilities ($P_\psi = 1 - P_\theta$) of victory derived in the previous chapter. We will go on in a moment to discuss the contingent profit functions $R_h(\theta)$ and $R_h(\psi)$, but first, we must emphasize the novelty of the investor's utility function, and its consistency with our theory of ideology.

By including both the expected utility for the investor if one candidate (say, Theta) is in office and, *separately*, the implications of that candidate's ideological stand for profits ($R(_\theta)$), we allow for some mix of economic and ideological giving. This implies no major mathematical difficulties, because the calculus will illustrate nicely the resultant trade-off between economic gain and what the investor believes (or feels he must act as if he believes) to be appropriate, or "good," public policy. But the calculus belies the complexity of the situation, for only rarely (and in times of conflict) will the ideological and the economic impetus for behavior diverge. Such a result is (probably) an equilibrium condition of a larger game that is, as yet, unspecified. It is nonetheless crucial to allow for the separate force of each influence to be felt, because (1) to assume interest and "justice" always coincide is too facile, and (2) to ignore the conflict is to deny ourselves a theory that can explain both peaceful realignment and revolution.

---

administration of its Political Action Committee is fixed and known in advance. However, across years, and elections, the intensity with which PAC donations are solicited from employees and managers is variable. In any case, the determination of the level of this budget requires that an explicit profit function be specified. Grier, Munger, and Roberts (1992) contains empirical work on the level of budget by industry.

We can now write out the entire maximization problem of the jth investor, and discuss its components separately:

$$u_h = P_\theta(\pi_\theta, \pi_\psi, e_\theta, e_\psi) \; \phi_h(\pi_\theta, R_h(\theta, \beta_{\theta h}(C_{\theta h}), B'_h))$$

$$+ P_\psi(\pi_\psi, \pi_\theta, e_\psi, e_\theta) \; \phi_h(\pi_\psi, R_h(\psi, \beta_{\psi h}(C\psi_h), B'_h)) \qquad (9.6)$$

where e_θ and e_ψ are the total expenditures by each of the two candidates. This expression for expected utility has several obvious, but interesting, features.

> First, investors do not necessarily contribute to the candidate they honestly prefer ideologically, because the utilities are discounted by the probabilities of winning.
>
> Second, and more important, investors may well not give to the candidate who would maximize their profits if he were elected, for the same reason. It makes no sense from either an ideological or a purely economic perspective to give to the candidate one most prefers if there is no chance that candidate will win.
>
> Third, it is possible that there is a trade-off in the investor's mind between political preference and profits. That is, one candidate may be preferable on ideological grounds, and the other superior purely in terms of expected net profits.

Investors, therefore, make contribution decisions using a sophisticated calculus that must account not just for their own preferences, but for the strategic actions of other contributors and for contributors' perceptions of voter preferences.

Let us assume that each candidate spends whatever new funds he receives, and that investment decisions are made under the simple Nash-Cournot assumption that others will not vary their contributions. This latter assumption is true only in equilibrium, but it allows us more easily to exposit the model. We assume, further, that investors optimize separately the other arguments in the profit functions R (for example, prices, output, plant size, investment, etc.). At this point, the candidates' positions π_θ and π_ψ are independent of the contribution allocation decision; we shall explore later in this chapter the consequences of endogenizing these positions. Finally, we assume that the probabilities of election are nondecreasing in the candidate's own expenditures, and nonincreasing in the opponent's. Under these circumstances, we can treat the kth investor's utility as an unconstrained maximization problem in contributions $C_{\theta h}$ and $C_{\psi h}$.

The first order conditions are:

$$\partial u_h / \partial C_{\theta h} = (\partial P_\theta / \partial e_\theta) \phi_h + P_\theta (\partial \phi_h / \partial R_h)[(\partial R_h / \partial \beta_{\theta h})(d\beta_{\theta h}/dc_{\theta h}) - 1]$$

$$+ (\partial P_\psi / \partial e_\theta) \phi_h + P_\psi (\partial \phi_h / \partial R_h)[(\partial R_h / \partial \beta_{\psi h})$$

$$\times (d\beta_{\psi h}/dC_{\theta h}) - 1] = 0 \qquad (9.7)$$

$$\partial u_h / \partial C_{\psi h} = (\partial P_\theta / \partial e_\psi) \phi_h + P_\theta (\partial \phi_h / \partial R_h)[(\partial R_h / \partial \beta_{\theta h})(d\beta_{\theta h}/dC_{\psi h}) - 1]$$

$$+ (\partial P_\psi / \partial e_\psi) \phi_h + P_\psi (\partial \phi_h / \partial R_h)[(\partial R_h / \partial \beta_{\psi h})$$

$$\times (d\beta_{\psi h}/dC_{\psi h}) - 1] = 0 \qquad (9.8)$$

where:

$\partial P_\theta / \partial e_\theta \geq 0$ (probability nondecreasing in candidate's own expenditures)

$\partial P_\psi / \partial e_\theta \leq 0$ (probability nonincreasing in opponent's expenditures)

$\partial P_\theta / \partial e_\psi \leq 0$

$\partial P_\psi / \partial e_\psi \geq 0$

$\partial \phi_h / \partial R_h \geq 0$ (utility nondecreasing in profit)

$\partial R_h / \partial \beta_{\theta h, \psi h} \geq 0$ (profit nondecreasing in private benefits)

$d\beta_{\theta h}/dC_{\psi h} \leq 0$ (private benefits nonincreasing in contributions to opponent due to possibility of retribution)

$d\beta_{\psi h}/dC_{\psi h} \geq 0$ (private benefits nondecreasing in contributions to candidate)

$d\beta_{\psi h}/dC_{\theta h} \leq 0$

$d\beta_{\theta h}/dC_{\theta h} \geq 0$

The two well-known interpretations of contributions (originating with Welch 1974) as "quid pro quo" and "ideological" both appear as natural interpretations of parts of our model. "Quid pro quo" contributions accept the identity of the candidate and seek to modify his behavior, in our case supplying different amounts of private benefits, β. "Ideological" contributors seek to change the outcome of the election by assisting the candidate they prefer, assuming his policy stands and allocation of benefits are fixed. Set the two first order conditions equal, and rearrange terms assuming $\partial R_h / \partial \beta_{\theta h} = \partial R_h / \partial \beta_{\psi h}$ (investors don't care which candidate gives them private benefits). Then, holding constant the ideological differences accounted for elsewhere in ϕ, we get:

$$
\frac{\partial \phi_k}{\partial R_k} \frac{\partial R_k}{\partial \beta_p} \left[P_\theta \left(\frac{d\beta_\theta}{dC_{\theta k}} - \frac{d\beta_\psi}{dC_{\psi k}} \right) + P_\psi \left(\frac{d\beta_\theta}{dC_{\psi k}} - \frac{d\beta_\psi}{dC_{\psi k}} \right) \right]
$$
$$
= \phi_k(\theta,.) \left(\frac{\partial P_\theta}{\partial C_{\theta k}} - \frac{\partial P_\theta}{\partial C_{\psi k}} \right) + \phi_k(\psi,.) \left(\frac{\partial P_\psi}{\partial C_{\psi k}} - \frac{\partial P_\psi}{\partial C_{\theta k}} \right)
$$

(9.9)

The left-hand side is the change in utility from profit, times the change in profit from private benefits, given the maximizing allocation of contributions based on the net increments in private benefits (benefits given in exchange for contributions minus benefits withheld for giving to the opponent). This is *exactly* what is meant by quid pro quo contributions: maximizing return based on which candidate promises the most, discounted by the fixed probabilities of his actually delivering it. The right-hand side is the alternative means of gaining from contributions, the ideological strategy. Taking the levels of utility (given what each candidate will do once in office) as fixed, the entrepreneur can affect the probabilities of election. Giving to both candidates will have no net effect, because the election is a zero-sum game, from the perspective of the candidates. Thus, the utility levels on the right-hand side are multiplied by the *difference* in the change in probabilities, given contribution levels $C_{\theta h}$ and $C_{\psi h}$. The entrepreneur trades off the ideological and quid pro quo motivations, and equates their marginal utilities.

This representation of the investor's decision problem is quite general, capturing the purely economic influences on the contribution allocation decision. The final task to be accomplished in this chapter is a discussion of the role of groups in "choosing" candidates and establishing protoparties. Parties, after all, require the existence of relatively well-established ideologies, and are not usefully conceived in isolation from the party system in which they exist. Groups, or factions, preexist parties, and act with parties to identify and choose candidates, even once the party system is well established.

Before the Election: The Choice of Candidates

The point of the mathematical exercise in the previous section is largely expositional: interest groups can, at most, affect the outcome of an election, and this only marginally, if attention is limited to the campaign, once the candidates are decided upon. The key questions then become (1) what individuals in the society are considered as potential candidates? and (2) of this group, how are some chosen over others?

In order to come up with even tentative answers, a simple thought experiment is required. Imagine a situation without parties, or even well-formed groups, where politics consists primarily of a striving for resources. The most likely structures around which groups will begin to coalesce are family units. The comparative success of these units derives from their cohesiveness, their physical and military skill, and the resources they control. After a more organized political system has been established, with some ideological principles to frame the terms of debate, more is required for success. The single most important new factor is a "candidate": unless the family group has a member possessing the force of personality, the charisma, and the simple willingness to work hard on purely "political" matters of coalition building, the group is not directly represented.

Imagine that all of the groups are otherwise of equal size, military strength, and wealth. In a nonpolitical world, they might combine in various coalitions for mutual defense, but have little need for a "candidate." Once they are part of some larger collectivity, be it nation, province, or city, particularly if that entity uses a majority rule choice mechanism, each group has a choice. If they have a candidate, they promote him, lauding his qualities to the other groups. If not, they choose which candidate from another group to support. Let us assume that, for each group, the best result (*a*) is that their candidate is elected, the next best (*b*) is that they run no candidate of their own but support another group's candidate who wins. The worst outcome (*c*) is either to support a losing candidate from another group, or to advance one's own candidate, only to have him rejected.

To flesh out this example, consider this description of traditional Arab tribal society by David Pryce-Jones.

> In tribal society, all male members are theoretically equal and capable of exercising authority. . . . In due course, the shiekh will grow old, his sons will hope to succeed, and each of them will challenge the other, being themselves challenged by others with similar aspirations. . . . each power holder embodies the wishes of his group and to that extent is endorsed by it. Should such endorsement be withheld for any reason, then the power holder is diminished and the possible challenger may emerge. . . . A tiny elite of family heads or patrons everywhere disposes of the available patrimony. . . . To take the everyday matter of wanting to obtain a job, a young man approaches the head of his family or clan, his patron. The head of the family is under obligation to do his very best to make sure his kinsman is given what he asks for. The honor of the

whole family is at stake. If the job is in the gift of someone from another clan or religion, complicated bargaining ensues, and a quid pro quo is sought. In the event of the job going to someone else, the patron becomes the object of shame, and his standing is under threat until such time as he can reestablish it by whatever means, and his young kinsman is satisfied. Placing him, the patron has the right to expect allegiance and loyalty in return, and so he himself is also taking a personal careerist step forward. Whether or not the young man deserved the job is no kind of consideration. . . . politics remains an essential business of promoting and protecting one's own kind. (Pryce-Jones 1991, 24–40)

The resulting game is depicted in figure 14. For each family group (I, II, and III), there are three strategies available: support your favorite son (1, 2, and 3, respectively), or pass over your own to support the son of either of the other two families. In order to depict the game as an extensive form, we arbitrarily assume I is the "senior" family and moves first, II second, and III last. Take as the decision rule 2/3 or 3/3. Choosing a son results in him ruling, and ties result in civil war. Given that each family has three strategies s available ($s \in \{1, 2, 3\}$), there are twenty-seven possible outcomes of the game. Interestingly, only six of the strategies are plausible, in the sense that they are rational strategies for the families to pursue.

We start with family I, who choose their own favorite son 1, 2, or 3; II then makes the same choice, and III follows last. The order is not crucial, for the results are symmetric. The six possible outcomes (with ordered triples representing strategies of I, II, III, respectively) are [1, 1, 1] (1 wins), [1, 2, 1] (1 wins), [1, 2, 2] (2 wins), [1, 3, 3] (3 wins), [2, 2, 2] (2 wins), and [3, 3, 3] (3 wins). There are three cases of unanimity, and one case each of a majority for 1, for 2, and for 3.

Let us make clear the informational assumptions under which the game is played. Each family knows the preferences of the others, but these are only in terms of the coalition that wins: $a > b > c$, where " $>$ " means "is preferred to." a means your son wins, b means the son of the family you support wins, and c means either your son loses or the son you support loses. No one knows the other families' preferences over sons, except that each likes its own best. The game is sequentially played, so I moves first, II moves after seeing I's move, and III moves after seeing both moves. One way to imagine the structure of the game is to envision a king (I) on his deathbed, announcing whether his son (1) has his blessing to rule, or if he chooses (2) or (3). A rider goes out from the castle, coming first to Duke II's fiefdom. Informed of the King's decision, II announces he will follow (1), advance his own son (2) as king, or propose (3) as king. The rider then travels to faraway Duchy III, where III chooses (1), (2), or (3). If any two or more choose (1), (1) is king. If there is a tie, civil war breaks out.

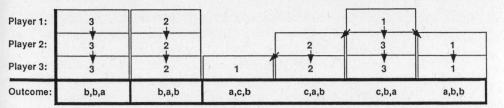

Player 1:	3	2			1	
Player 2:	3	2		2	3	1
Player 3:	3	2	1	2	3	1
Outcome:	b,b,a	b,a,b	a,c,b	c,a,b	c,b,a	a,b,b

Legend: a: your son wins
b: you support the winner (someone else's son)
c: you support the loser, or your son loses

Fig. 14. Choice of candidates by family groups

I's decision is conditioned on what he expects II and III to do, but he knows only that they have preferences $a > b > c$. Interestingly, if he does not choose his own son (1), the game is effectively over. Say he picks (2). Then II chooses (2), and III must choose (2) or be left out (remember, $b > c$). The outcome is [2, 2, 2], or unanimous support for (2). Say, instead, I picks (3). II is apparently faced with a choice among all three, but he knows III will pick his own son (3), so II picks (3) and the outcome is [3, 3, 3]. The eighteen possible outcomes in the lower two branches reduce to 2 "unanimous" choices, even though they are unanimous only in the sense of strategic voting.

If I chooses (1), then any one of the three sons might be chosen depending on the choices of II and III. Notice, however, that only two outcomes {[1, 1, 1] [1, 2, 1]}, are possible if I knows the actual preference rankings of II and III. Otherwise, I would never select his own son because the results [1, 2, 2] and [1, 3, 3] result in payoff c for I. Because we have assumed no such knowledge, we leave the other outcomes on the tree. It is important to note, however, that all of the nonunanimous outcomes cannot be supported as full-information equilibria, because in each case the dissenter would like to change his vote: he "regrets" his choice.

This game helps us to illustrate both the benefits and costs of advancing a candidate, particularly if that candidate must pass some sort of test, be it martial combat, a debate, or simply the exertion and informational stresses of a campaign against an opponent. The expense of advancing and financing a candidate is lost if the candidate is not persuasive and charismatic. Better, then, to support another group's candidate, who passes this absolute test, even though his expected policy positions are relatively less preferred. Best of all, of course, is to advance and finance a champion and have him win. In the context of our thought experiment, the son chosen king must actually rule effectively, or all three families are worse off. In the context of choosing a candidate, the goal is to win not just the primary, but also the general election.

The point of this example for the choice of candidates is that the choice is not simply over policy. Another factor, very difficult to model, but of clear importance to the process, is the availability of a candidate others will accept. It is not enough that he espouse policies others favor; he must also be counted on to be willing and able to implement them. More than this, in a world where uncertainty is rife and the nature of the issues themselves is unclear even a year into the future, the leader must project confidence in his own ability, and a set of ideas that summarize his philosophy of governing that appeal to the polity. These ideas, of course, are his ideology.

Groups and Candidates

The choice of a representative to serve in an elective office has two stages. The first is the choice of candidates who are considered genuine, possessing a realistic chance of winning. The second is the choice among these candidates. The role of groups in influencing the second stage has been widely studied, and in this chapter we have offered a formal model of group influence through investment in the candidates.

The first stage is much more difficult to analyze, because it is so idiosyncratic. Yet this stage has by far the greater influence, because it determines the menu of choice. The answers to the question "where do candidates come from" that we are able to offer is only preliminary. Still, we can outline the parameters likely to be important: groups, ideologies, and personalities.

Groups are important in that they boost or retard the advancement of proto-candidates. In many societies, the family unit is the basic building block of political power. There need be no "vote" in the stylized sense we are accustomed to imagining for political decision making, yet the elite families at the top of a society exercise a clear set of vetoes and proposals. Each family, and later, each group, in the more amorphous sense of advanced democracies, has the choice of advancing one of its own members or supporting the advancement of someone else. The reason the latter choice may be attractive is simple, but theoretically intractable: the group may have no one qualified to be a candidate. Rather than advance someone who will certainly not win (even though if they won, the policies they would implement are the best the group could hope for), the group supports another group who does have a candidate. This choice appears irrational from the perspective of an outsider, but is optimal, given constraints that may well be known only from the perspective of the choosers.

Ideologies, as we have noted before, serve to legitimize what a group wants to do anyway, be it to maintain or overturn the status quo. The argument "because it would be in our interest" is not sufficient to persuade the listener, so the terms of debate must derive from the ideological cleavage that organizes political discourse. But this means that groups are not free to implement any set of policies that please them, or to propose modifications that clearly *would* be in their interest. The power of groups is their power to veto, to protect the status quo, and to prevent modifications in policy.

Finally, we consider candidates. Napoleon Bonaparte once said, not without a certain pride, that he had the ability to make men willing to die for little pieces of ribbon. More to the point, he asserted: "What is the throne? A bit of wood gilded and covered with velvet. I am the state—I alone am here the representative of the people" (speech before the Senate, 1814, quoted in Bartlett, 420, no. 11).[9] The act of holding office confers on the holder only the patina of the authority a leader must possess. In order not to be found out, and ridiculed, a person must have the qualities of leadership, the charisma and personal bearing that, themselves, confer authority and that the office does no more than give official status. A "candidate" is therefore much more than a person standing for office. He or she must possess the qualities that make human beings willing to follow, to sacrifice, even to die, for the little pieces of ribbon that are the leader's to hand out. Such people cannot simply be manufactured or molded; they are rare. More rare still is one who has these qualities and embraces the particular ideology that a group seeks to advance.

This scarcity of candidates is an overlooked, but crucially important, aspect of the electoral process. Groups must choose among candidates, with the qualities that make them leaders, who have long ago publicly and consistently embraced the ideology the group supports. Once this choice is made, the ability of the group to influence the outcome of the election is only marginal, though, as we have shown, it can be much more precisely stated. Thus, the most important role of groups may be their ability to find, nurture, and groom candidates. If the only "candidates" are those interests groups support, the ideological underpinning of electoral contests is greatly strengthened.

Summary and Conclusion

In this chapter, we have sought to cover a number of quite disparate topics. First, the classic literature on pluralism was reviewed to give some contrast to the normative theory of democracy underpinning political choice. Second, we outlined a simple model of investors/groups seeking to influence the outcome of electoral races between candidates over whom the investors possess both ideological and profit-maximizing preferences. These two factors are allowed to differ in principle, though they may rarely diverge in fact.

Last, as an illustrative digression, we considered a means by which

---

9. The "I am the state" quotation is often attributed to Benito Mussolini, who did say it several times. Whether he was aware of Napoleon's words is not known.

candidates, as types of individuals combining both ideological commitments and leadership qualities, might be nurtured and advanced by groups. The probabilistic model of voting allows us to account for both of these influences, though only implicitly.

The next chapter draws together all of the separate strands of reasoning we have created so far.

CHAPTER 10

The Integrated Model of Politicians, Voters, and Interest Groups

So far, we have identified only pieces of a complete model of politics. We have claimed that ideology is the means by which communication takes place, and the basis of political understanding. Ideology is not a *substitute* for rationality; it is the way citizens think about political life precisely because they purposively seek the best alternative in making political choices. The role of parties as collections of individuals united by a broad ideology was advanced, and the difference between a party and its ideology discussed. We have chosen probabilistic voting as an important theoretical basis for representing choice by citizens. Its advantages are that it allows for abstention, and directly incorporates uncertainty from the perspective of the observer. Finally, we have outlined the role of interest groups in the campaign process as providers of money and other resources parties require in the campaign.

In this chapter, we combine all of the disparate components, and examine the implications of the overall model for our understanding of political choices. Along the way, we are able to answer a number of questions that have troubled scholars. First, why does it cost so much to campaign? Second, a constant complaint heard in present campaigns is that politicians never talk about "issues." What (if any) reforms are likely to improve the process of campaigning by creating more and better information about issues? Finally, we wish to be able to discuss the role of the campaign in influencing the political community, as discussed by Taylor (1976, 1982) and Schofield (1985a). Schofield describes "community" as follows:

> The key features of community are: (i) shared common beliefs or norms, (ii) direct and complex relations among members, (iii) reciprocity. Communications is not a key aspect since people may communicate while sharing hardly any norms. On the other hand, of course, shared norms may be reinforced through communication. (Schofield 1985a, 217)

Politicians may campaign in such a way that communication takes place, and voters are "informed," but community is destroyed by negative messages and constant misrepresentation. Community is the basis for the credibility and workability of the political system, and plays an important role in influencing the willingness of members of society to trust one another and work together. Consequently, there may be a conflict between the individual competitive incentives politicians face (win through "informing") and the broader desires and needs of the community these politicians are vying to serve.

The basic logic of the integrated model in this chapter is that candidates campaign against each other in the context of an explicit game. Their positions in the ideological space, deriving from efforts to associate themselves with a party or other kind of platform, give them different advantages regarding the preferences of voters and the preferences of interest groups. To foreshadow the results we find, the prediction of the model is a constantly increasing spiral of expenditures, but with no electoral gain by candidates, and no informational benefits to citizens in making voting decisions.

The chapter is organized as follows. We first consider the role of information in the campaign. The second section reprises the spatial model of voter choice between candidates. The third section incorporates the model of investor contributions as contingent claims. Then we investigate the form of the simple expenditure game between candidates, and present the equilibrium result of this game.

"Informing" and "Campaigning"

The difficulties with modeling the use of information by voters are articulated by Denzau and Munger (1986) in their comparison of rational ignorance and "civics class" full information assumptions about voters. If voters are ignorant, and neither candidate has an advantage in credibility or position, then the candidate spending the most must win, and elections are only fund-raising contests. The alternative of full information is even less palatable: advertising can have no effect whatsoever, except through bribery. The fundamental question, raised previously in chapter 9, is: Why does money matter in electoral campaigns where direct bribery of voters is not allowed?

Austen-Smith (1987a) presents a partial answer, which has since been elaborated by Hinich and Munger (1989) and Cameron and Enelow (1992). In Austen-Smith's theory of electoral competition, interest groups compete for political favors by contributing to candidates, and candidates spend the money to affect voter decisions. The most important question is how money influences the voting decision. Austen-Smith's answer is:

> while candidates adopt and state the positions with which they contest the election, they cannot do so without ambiguity. People learn of candidates' positions through the various media, in political debate, and so on.

Such intervening variables *introduce noise into the signal* sent by a candidate, who must then devote resources to articulating a position. (Austen-Smith 1987, 126; emphasis added)

Succinctly, the role of campaign contributions/expenditures is to reduce the variance of voters' perceptions of candidate positions. Austen-Smith does not fully develop this insight, because he restricts the focus of each candidate's expenditures to reducing his own variance. Hinich and Munger (1989), and later Cameron and Enelow (1992), considered the implications of allowing expenditures to be focused *either* on reducing one's own variance, or increasing that of the opponent. An obvious, and more realistic, extension is a model of voter choice based on party means, where messages from the candidates affect voters' perceptions of the candidates' positions relative to the prior distribution voters bring to the campaign. Later in this chapter, we outline such a model, and its implications for the study of political choice. But first we reexamine the justifications for using a spatial representation for campaigns.

The Classical and Probabilistic Models of Spatial Voter Choice

Although we have discussed the classical spatial model at length in previous chapters, it is useful to restate the key assumptions of the classical model, particularly as regards voters' use of information, and contrast this approach with the one taken here. The classical assumptions are that voters are perfectly informed about (*a*) their own preferences on policy (meaning they understand the implications of policies by government for their own welfare), (*b*) the stated positions of candidates, and (*c*) the precise likelihood that those stated positions will be the actual positions of the candidates, once they are in office. As was shown in chapter 3, under these circumstances, the voters can choose among candidates based on a loss function that measures the divergence between each candidate's position and the voter's own ideal point.

The classical model, by assuming voters react only to policy platforms, makes two rather extreme implicit presumptions about voter behavior. First, there exists a sharp discontinuity in the likelihood that a voter votes for a particular candidate based on a knife-edge comparison of the weighted Euclidean distance between the voter's ideal and each platform. Except in the case of absolute indifference (where the voter, in effect, flips a coin), behavior is deterministic. Second, only the asserted platforms of the candidates are relevant to the voting decision. Candidates cannot differ in terms of the credibility of their commitments to a particular platform, and voters do not vote based on character and leadership qualities that make a candidate appear well suited to react to crises or respond to unforeseen issues.

A more realistic treatment of voter choice, relaxing several of the restrictive assumptions of the classical model, is probabilistic voting, where voters individually choose according to the classical model, but an observer cannot determine with certainty how any one individual will behave. An important advantage of this approach is that it incorporates nonpolicy characteristics of candidates, such as character, credibility, and leadership. Empirical research on the importance of nonpolicy characteristics (Enelow and Hinich 1982b) argues strongly for its inclusion, and the probabilistic approach appears to be the most parsimonious way of accomplishing this. The likelihood of voting for the "closest" candidate is a continuous, monotonically decreasing function of the difference between the voter's ideal and the positions of the two candidates, rather than a step function where the only outcomes are a certain vote for Theta, a coin flip, or a certain vote for Psi.

As was shown in chapter 8, it is quite straightforward to integrate the theory of probabilistic voting with the spatial theory of ideology. In this chapter, to lay out a more general model, we will make the following assumptions. Voters have preferences over positions in the n-dimensional policy space $\mathbf{\Omega}$, so that (a) each voter i's ideal point $\mathbf{x}_i$ is an $n \times 1$ column vector of preferred positions, and (b) each voter evaluates candidates based on the weighted Euclidean distance between the expected position of that candidate and $\mathbf{x}_i$. The two candidates, Theta and Psi, have ideological positions on a recovered, implicit dimension Π. These positions are denoted π_θ and π_ψ, respectively. Finally, voters use their perceptions of the mappings from the ideological dimension Π to the policy space ω to arrive at their predictions of candidate positions: $\boldsymbol{\omega}_\theta$ and $\boldsymbol{\omega}_\psi$.

Two questions must be answered immediately: Where do voter perceptions of π_θ and π_ψ come from? How do these perceptions change? The verbal answer is that voters associate Theta and Psi with their respective party labels (that is, the "image," to use Sartori's language, of the party in voters' minds) at the outset. But as voters hear candidate-specific messages from the two candidates, both self-aggrandizing and mudslinging, each voter modifies, or updates, these "image" perceptions. To present this process more formally, we write out the following model.

For expositional ease, first assume voters are certain about the ideological locations of the candidates. Then, for voter i:

$$\boldsymbol{\omega}_\theta = \pi_\theta \mathbf{v} = (\pi_\theta v_1, \ \pi_\theta v_2, \ \ldots, \ \pi_\theta v_n) \tag{10.1a}$$

$$\boldsymbol{\omega}_\psi = \pi_\psi \mathbf{v} \tag{10.1b}$$

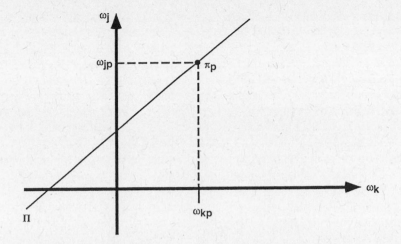

Fig. 15. The ideological space overlaid on the policy space

The relation between candidate position on the predictive dimension and his imputed policy stand is depicted in figure 15 for the case of two dimensions, where Π is projected onto the two dimensions ω_1 and ω_2. (This figure is repeated from chap. 6.)

In the case of certainty, no campaign is necessary, or even possible. The actions of politicians are common knowledge, in the sense game theorists mean.[1] To create a setting where campaigns make sense, we must admit uncertainty. Of course uncertainty is not just one concept, but many, and there are a variety of ways of incorporating these different notions of uncertainty, as we have discussed over and over in the preceding chapters. One possibility is to allow voters to know what candidates claim they will do, but to leave voters wondering whether candidates are telling the truth, as has been suggested in the work of Austen-Smith, Banks, and others. Other possibilities for incorporating uncertainty include changes in the mean, or variance, of the positions of candidates along the ideological dimension. The most extensive, and most difficult to model, types of uncertainty in our model involve lack of knowledge about the implications of an ideological position for concrete policies, and, ultimately for utility. The mapping terms (v_{ij}) may be highly variable on any issue j, so that voter i is uncertain what the specific policy implications of an ideological position are. If voters are less than fully informed about what the economic and personal implications of a policy are, they may also be

---

1. Technically, the information sets of all agents contain the same elements, in the same form.

uncertain about their own policy preferences, so that $\mathbf{x}_i$ would be known only with error, at least *ex ante*.

We will focus only on the uncertainties associated with candidate positions. Uncertainty about mappings, or about the voters' own preferences for policies, given problems of interpreting their effects, are probably important real-world phenomena, but make the presentation unmanageable. Each candidate is perceived by each voter in our model as a *distribution* of possible positions along the ideological dimension. Candidates can affect this distribution by presenting campaign messages to the voters; voters recognize that the actual ideological position, and, ultimately, the policy of government, of each candidate (if elected) is a draw from this distribution.

An obvious approach to generating these distributions is to allow updating; the simplest assumption is the use of Bayes's rule.[2] The logic of such a model is elementary, though it turns out to be computationally complex. If voters know *nothing* about a candidate except party affiliation, it makes sense that voters would conceive the candidate's position to be a random variable drawn from a distribution. The distribution is derived from the voter's experience with the party, with the mean of the distribution being the average position party candidates have taken in the past, and the dispersion around this mean deriving from how unified the party is around the mean. The voter knows that there are different factions within the party (for example, liberal and conservative wings within the Democratic party in the United States), but has no prior knowledge of the faction to which the candidate belongs. Furthermore, it may not even be clear which faction is going to dominate the party after the election, so the voter is faced with incomplete information, and must use whatever data are available to update prior beliefs.

Let us take the random variables voter i associates with two candidates, whose party affiliation (but nothing else) is known, to be P and C. Define the *prior distributions* voter i associates with each party (call the parties Pro and Con) as $f_i(\text{Pro})$ and $f_i(\text{Con})$. These distributions could be the actual relative frequencies of candidates from these parties, the relative frequencies of platforms over time, or the voter's perception of the parties' activities once in office, regardless of campaign rhetoric. Because the distributions are idiosyncratic (i.e., $f_i(\text{Pro}) \neq f_i(\text{Con})$, $f_i(\text{Pro}) \neq f_j(\text{Pro})$, and so on), different voters may arrive at their priors through different means. All that is required is that each voter i have some prior distribution over the expected actions of the two parties. We therefore have $P \in f_i(\text{Pro})$, and $C \in f_i(\text{Con})$ (table 9).

---

2. Bayesian statistical inference is an alternative conception of the basic definition of people's perceptions of probability distributions. Specifically, it is assumed that individuals' beliefs about events reflect prior beliefs that are updated in light of subsequent experience. This updating, based on "Bayes's rule," results in a posterior distribution that reflects all available information.

**TABLE 9.   Discrete Probability Distribution Functions
for Factions in "Pro" (Leftist) Party**

Position	Probability for Right Faction	Probability for Left Faction
−1 (Extreme Left)	0.4	0.7
0 (Center)	0.5	0.3
1 (Extreme Right)	0.1	0.0

Note: Example of updating process: Voter knows candidate is from "Pro" party, but doesn't know if candidate is from left or right faction, which are of equal size and strength in the party. If the candidate takes position "0," he has a probability of 0.375 of being from the left faction, and 0.625 of being from the right faction. If he takes position "−1," he has probability 0.636 of being from the left faction, and 0.364 of being from the right.

The mechanics of the Bayesian approach are well known; we will give only the outline of the procedure here. The voter is interested in the final outcome, or "true" ideological position of the candidates. The outcomes of interest are therefore the projected ideological positions $\hat{\pi}_\theta$ and $\hat{\pi}_\psi$. But the voter must predict what the candidates will do, based on (1) what Psi's party (Con), and Theta's party (Pro), have done in the past, and (2) any information the voter can obtain about what Psi and Theta will do once in office, given that he may be a member of a particular faction of Con. Thus, the distribution of the conditional, or posterior, distributions for outcomes can be written:[3]

$$\hat{\pi}_\psi \sim N(\mu_C, \sigma_\psi^2)$$

$$\hat{\pi}_\theta \sim N(\mu_P, \sigma_\theta^2)$$

The link between the conditional distributions and the prior distributions on the parties is Bayes's Rule. Assume that the prior distributions are:

$$\mu_C \sim N(\mu_{Con}, \sigma_{Con}^2)$$

$$\mu_P \sim N(\mu_{Pro}, \sigma_{Pro}^2)$$

That is, the means of the random variables μ_C and μ_P are drawn from a normal distribution based on the means and variances of the entire parties Con and Pro, respectively. Now we can write the mean and variance of the distribution of the *updated* $\bar{\mu}_C$ conditional on $\hat{\pi}_\psi$ (the definitions for Theta are analogous):

---

3. The derivation of the posterior distributions using Bayes's rule is tedious, but straightforward, and is not given here. It involves completing the square of the multivariate normal.

$$E(\bar{\mu}_C \mid \hat{\pi}_\psi) = \left(\frac{\sigma^2_{Con}\mu_C + \sigma^2_\psi\mu_{Con}}{\sigma^2_\psi + \sigma^2_{Con}} \right) \tag{10.2}$$

$$Var(\bar{\mu}_C \mid \hat{\pi}_\psi) = \frac{1}{\dfrac{1}{\sigma^2_\psi} + \dfrac{1}{\sigma^2_{Con}}} \tag{10.3}$$

Another way of thinking of the updating process is that the posterior probability densities of $\hat{\pi}_\theta$ and $\hat{\pi}_\psi$ are the conditional densities of that random variable, given that the candidates came from the parties Pro and Con, respectively. Since the voter knows something about the distribution of candidates who carry these party labels, there is some expectation of what each will do. The campaign gives the candidates a chance to affect these prior expectations, both by advertising on their own behalf and by attacking their opponents.

The parameters for π_θ are analogously defined. These mean and variance terms in the posterior normal distributions are the focus of the campaign. They are partially a function of the entire histories of each of the two parties, of course, represented by the mean and variance the voter associates with the party. But voter expectations are also influenced by information on the mean and variance of the particular candidate. We will write out the expected value calculation of the voter who uses the Bayesian updating rule, though to simplify notation we will substitute μ_ψ and μ_θ for the updated means from equation 10.2, and σ_ψ and σ_θ for the updated variances from equation 10.3. We will then discuss the role of interest groups in influencing the campaign.

We rewrite equations 10.1 and 10.2 to reflect the fact that voter perceptions are uncertain and described by the posterior parameters of the normal distribution derived using Bayes's rule. For voter i:

$$\hat{\omega}_{\theta i} = \hat{\pi}_{\theta i}v \tag{10.4}$$

$$\hat{\omega}_{\psi i} = \hat{\pi}_{\psi i}v \tag{10.5}$$

Notice that the v terms, or mappings, are not subscripted here by voter; *only the posterior distributions of candidate positions are voter-specific.*

Voters acquire information about the candidates from campaign advertising, both positive (self-aggrandizing) and negative (mudslinging). Although changing the mean of the posterior distribution is possible, we will assume that the campaign focuses on variance. However, campaigns focus on variance in two distinct ways, and it is useful to distinguish them.

Candidates and their campaign workers *can spend resources to reduce the variance of their "self" (s) position* by making self-aggrandizing and positive statements. For example, photo opportunities of the (usually) great man with his wife (of many years) and children (numerous, happy, and well adjusted), or testimonials from older and well-known public figures, suggest to voters a candidate who is stable, committed, and a good leader.

Campaigns can also *spend resources to increase the variance of their "opponent's" (o) position* by slinging mud and questioning the opponent's character. Campaigns are full of statements that the opponent is "not from the mainstream" of his or her party, or is an "extreme" liberal or conservative. Such claims are backed with highly selective "evidence" of this extremism (one incident, in the distant past, where the opponent voted in a certain way, belonged to an organization, or went to a meeting where people of extreme views spoke, etc.). The intention of these claims is clearly to make people less certain about the opponent's true intentions and abilities if voters should be so foolish as to vote him or her into office.

In terms of the implications of self (*s*) and opponent (*o*) spending:

$$\sigma_\theta^2 = f_\theta(s_\theta, o_\psi), \ \partial f_\theta / \partial s_\theta < 0, \ \partial f_\theta / \partial o_\psi > 0 \tag{10.6}$$

$$\sigma_\psi^2 = f_\psi(s_\psi, o_\theta), \ \partial f_\psi / \partial s_\psi < 0, \ \partial f_\psi / \partial o_\theta > 0 \tag{10.7}$$

We can now define the *i*th voter's spatial utility function and net candidate differential (still defined as the value of Theta over Psi) NCD_i:

$$u_i = u_i[\hat{\omega}_{\theta i} - \mathbf{x}_i] \text{ if Theta is elected} \tag{10.8}$$

$$u_i = u_i[\hat{\omega}_{\psi i} - \mathbf{x}_i] \text{ if Psi is elected} \tag{10.9}$$

$$NCD_i = u_i[\hat{\omega}_{\theta i} - \mathbf{x}_i] - u_i[\hat{\omega}_{\psi i} - \mathbf{x}_i] \tag{10.10}$$

Substituting for $\hat{\omega}_\theta$ and $\hat{\omega}_\psi$, using the Bayesian posterior distribution parameters for mean and variance and assuming quadratic utility, we get the following series of expressions:

$$u_i = -[\hat{\pi}_\theta \mathbf{v} - \mathbf{x}_i]^2 \text{ or } u_i = -[\hat{\pi}_\psi \mathbf{v} - \mathbf{x}_i]^2 \tag{10.11}$$

(where the $[\hat{\pi}_\theta \mathbf{v} - \mathbf{x}_i]^2$ notation continues to mean $\Sigma_{j=1}^m (\hat{\omega}_{\theta j} - x_j)^2$ over the *m*-dimensional policy space). Taking expectations, after simultaneously adding and subtracting means:

$$E(u_i(\theta)) = -E(\mathbf{v}(\hat{\pi}_\theta - \mu_\theta) + \mathbf{v}\mu_\theta - \mathbf{x}_i)^2$$

$$= -(\mathbf{v}\mu_\theta - \mathbf{x}_i)^2 - \mathbf{v}^2\sigma_\theta^2 \qquad (10.12)$$

$$E(u_i(\psi)) = -E(\mathbf{v}(\hat{\pi}_\psi - \mu_\psi) + \mathbf{v}\mu_\psi - \mathbf{x}_i)^2$$

$$= -(\mathbf{v}\mu_\psi - \mathbf{x}_i)^2 - \mathbf{v}^2\sigma_\psi^2 \qquad (10.13)$$

$$NCD_i = -(\mathbf{v}\mu_\theta - \mathbf{x}_i)^2 + (\mathbf{v}\mu_\psi - \mathbf{x}_i)^2 + \mathbf{v}^2\delta_i$$

$$\text{where } \delta_i = \sigma_{i\psi}^2 (s_\psi, o_\theta) - \sigma_{i\theta}^2(s_\theta, o_\psi) \qquad (10.14)$$

Two simple, illustrative results can be stated immediately. Suppose, for voter i, $\mathbf{v}\mu_\theta = \mathbf{v}\mu_\psi = \mathbf{x}_i$, or both candidates' distributions of ideological positions are centered on $\mathbf{x}_i$. Then

$$NCD_i = -(0)^2 + (0)^2 + \mathbf{v}^2\delta_i = \delta_i\Sigma_{k=1}^m v_k^2 \qquad (10.15)$$

The first result can then be stated like this: *If the two candidates take what look like identical ideological positions, the voter will choose the candidate with the lower variance.*

The second result is just as obvious from the model, but contains an important intuitive point: *The lower the utility of the voter, the higher the variance of the candidate he chooses. Thus, even if both candidates pledge to pursue exactly the voter's ideal point if elected, the utility of the voter is reduced by negative advertising if the consequence of negative advertising is to increase the perceived variance of both candidates' positions.* Interestingly, the *larger* the mapping terms v_k on the m issues, the *lower* the voter's utility. The logic underpinning this conclusion is straightforward. The larger the v_k, the more related the voter's perception of ideological position is to actual policy. Since small changes in ideology cause big changes in policy, variance in ideology produces magnified variance in expected policy. The greater the relation between ideology and policy, the greater the increase in variance. If the expected NCD_i is positive, and voter i behaves deterministically, she votes for Theta; if NCD_i is negative, she votes for Psi; and she abstains if the expected difference is zero. Candidates seek electoral victory, implied by $V_p > 0.5$, where $V_\psi = 1 - V_\theta$. The interpretation Hinich (1977b) attaches to the random variable V_θ is the proportion of voters with ideal x_i who vote for Theta, summed across all ideal points.[4] If F is a population cumulative

---

4. Voters whose preferred positions are closer to π_θ are more likely to vote for Theta than for Psi, but given the other, unobservable, characteristics of the candidate (character, integrity,

density function for the likelihood a particular voter votes for Theta, given NCD_i, then Theta seeks to maximize this function:

$$V_\theta(s_\theta, o_\theta, s_\psi, o_\psi) = \Sigma_i[F(-[\hat{\omega}_\theta i - \mathbf{x}_i]^2 + [\hat{\omega}_{\psi i} - \mathbf{x}_i]^2 + \mathbf{v}^2\delta_i)] \qquad (10.16)$$

The expected plurality function is, like the individual variance terms that are its most important components, concave in s and convex in o.

Finally, we must identify the source of the funds to be spent. We assume that candidates have no funds of their own, and cannot borrow, but must solicit contributions C_j from the H contributor/investors. Total campaign *expenditures e* (the sum of o_p and s_p, for each candidate p) are constrained by the amount they receive in total *contributions C*:

$$e_\theta \leq \Sigma_{h=1}^H C_{\theta h}, \text{ and } e_\psi \leq \Sigma_{h=1}^H C_{\psi h} \qquad (10.17)$$

Thus, we now turn to integrating contributors into the model.

Contributors

As was discussed in chapter 9, the contributors' problem is to maximize the net expected return from political investment, assuming that the investor can borrow additional money beyond the budget, or that leftover budget can be invested at the next best rate of return. Of course, if this "next best" rate of return exceeds that available in political activity, then the investor contributes nothing to either candidate. We posit four characteristics of political participation relevant to the hth investor's utility function ϕ_h: (1) perceived candidate positions ($\hat{\pi}_{\theta h}, \hat{\pi}_{\psi h}$);[5] (2) private benefits (β_θ, β_ψ) offered in exchange for contributions; (3) borrowing/leftover budget (B'_θ, B'_ψ); and (4) subjective *ex ante* probability that each candidate will win $P_{\theta h}, P_{\psi h}$. Let us consider each of the four in turn.

Perceived positions $\hat{\pi}_{\theta h}, \hat{\pi}_{\psi h}$. We assume that each investor h, like each voter i, maps candidate positions along the predictive dimension onto the policy space with a transformation vector, denoted w_h, and with prior expectations updated according to Bayes's rule.

---

commitment, leadership ability) we cannot treat voter choice as being determined solely by the weighted Euclidean distance. We can represent the voting choice probabilistically, rather than deterministically.

5. It is possible to derive contributor perceptions using a Bayesian approach analogous to that used by voters. But since there is no application of these parameters beyond our assumption that contributors on average have lower variances in their perceptions, we drop this derivation. See Hinich and Munger (1989) and Cameron and Enelow (1991).

$$\hat{\omega}_{\theta h} = \hat{\pi}_{\theta h} \mathbf{w}_h \tag{10.18}$$

$$\hat{\omega}_{\psi h} = \hat{\pi}_{\psi h} \mathbf{w}_h$$

It is plausible to assume that, for the posterior distributions, $\sigma_{i\theta}^2 \geq \sigma_{h\theta}^2$ and $\sigma_{i\psi}^2 \geq \sigma_{h\psi}^2$ (contributors' perceptions have variance no larger, and perhaps smaller, than the perceived variance for voters).

Private benefits $\beta_{\theta h}(C_{\theta h})$, $\beta_{\psi h}(C_{\psi h})$. Each candidate makes available to investors private benefits that affect their wealth positions; these benefits are awarded to investors based on the investors' contributions C_{ph}. While the level of provision of such benefits may correlate with candidate ideologies π_θ and π_ψ, private benefits are nonpublic.[6] Each β_h must therefore be excludable (the candidate can, with some cost, feasibly withhold the benefit from some or all potential recipients), and have a positive marginal cost of provision, from the candidates' perspectives. This positive marginal cost of provision may be no more than the shadow price or opportunity cost of benefit, based on the fact that each candidate p has only a fixed stock ($\overline{\beta}_p$) of private benefits to allocate. We assume, however, that at the margin, such particularistic benefits (particularly access) create only a negligible increment to the total tax bill, and that we can ignore the $\overline{\beta}$'s as components of public policy Ω.

Borrowing/leftover budget B'. Recall from chapter 9 that the investor's budget is defined as:

$$B'_h = I_h - C_{\theta h} - C_\psi h \tag{10.19}$$

where I_h is the total amount allocated by the investor h to political activity. Thus, if $B'_h < 0$, the investor has borrowed money ($C_{\theta h} + C_{\psi h} I_h$); if $B'_h > 0$, then h has B' dollars to invest in other races or the next most profitable business investment.

Probabilities of election $P_{\theta h}$ and $P_{\psi h}$. Each prospective investor knows that the election will have one of two outcomes: Theta wins (occurring with probability $P_{\theta h}$) or Psi wins ($P_{\psi h} = 1 - P_{\theta h}$). Because of differences in information about voters, and priors about $\hat{\pi}_{\theta h}$ and $\hat{\pi}_{\psi h}$, these assessments may differ across investors. Further, though $P_{\theta h}$ and $P_{\psi h}$ are, in principle, endogenous to the model, we assume that the marginal electoral impact of each contribution is negligible. Hence, $P_{\theta h}$ and $P_{\psi h}$ are *exogenous* inputs to the decision calculus of investors acting alone or in small coalitions.

Thus, the investor's problem (dropping the h subscript to simplify nota-

---

6. The notion of "private," or "service-induced" contributions has been explored in Baron (1989a, 1989b) and Hinich and Munger (1989), and discussed in the review in Cameron and Morton (1991).

tion) is to invest his funds C_θ and C_ψ in a single race to maximize net expected return Γ:

$$\Gamma(C_\theta, C_\psi) = P_{\theta h}\phi(\hat{\pi}_\theta, \beta_\theta(C_\theta), B') + P_\psi h\phi(\hat{\pi}_\psi, \beta_\psi(C_\psi), B') \quad (10.20)$$

where $\phi(.)$ is concave in β_θ and β_ψ.[7]

To establish the concavity of the objective function Γ, take first and second derivatives with respect to C_θ (the case for C_ψ is symmetric):

$$\frac{\partial \Gamma}{\partial C_\theta} = P_\theta \frac{\partial \phi}{\partial \beta_\theta} \frac{\partial \beta_\theta}{\partial C_\theta} - \frac{\partial \phi}{\partial B'} \geq 0 \quad (10.21)$$

$$\frac{\partial^2 \Gamma}{\partial C_\theta^2} = P_\theta \left[\frac{\partial^2 \phi}{\partial \beta_\theta^2} \left(\frac{\partial \beta_\theta}{\partial C_\theta} \right)^2 + \frac{\partial \phi}{\partial \beta_\theta} \frac{\partial^2 \beta_\theta}{\partial C_\theta^2} - \frac{\partial^2 \phi}{\partial \beta_\theta \partial B'} \frac{\partial \beta_\theta}{\partial C_\theta} \right] + \frac{\partial^2 \phi}{\partial (B')^2} \quad (10.22)$$

For the first derivative, equation 10.21 establishes nonnegativity. Either Γ is increasing in C_θ or the opportunity cost rate of return ($\partial \phi / \partial B'$) is so high that the result is a nonparticipating corner solution. The second derivative is more complex: the first, second, and fourth terms are negative, as required, but the cross-partial for β_θ and B' may be positive. This term captures the influence of private favors on the opportunity cost rate of return. If private favors raise (or reduce only slightly) the opportunity cost rate of return, the expression in equation 10.22 is strictly negative, which is sufficient to establish concavity.

We turn now to a consideration of the strategic interactions of candidate activities, given the behavior of voters and contributors outlined above.

The Structure of the Game and Characterization of Equilibrium

Two aspects of the game between candidates require further exposition before we proceed to the existence results in the next section: (1) Fixed candidate positions. Candidates are not free to choose voters' perceptions, which derive from prior experience and their understanding of the linkages between policy and ideology. Instead, Theta and Psi must rely on attempts to depict their fixed records in a more propitious light. (2) Fixed election probabilities, from the perspective of contributors. We are treating election probabilities as invariant to the individual contribution decisions, though clearly, in the aggregate, contributions partly determine the plurality *ex post*. Thus, there is no game

---

7. The opportunity cost return embodied by B' accounts for investment in alternative projects, including other races.

among contributors. Although economic interests may not be indifferent between the outcomes Theta wins and Psi wins, the election is beyond their individual control, and there are no strategic factors in the contribution decision, except maximization of wealth.

The conceptual form of the game is depicted in figure 16. To cast the complex political interaction outlined above as a game, we must formally characterize the objective functions and strategy sets of Theta and Psi. Assuming Cournot-Nash behavior, and focusing on Theta, the candidate seeks to maximize:

$$V_\theta(s_\theta, \bar{s}_\psi, o_\theta, \bar{o}_\psi) + \lambda(e_\theta^* - s_\theta - o_\theta) \tag{10.23}$$

where $\bar{s}_\psi$ is the level of the opponent's spending on reducing the variance associated with Psi's position, $\bar{o}_\psi$ is Psi's spending devoted to increasing the noise associated with Theta's political messages, and e_θ^* is the maximum quantity of electoral resources available to be allocated between these two functions (* hereafter denotes an optimum, or equilibrium, condition). The multiplier λ is the shadow price of money to be spent on the campaign, or the increase in expected plurality deriving from a \$1 increase in money obtained in exchange for private benefits.

We do not consider the strategic elements of candidate pledges in competing for contributions from the same prospective investors, though such competitive elements are likely to shape real-world allocation strategies. For present purposes, it is sufficient that the candidates maximize the resources e_θ^* and e_ψ^* available to them. For Theta:

$$e_\theta^* = \Sigma_{h=1}^{H} C_{\theta h}(\beta_{\theta h}^*) \tag{10.24}$$

$$\bar{\beta}_\theta \geq \Sigma_{h=1}^{H} \beta_{\theta h}^* \tag{10.25}$$

The formal solution to the problem takes the form of an H-dimensional vector of private benefit allocations and the associated shadow price:

$$\beta_\theta^* = (\beta_{\theta 1}^*, \beta_{\theta 2}^*, \ldots, \beta_{\theta m}^*, \lambda^*) \tag{10.26}$$

This allocation represents the contribution-maximizing strategy, but is not strategic in any useful sense. Rather, the candidate takes these resources and turns to the next stage of his campaign: how to allocate the resources between "self" and "opponent" expenditures.

The existence of the solutions β_θ^* and β_ψ^* is easily demonstrated. The strategy set of private benefits available for allocation among competing po-

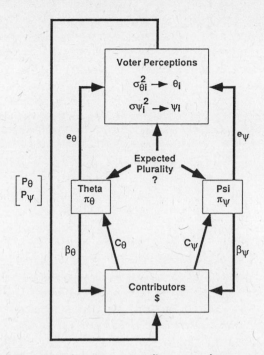

Fig. 16. The conceptual variance/expenditure game between candidates

tential contributors is compact and convex, so that we need only show that the vote function is concave in its argument. This result follows from Enelow and Hinich (1989a), Theorem I, assuming that the following four conditions hold: (1) the voter utility functions U_i are jointly concave in all arguments; (2) the cumulative distribution function F is defined over any of the broad class of densities known as PF2 densities (which includes the normal, exponential, gamma, binomial, poisson, and virtually every other density function used in the statistics or modeling literature); (3) additionally, the contributor objective functions must be strictly concave, but this was demonstrated by equations 10.21 and 10.22 above; and (4) the variances associated with voter perceptions of the two candidates must be jointly concave in its arguments (the four expenditure variables) as we assumed above in equation 10.22.

Having informally demonstrated the existence of a set of solutions to the individual maximization problems of Theta (given arbitrary C_ψ) and Psi (given arbitrary C_θ), we now turn to the main existence result. We formally state our assumptions and the existence theorem, as well as two corollaries, the proofs of which are presented in the appendix to this chapter.

Assumption 1. *At least one contributor contributes to at least one candidate.*

Assumption 2. ϕ_h *is concave in* C_θ, *given* $\overline{C}_\psi$, *and in* C_ψ, *given* $\overline{C}_\theta$, *for each contributor.*

Assumption 3. *The choice sets* e_θ *and* e_ψ *are convex and compact.*

Assumption 4. F *is strictly concave in* s_θ *and* o_θ, *and strictly convex in* s_ψ *and* o_ψ.

Assumption 5. *The distributions representing voter perceptions of the candidates have expected values relatively close compared to their variances. If this condition is met, it implies* V_θ *and* V_ψ *are concave.*[8]

The most interesting and controversial of these requirements turns out to be Assumption 5; the others are largely trivial. Assumption 2 and Assumption 4 simply require that the individual maximization problems faced by contributors and candidates, respectively, have solutions. Assumption 1 is necessary for any game to exist at all (since candidates strategize over spending, there must be some money to spend), and Assumption 3 is, in essence, a restatement of the definition of the e_θ, e_ψ sets as the sums over the (nonempty, by Assumption 1) sets of $C_{\theta h}$, $C_{\psi h}$. We will return to Assumption 5 in a moment; in the meantime, let us simply state the obvious result.

Existence Theorem. *Assumptions 1–5 imply the existence of a unique Nash equilibrium to the campaign expenditure game.*

As has been pointed out by innumerable researchers, the existence of equilibrium in majority rule voting games is highly problematic. The particular approach we have taken, using the probabilistic voting approach, solves some problems and creates others. The problems probabilistic voting solves include the problem of incorporating variable turnout, and smoothing the highly discontinuous outcomes of classical choice theory. The problem with the probabilistic approach, as Slutsky (1975) points out, is the choice from the set of distributions that might represent voter choice. Some distributions create equilibria, it is true; some prevent it. There is certainly no equilibrium

---

8. Slutsky (1975, 292, 303) points out that the early probabilistic voting existence theorems (Hinich, Ledyard, and Ordeshook 1972, 1973) required conditions on the probability distribution of abstention and voting that were "ad hoc. . . . For all the possible shapes not equivalent to the Hinich, Ledyard, and Ordeshook assumptions there will not in general exist a majority equilibrium." See also Enelow and Hinich (1989b).

result deriving from the probabilistic approach that is in any way general, any more than equilibrium is generally found in the classical spatial approach.

But there is one other problem that Assumption 5 highlights. It is discussed formally in the appendix to this chapter, but is worth reviewing verbally here. If each candidate's likely position is perceived as a random variable drawn from a distribution, then the *relative* forms of those distributions require an additional set of restrictions for an equilibrium to exist. These restrictions are interesting, and important, because they are quite counterintuitive. In fact, the nature of the assumption has fundamental implications for the study of comparative politics, or of one political culture over long time periods. To restate Assumption 5 more clearly:

> *Narrow choices, or noisy choices, create equilibria, even in multidimensional spaces; diverse choices, and certain choices, prevent equilibria, even in unidimensional spaces. In a polarized political system, with well-defined parties and firmly established ideologies, Condorcet cycles are immanent. In political systems without polarization, or where ideologies are only loosely and murkily related to concrete policy choices, stability reigns.*

The following two corollaries are extensions of the main existence theorem. In examining these results, we seek only to illustrate some immediate consequences, rather than to exhaustively explore the implications of the model. We assume candidates perceive voters as voting probabilistically, so that (as suggested by Enelow and Hinich [1984a]) platforms converge to $\pi_\theta = \pi_\psi$. This assumption allows us to focus on the gaming aspects of the process, and is not crucial to the applicability of the model.

Corollary I. *If $\pi_\theta = \pi_\psi$, $\beta_\theta = \beta_\psi$, $\sigma^2_{\theta i} = \sigma^2_{\psi i}$, and Assumptions 1–5 are true, then $e^*_\theta = e^*_\psi$, $o^*_\theta = o^*_\psi$, $s^*_\psi = s^*_\theta$, and $\delta_i = 0$ for each voter.*

Corollary II. *If $\pi_\theta = \pi_\psi$, $\beta_\theta = \beta_\psi$, $\sigma^2_{\theta i}(.) = \sigma^2_{\psi i}(.)$ for each voter i, Assumptions 1–5 are true, and f(.) is symmetric around f(0), then once again all expenditures and strategy variables are identical, $\delta_i = 0$, and the optimal strategies yield $V^*_\theta = V^*_\psi = 0.5$, or equal expected vote totals for each candidate.*

In other words, if neither has an advantage in terms of policy, the technology of changing variance by advertising, or the private benefits to be offered, then the allocational strategies will be the same, because the game is formally symmetric. The result is a continuous strategy Prisoner's Dilemma: each candidate exhausts his electoral resources (private benefits) for exactly zero net gain. In short, the result implied by Corollary I is akin to what the Red Queen told Alice: in the absence of differentiation between candidates, "it takes all the running you can do, to keep in the same place. If you want to get somewhere else, you must run at least twice as fast as that!"[9] The reason is that each can respond to expenditures by the other with exactly matching, offsetting spending. Since strategies are defined over a difference term (δ) and strategies are symmetric, the net impact is zero, and candidates cannot improve their expected pluralities. This is true *no matter how many private benefits*, up to and including the Gross National Product, the two candidates have to give out.

The symmetric game where neither candidate has an advantage and spends whatever he or she can for no electoral gain has at least one clear real-world application: open seats in the United States Congress. In these races, far more money is spent than in the average campaign, where there is an incumbent. The reason for this is that when there is an incumbent, voters have knowledge of the likely mean policy, and direct experience on the associated variance of the legislator's activities in office.

The intuitive situation in an open-seat race can be depicted in figure 17, where the optimal spending of candidate Theta is on the vertical axis, and the optimal spending of Psi is on the horizontal axis. Let us suppose that Theta begins by spending e_1^*; the best response in the symmetric game is for Psi to spend e_2^*. But the outcome of the election is exactly the same as if no money had been spent at all! The 45-degree line through the origin describes the set of races where the outcome is a tie (in effect, voters choose randomly between Theta and Psi).

All equilibria of the symmetric game lie along this 45-degree line, and represent expenditures on rallies, commercials, and other trappings of campaigns that (in equilibrium) have no impact on the election. The problem for society is not the money that is wasted in such pointless campaigns. After all, this money is not really "wasted," but is transferred from contributors to the media, owners of restaurants and conference facilities, and owners of other factors used in campaigns.

Even when the race is not for an open seat, however, there is cause for concern about the informative capacity of elections. In order to see this, let us write out the full solution to the candidates' maximization problem. Reproducing equation 10.23 above, but writing out each of the terms as given in equations 10.16 and 10.24–10.26, the maximization problem of Theta is:

---

9. From Charles Lutwidge Dodgson ("Lewis Carroll"), *Through the Looking Glass*, 1872, chapter 2.

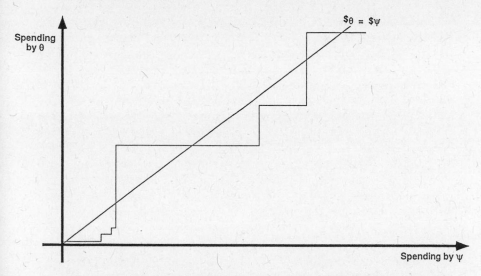

Fig. 17. The symmetric spending game with no constraints on political favors

$$\text{Max: } \Sigma_i[F((\hat{\omega}_{\psi i} - x_i)^2 - (\hat{\omega}_{\theta i} - \mathbf{x}_i)^2 + \sigma^2_{i\psi}(\bar{s}_{\psi}, o_{\theta})$$

$$- \sigma^2_{i\theta}(s_{\theta}, \bar{o}_{\psi}))] + \lambda([\Sigma_h C_{\theta h}(\beta^*_{\theta h})] - s_{\theta} - o_{\theta}) \qquad (10.27)$$

where, as before, β^* is the solution vector to the contribution maximization problem, and the contribution supply $(C_i(\beta_{\theta i}))$ functions are the inverses of the demand for policy functions in the contributor objective functions from equation 10.20:

$$\Gamma(C_{\theta}, C_{\psi}) = P_{\theta h}\phi(\hat{\pi}_{\theta}, \beta_{\theta}(C_{\theta}), B) + P_{\psi h}\phi(\hat{\pi}_{\psi}, \beta_{\psi}(C_{\psi}), B') \qquad (10.28)$$

To solve this problem, we take the first derivatives with respect to the two strategy variables o_{θ} and s_{θ} and the shadow price λ. The three first-order conditions of this problem are then set equal to zero, implying that at a maximum:

$$\partial\sigma^2_{\theta i}/\partial o_{\theta} = -\partial\sigma^2_{\psi i}/\partial s_{\theta} = \lambda \qquad (10.29)$$

This expression requires that the last dollar allocated by the candidate must *increase* the opponent's variance by the same amount that it *reduces* his own, and that the electoral value of this last dollar is the shadow price of additional funds λ. Equation 10.27 is true of any maximum, but it is of particular interest to us in this section in our consideration of incumbency and campaign finance laws.

In the existence theorem and corollaries above, we assumed that the technologies of reducing one's own variance and increasing that of one's opponent were concave, symmetric, and identical. There is no reason to believe that these conditions are general, however. First, there may be differences between two candidates in the expenditures required to convince voters of the plausibility of a given reduction or increase in the noise associated with the two positions. Second, as Alesina and Cukierman (1987), Page (1976), and Shepsle (1972) suggest, the symmetry condition is unlikely to hold. It is easier (more precisely, for our purposes, cheaper) to cloud the likely position of an opponent than to illuminate and focus on one's own position, implying a strategy of "ambiguity." To the extent that it is comparatively cheaper to campaign negatively (i.e., attack one's opponent), then equation 10.27 above indicates that positive, self-oriented campaigning will be observed (if at all) only if the available budget, e^*, is large enough to equalize the marginal electoral gains. It is entirely possible that, for poorly financed campaigns with a candidate known to voters, the equalities in equation 10.27 do not hold, and all money is spent on negative campaigning, or o_θ and o_ψ. Alternately, if the candidate is unknown, the opposite corner solution is implied: all money in a limited campaign is spent on establishing name recognition and reducing the very large variance associated with a political neophyte. We will not consider further either of these two corner solutions, but certainly do not rule them out as empirical possibilities.

The asymmetry in the technologies of using positive versus negative campaigning to affect elections becomes especially important in light of the discussion earlier in this chapter regarding voter utility in high variance races. To recapitulate, we found that (1) voters will choose the lower variance candidate if positions are similar, or are equidistant from the center of the distribution of voters, but (2) the higher the variance of the perception of each candidate's actions, the worse off *all* voters are. In the limit, the very community of understanding on which any political system depends can be destroyed or changed by negative advertising.

It is important to point out that there is no logical contradiction here in individual agents' actions. In fact, it is *because* the actions are individually rational, but harmful to the collective interest, that there is a Prisoner's Dilemma problem. Candidates who use negative campaigning are more likely to win, all else equal and across many races, than those who emphasize positive themes or (worst of all!) "stick to the issues." The problem for society is created when *both* candidates act on the incentives to use negative campaigning. Neither candidate realizes any net electoral gain, though each does better than if he had stayed positive, but the campaign itself imposes enormous and uncompensated utility losses on voters. Voters are made worse off by the breakdown of trust and communication, or (more precisely) by the increase in variability of their own perceptions of the implications of a particular ideological position for policy outcomes. In the stylized world of the model we have presented, this situation is an equilibrium that is quite clearly not a Pareto optimum, *for the society*.[10] Voters would be better off if campaigns were outlawed and choices were made strictly based on broad ideological cues, such as party labels.

One should not go too far, however, in interpreting these results as having direct policy implications. The expense, the furor, and (often) the sheer tackiness of elections is the price citizens in a democracy must pay for having choices. There is no legitimate alternative to the decision by the majority on who will lead them. As Herbert Spencer, in his *First Principles* (1861), said, "The fact disclosed by a survey of the past that majorities have been wrong must not blind us to the complementary fact that majorities have usually not been entirely wrong."

Finally, we are left with the question of how to address incumbency and account for its effects in the model we have written out in this chapter. There are at least two ways that incumbency can be imbedded in the model. First, it seems plausible to imagine that incumbents could promise greater levels of private benefits to potential contributors, primarily because incumbents have known, secure committee assignments and seniority. Even if a challenger is fortunate enough to be named to the same committee as the person he defeated, he will have none of the experience and institutional assets associated with seniority. Second, the incumbent has a known record, a set of votes, and a reputation for delivering on previous promises of private benefits. Further, the incumbent is likely to be able to deliver immediately, while challengers will almost certainly have to wait until they are in office. For either case, the variance of the challenger's position will always be higher for a given level of expenditure. Challengers must spend more money to achieve a similar level of variance, even if the marginal reduction of variance for challengers may be higher from each dollar spent.

In the notation of our model, and making Theta the incumbent and Psi the challenger, we have:

$$\overline{\beta}_\theta \gg \overline{\beta}_\psi \qquad\qquad (10.30)$$

$$\sigma^2_{i\theta}(.) \ll \sigma^2_{i\psi}(.) \text{ if } e_\theta \approx e_\psi \qquad\qquad (10.31)$$

---

10. It is possible to claim that, *for the candidates*, the outcome is a Pareto optimum, since they have no gain or loss either way. The optimality condition is more properly defined for the society as a whole, however, since it is voters making the choices.

The first condition reflects the fact that the incumbent has more experience, and more "favors" available to promise. The second condition simply formalizes the assumption, common in the elections literature, that the incumbent is better known than the challenger. In either case, the incumbent must win ($V_\theta > 0.5$) as long as the two platforms are approximately equal, because it will be impossible for the challenger to outspend the incumbent.

However, a dramatic change in either of two areas can force incumbents out of office. First, individual voters' perceptions of a candidate's character, performance, or other volatile factors influencing the shape of the voting probability distribution can hurt an incumbent or remove a candidate who was once perceived as a front-runner (witness the precipitous decline of Gary Hart's popularity in 1988, the collapse of George Bush's lead in 1991, or Bill Clinton's problems with consistency and focus immediately after taking office). Likewise, an apparently invulnerable party may lose power very quickly, as in the case of Japan's Liberal Democratic party in 1993. Second, a "realignment" (exogenous change in the mapping parameters $\mathbf{v}_i$) will cause incumbents to lose, because they have difficulty changing their perceived positions along the predictive dimension. Thus, our prediction is that incumbents should never lose if they maintain their image as being trustworthy and consistent, and the system is in equilibrium. When this prediction is wrong, incumbents will not lose piecemeal; they will lose in bunches, as the system cycles among different polarized ideological positions.

Campaigns, Communication, and Community

It is useful to restate the logic of strategic interaction that underlies the predictions of the model outlined above. The three sets of agents we consider are wealth/utility-maximizing contributors, utility-maximizing voters, and two expected plurality-maximizing candidates who have positions along a left-right ideological or predictive dimension. Voters map the candidates' positions along this single dimension onto the policy space, over which they have preferences and a well-defined ideal point. This mapping, however, is accomplished only with idiosyncratic priors updated according to Bayes's rule. It is the variance of the posterior distributions that candidates seek to affect through their campaign expenditures, with the money for these efforts coming from contributors.

The explicit game matches candidates seeking to influence the difference in voters' perceptions of the errors associated with the two candidate positions. In this regard, expenditures on affecting variance have symmetric effects on expected plurality: an increase in the opponent's variance is exactly the same as a similar decrease in your own. Our results suggest that there exist reasonable conditions under which such a game has at least one equilibrium. Further, if the two candidates are identical, each will spend the same amount, and if the probability distribution describing voter behavior is symmetric, then the two candidates will split the vote. This suggests, for example, that open-seat elections will be very close and spending will be very high, unless one of the candidates has a clear and established reputation acquired in other office or public life.

On the other hand, if one candidate is an incumbent, there may be no amount of spending that will cause the challenger to win, provided that the incumbent can match it. The game, in our model, implies that electoral competition can result in extremely close races at either high or low levels of expenditure, but that the individual incentive to spend more will create an upward spiral of spending and response spending. Thus, our results do not paint an optimistic picture for the chances for reform of the campaign finance process. Restrictions on spending or contributions tend to benefit incumbents, reducing competition and insulating officials from the electoral forces that assure accountability. The alternative is little better, however, since the absence of such restrictions imply that an ever-expanding quantity of resources will be spent on elections. Worse, such a result implies no real consequent increase in competitiveness, because incumbents can still win by simply matching the challenger's spending.

Finally, and most important, we wish to consider the implications of these results for the political system in which campaigns take place. To pursue this inquiry, we must detour a moment to consider the real point of the whole enterprise of the campaign. From the perspective of the candidates, the goal of the campaign is to win the office being contested. From the perspective of voters, the goal of the campaign is to choose the best candidate. Obviously, only one candidate can win; under what circumstances is the winner the "best"?

In earlier chapters, we have argued that ideology serves a number of functions that make it the means by which candidates communicate about political choices, and the means by which voters make those choices. Schofield (1985a) identifies the primary problem of achieving cooperation in a community in the following question:

> What is the minimal amount that one agent must know in a given milieu about the beliefs and wants of other agents, to be able to form coherent notions about their behavior, and for this knowledge to be communicable to the others? It seems to me that this problem is at the heart of any analysis of community, convention, and cooperation. (Schofield 1985a, 219)

In this chapter, we have considered the role of the campaign in providing voters with information about "the beliefs and wants of other agents, to be able to form coherent notions about their behavior." Our conclusion is that, to the extent that campaigns deal in persuasion about commitment to ideology, the technology of the modern campaign destroys communication, and therefore community, rather than improving it.[11]

The reason is that candidates, whose goal is to win, find it in their interest to focus much (maybe most) of their resources on negative campaigning. By increasing the variance of the posterior distribution voters perceive as describing the opponent, each candidate can improve his chances of winning. Unfortunately, the aggregate effects of this mudslinging are pernicious: since both candidates have access to the media technology required for negative advertising, neither candidate is really better off. Voters are worse off, however, as the variance of their perceptions of the candidate distributions is increased. As we showed earlier, this means that voters' utilities are lower, without any associated electoral gain for candidates. Campaign results are not Pareto optimal.

Schofield (1985), summarizing Taylor (1982), lists three key features of "community":

shared common beliefs or norms
direct and complex relations among members
reciprocity

Within a community, it is possible to achieve collective, apparently altruistic, ends because what Schofield calls the "common knowledge basis of cooperation" is satisfied. As Schofield points out:

The fundamental theoretical problem underlying the question of cooperation is the manner by which individuals attain knowledge of each others' preferences and likely behavior. Moreover, the problem is one of common knowledge, since each individual, i, is required not only to have information about others' preferences, but also to know that the others have knowledge of i's own preferences and strategies. (Schofield 1985, 218)

We have argued, in effect, that "community" is a sufficient basis for cooperation, but is not necessary. Ideology provides an alternative means by which the common knowledge basis of cooperation can be achieved. Common knowledge of this sort is itself a collective good, however, and is subject

---

11. Interestingly, this is a point partially predicted by Key (1961).

to depreciation because of the incentives facing candidates who want to win, for negative campaigning serves the candidate but hurts the electorate. The ultimate effect is the erosion of the common knowledge basis for cooperation, as ideological messages lose their meaning, and campaigns lose their importance as a means for making effective and wise political choices.

APPENDIX: PROOFS OF THE EXISTENCE THEOREM AND COROLLARIES

Existence Theorem:
The formal statement of Assumption 5 is given by Enelow and Hinich (1989b, 106), Theorem 1. In the notation of this book, Assumption 5 can be interpreted as requiring that the following condition be satisfied:

$$1/[a(\omega_\theta - x)]^2 \geq [(\omega_\theta - x)^2 - (\omega_\psi)^2] / 2\sigma^2 \qquad \text{(10 App. 1)}$$

where a is the relevant salience parameter from the A matrix in the voter's utility function, and σ^2 is the variance of any "normally distributed random element" (Enelow and Hinich 1989b,102) that is assumed to differ idiosyncratically across voters. This condition is general, and therefore includes the cases where the errors in the understanding of voters of the implications of ideology for policy differ, and the case where voters have different perceptions of the variances of different candidates.

Then, given Assumptions 1–5, we know from Owen (1982, Theorem IV.6.2) that a pure strategy equilibrium exists; if the expected plurality function V is strictly concave, then a unique pure strategy equilibrium exists in expenditures. Assumptions 1–3 and 5 have already been demonstrated. Thus, we must only justify Assumption 4, and the theorem follows immediately from the theorem proved by Owen (1982). Enelow and Hinich demonstrate the concavity of the expected plurality function in policy choices. The relevant expected plurality for the present problem is:

$$V_\theta(s_\theta, o_\theta, s_\psi, o_\psi) = \sigma_i[F(-(\pi_{\theta i} - x_i)^2 + (\pi_{\psi i} - x_i)^2 + v^2\delta_i] \qquad \text{(10 App. 2)}$$

Since the summation is over voters, and the sum of concave functions is, itself, concave, we need only establish that equation 10 App. 2) is concave for arbitrary i. For any particular voter, the concavity of f(.) is established by Enelow and Hinich (1994) if $\delta_i = 0$. This result will still follow, so long as δ_i is concave in the strategy variables e_θ and e_ψ. Recall that δ_i is:

$$\delta_i = \sigma^2_{i\psi}(s_\psi, o_\theta) - \sigma^2_{i\theta}(s_\theta, o_\psi) \qquad \text{(10 App. 3)}$$

where:

$$\frac{\partial V_\theta}{\partial s_\theta} > 0 \quad \frac{\partial V_\theta}{\partial s_\psi} < 0 \quad \frac{\partial V_\theta}{\partial o_\theta} > 0 \quad \frac{\partial V_\theta}{\partial o_\psi} < 0 \qquad \text{(10 App. 4)}$$

and

$$\frac{\partial^2 V_\theta}{\partial s_\theta^2} < 0 \qquad \frac{\partial^2 V_\theta}{\partial s_\psi^2} > 0 \qquad \frac{\partial^2 V_\theta}{\partial o_\theta^2} < 0 \qquad \frac{\partial^2 V_\theta}{\partial o_\psi^2} > 0 \qquad\qquad (10 \text{ App. } 5)$$

*But (10 App. 2) is therefore the sum of products involving scalars and concave functions of the strategy variables, and is concave. (**Q.E.D.**)*

Corollary I:

*Suppose the corollary is false, or that $e_\theta \neq e_\psi$. Given that the two variances, both functions of expenditures, are concave, we know that δ, a sum of concave functions, is concave, and $V(.)$ is therefore concave in expenditures. Suppose Theta spends less; then $\sigma_\theta^2(.) > \sigma_\psi^2(.)$, $\delta < 0$, and $V(.) < 0.5$, indicating a loss for Theta. Since Theta could spend more if he allocated more of his private benefits to attracting funds, this cannot be an equilibrium. Theta can do better than Psi only if he spends more, yet both have the same quantity of resources to allocate. As long as the ability of the two candidates to affect their own variance and that of their opponent is identical ($\sigma_\theta^2(.) = \sigma_\psi^2(.)$ for the same levels of own and opponents' total expenditure and mix between mudslinging and aggrandizement), each candidate must dissipate all his resources. Alternatively, suppose $s_\theta \neq s_\psi$; one candidate must, then, not be maximizing his plurality, since the first order conditions of the maximization problem imply equal marginal impacts for s and o spending, and if the two candidates are identical, they must arrive at the same solutions. (**Q.E.D.**)*

Corollary II:

Assuming that f is symmetric around $f(0)$ means that equal departures in either direction from zero expected policy difference ($E(NCD_i) = 0$) are equivalent in probability terms. The only addition to the equilibrium in Corollary II is that the two candidates tie in expected vote, or:
$$1 - F(NCD_i = 0, \delta = 0) = F(NCD_i = 0, \delta = 0) = 0.5. \text{ (**Q.E.D.**)}$$

CHAPTER 11

The Implications of Ideology for Political Choice

TOKYO—Japan may be on the threshold of its first major political change in almost 40 years, but only if voters abandon the security of old ways. The major players in the political drama unfolding ahead of Sunday's parliamentary election are portraying the choices facing Japanese voters in terms of good vs. evil, chaos vs. continuity. . . . "Stability or confusion—which will *you* choose?" asks a [Liberal Democratic party] flier. "Can we really trust Japan to the opposition?"
        —Associated Press news story, Friday, July 17, 1993

We are now ready to ask the questions that we claimed, at the outset, could only be answered by a theory of ideology. Why is political conflict so rarely a "rational" debate over policy, and so often a battle between good and evil? Why do some societies prosper and others, with similar natural resources, space, and population, languish? How can Japan, in this century, and England and the Netherlands, in the previous two, build prodigious wealth and power with virtually no natural resources? How can resource-rich Brazil and Argentina, or Russia of either 1893 or 1993, flounder in a static, third-world system of barter and government-organized theft?

In any society, there is a basic tension between altruism and egoism as a motivation for the actions of citizens. If we were to design a society and its rules and morals, two basic sets of questions would have to be addressed. First, do societies prosper more if their citizens act altruistically (for the good of the group), or selfishly (for their individual benefit)? Should societies try to indoctrinate citizens to believe that there is no difference between group and individual goals? After all, when selfish actions benefit the group, the conflicts that create political crisis, and the transaction costs that create economic stasis, are greatly reduced.

Let us suppose, for the sake of argument, that societies might want to affect the way that citizens conceive of their place in that society. The second question then becomes one of strategy. How does a society choose the basic values of its citizens and their choices between altruistic and egoistic actions? If such a strategic choice is impossible, we may still usefully ask what it is about a society that causes, intentionally or not, the attitudes its citizens have

221

toward themselves and the collective group. The reader will, no doubt, suspect that our answer is that such attitudes are related to the culture of the society, and that this culture determines the ideologies that rule the political system. The connection between culture, ideology, and prosperity has, until now, been woefully neglected in the social sciences as an analytic means of understanding human progress. To make the case for ideology complete, we must offer some argument for why the role we have claimed for morals and emotion is such an important part of the theory. Before doing this explicitly, it is meet to consider the concepts of altruism and egoism more generally.

Egoism and Altruism

We begin by defining two competing motives for individual action: egoism and altruism. Egoism holds that the only proper motive for human behavior is self-interest; altruism is the doctrine that human action is properly motivated only by concern for others. Any society's wealth and welfare are a consequence of the choices by individuals to act on one or the other of these motives.[1]

Citizens' actions perceived to serve both the society and the individual may be "best," but such an observation begs the question. If there is no conflict, it can only be because there is no difference: If an action serves both goals, then selfishness benefits others at least as much, and possibly more, than action putatively motivated by a desire to benefit others. Such an outcome is a happy event, but one that requires great planning or good fortune. To understand better the conflict between egoism and altruism, consider the following two illustrations.

(A) A foxhole, with five soldiers in it, has a fragmentation grenade thrown into it. None of the five soldiers has time to jump out of the foxhole; each has just enough time to jump on the grenade before it explodes. If no one leaps on the grenade, all will surely die. There is no time to draw lots, or communicate in any way.

(B) A lifeboat, with five sailors in it, has enough water for four to survive the week it will take to reach safety. If all five stay in the boat, all five will surely die of thirst. The water is full of sharks, so any who leave the boat will be eaten. There is no chance of rescue by other ships.

Let us now compare the results under egoism and altruism for our two stylized "societies." In the foxhole, egoism causes destruction of the whole group: no one acts, and all die. Altruism implies that each soldier tries to jump on the grenade. The largest, strongest, and fastest soldier jumps first (at least on average, if there are many such "societies"), while the other four survive.

---

1. A number of important works have been written on this question, including three which take widely differing perspectives: Baier (1958), Ardrey (1970), and Dawkins (1976).

Altruism is the better of the two simple alternatives, *both for the group and for each individual*. After all, even the one person who is killed is no worse off, his (scanty) remains are honored, and his family is cared for. If there are many of these foxhole societies, then the "competition" among them is almost trivial. Very quickly, only altruistic societies remain, though the societies that survive all lose their largest, fastest, and best soldiers. If foxhole societies have to compete against one another for resources, the successful ones will do so without their best members.

In the lifeboat, assume communication is again impossible, since otherwise the settings are not comparable. That is, imagine each sailor must decide immediately and simultaneously whether to leap out into the sharks, or stay in the boat. Now, altruism means all five are eaten by monsters of the sea; egoism implies each sailor tries to throw his neighbor out. Assume everyone pushes until at least one (there may be excessive, selfish zeal disguised as a desire to save the group) sailor is in the water. Then there will be no more than four people in the boat, and they will survive.

Further, since the form of selection of the sacrifice is the application of physical force, the person(s) thrown out will be smallest and weakest. It may have been better to throw out only one person, but we are confident that at least some sailors will survive, if they are egoists. Further, those who do survive are the strongest and the most resourceful. The result is, therefore, different from the foxhole example. If lifeboat societies have to compete for dock space when they finally arrive on land, egoist boats will win out. Altruist societies are simply empty boats, while egoist boats are peopled by the strong.

A more realistic scenario, in the lifeboat, is the possibility of drawing lots, but this requires some ability to talk and unanimously agree on an arrangement that benefits the society. The result is the sacrifice of one individual, whose identity is unknown at the time of the agreement. We can pose, as the altruistic alternative, a universal lottery (i.e., one that involves all five sailors), where each consents to go over the side if he loses. Egoism again implies throwing one out, though this time after arguing the merits and weaknesses of each person. Such an agreement might not require unanimous agreement, but be four against one, or even three against two (i.e., simple majority rule!). The difference is that altruism requires consent of all (including the throwee), and egoism requires only the agreement of the throwers. Both create the same outcome, in terms of the number of survivors (four). Egoism, again, consciously selects the smallest and weakest person as the one who is easiest to throw out or poses the smallest loss to the society.[2]

If there are many lifeboats, and they are forced to fight one another, the egoist societies will, on average, win out, because they have selected for

---

2. Of course, "egoism" might just as well choose the ugliest, or Jewish, or African, or Caucasian, or female, member of the group for sacrifice.

strength. Adding a layer of complexity, if some societies are lifeboat societies and some are foxholes, then (assuming the two groups are otherwise similar) surviving lifeboats will win conflicts over surviving foxholes. The reason is that foxholes, to survive, must select out their best and strongest to die. Lifeboats, to survive, first within the lifeboat, and then in conflict with other surviving lifeboats, destroy only their weakest and smallest.

Let us allow that all societies face some decisions analogous to the foxhole, and some analogous to the lifeboat. Then, under these abstract conditions, egoism would win out, not because it is morally superior, but because the ideology on which it is based is competitively superior. The form of the competition is quite complex, and quite different from the internal political competition we have addressed so far. Two recent works, Gauthier (1986) and Frank (1988) have considered the importance of individual rationality and morals for understanding the results we expect from societies, and it is worth considering each for a moment.

Gauthier argues that an important attribute of "rational" action is the action's context. In particular, it is possible to define a concept of morality that represents constraints on the individual's ability, and even desire, to act in what would otherwise be self-interest. The moral aspect of these constraints is precisely in their inducement to be concerned with the welfare of others in choosing an action. The problem comes (as in our lifeboat example) when a member of the society who has accepted the societal constraints on individual action, in principle, reneges, if it is in their practical self-interest to do so. As in our lifeboat example, each citizen is willing to participate in the lottery, but the citizen who loses and must swim for it quite possibly will have second thoughts. Although the *agreement* was mutually beneficial, the outcome of the agreement benefited some more than others.

The important point that Gauthier makes is that the *ex ante* contract, or agreement on morals to constrain individual action from self-interest, may be tenuous. The ability of the market, or market-like institutions, to create wealth and preserve freedom, may get more credit than it is due if we neglect the harmful, Pareto-inferior, but self-interested, actions individuals might take without moral constraints. The moral basis, and emphasis, of whatever ideology forms the social orthodoxy circumscribe the ability of individuals to achieve cooperative solutions.

Frank's (1988) claim is that the self-interested thing to do may be an action that appears altruistic, or even simply irrational. The soldier's decision to jump on the grenade may be the result of indoctrination: members of the foxhole "society" are trained to feel fury at the enemy's attempt to kill them, and to leap without conscious thought to stamp out the threat. If all agree to have their emotions tampered with in this way, *all* are better off, it is true. But so is every individual. Harking back to Gauthier's point, the "first-best" solution is to have everyone else jump, while you maintain control and hold back. This solution is unattainable, for if you are a known shirker, you will not be tolerated in the foxhole, or might even be tossed out of the foxhole (out where there are many grenades) by your angry comrades. The "second-best" solution is to enter the agreement and act on it without thinking.

It is important to emphasize that the decision to act is no longer "rational," in the usual sense, in Frank's framework. The decision to be indoctrinated into the mind-set of the soldier may have been conscious, but the whole point of the training is to rob oneself of any will to act otherwise. Sometimes this may have mutually beneficial effects, as in the grenade in the foxhole example. In other cases, we may see the futile charge of doomed men against an impregnable position because the orders were confused or simply mistaken. Frank's argument is not that it is instrumentally rational to behave irrationally. Rather, he points out that many irrational actions have important survival values. Organizations able to create norms of behavior (which we have called ideologies) that encourage such "irrationality" have a powerful advantage in competing with purely egoistic groups.

The role of ideology in a society is to choose the beliefs and ethical norms of citizens. Later in this chapter, we will examine the Marxian response to this perspective, but for now, we go on to the second question discussed above. How do ideologies influence the choices of citizens between egoism and altruism, and what are the implications of ideologies for the prosperity of real-world societies?

Egoism, Altruism, and Prosperity

> Every individual necessarily labors to render the annual revenue of the society as great as he can. He generally indeed neither intends to promote the public interest, nor knows how much he is promoting it. . . . He intends only his own gain, and he is in this, as in many other cases, led by an invisible hand to promote an end which was no part of his intention. . . . By pursuing his own interest he frequently promotes that of the society more effectually than when he really intends to promote it. I have never known much good done by those who affected to trade for the public good.
>   —A. Smith, *An Inquiry into the Nature and Causes of the Wealth of Nations*, 1776, book iv, chapter 2

Smith's famous claims for the reconciliation of the desire for individual gain and the realization of societal benefit through the action of the market are now hackneyed; at the time they were revolutionary. Combined with Smith's other great work, *A Theory of Moral Sentiments* (1759), and resting on the earlier contributions of Hobbes, Locke, and Hume, there seemed to be an answer to the egoism/altruism conundrum in explaining the growth and prosperity of societies. While not universally accepted, the answer Smith gave has not been greatly elaborated until recently.

Recent work has not argued that Smith was wrong, only that the perspective on the interaction between markets and the basic values of the society was incomplete. What was left out was, and is, ideology. One version of Smith's argument, taking ideology into account, might go like this. The prosperity of societies depends on the aggregate implications of the responses of individuals to the incentives and moral precepts that the society creates. The competition among societies to command resources and secure wealth is, of course, much more complex than our foxhole/lifeboat examples. Still, the characteristics that create growth and success (or cause failure) can be found in societies' basic values, or ideologies. Most important, for the purposes of our inquiry on egoism and altruism, it may be impossible to make accurate guesses about which set of societal norms is likely to result in a more prosperous or powerful society. This is particularly so when those guesses are based solely on the physical resources that the society commands.

However, societies that create and nurture an ideological linkage between moral action for individuals and practical consequence for all, or at least many, will prosper. One way (and there may be many others) of achieving this, under certain circumstances that are not yet well understood, is to organize a system of ownership that depends on private property, and an infrastructure of transaction that depends on prices for the transmission of information about scarcity and rents. But these arrangements, which Douglass North would call "institutions," are not sufficient to ensure prosperity; they may also not be necessary. What *is* necessary is that the prevailing ideology of the society encourage individual acts that are Pareto-improving, and that this ideology be widely accepted as legitimate and ethically defensible.

From this perspective, what Adam Smith did was to explain why a particular arrangement (we might call it capitalism) worked well to create prosperity.[3] There is little in Smith, however, that addresses the more fundamental question: Why does capitalism so often answer the needs of the ideology sought by elites who control political and economic power? That answer has been offered, separately, by several scholars, including Max Weber, in his treatise on the role of Protestantism and the "work ethic" in supporting and protecting capitalism. If challenged to explain why England prospered and Spain withered in the eighteenth century, a correct, but useless, answer would be that England relied on the market and Spain remained largely feudal. The only important reason England changed to a market system is that the Angli-

---

3. It is worth noting that Marx and Engels clearly agreed with Smith on the advantages of capitalism, *for accumulation*. This is the reason that Marx considered industrial capitalism an unavoidable step in the transformation from fuedalism to socialism.

can church allowed it. The only good explanation of why Spain remained feudal is that the Catholic church and the feudal political hierarchy, together, blocked what would have been a Pareto-improving move to the market system. It didn't matter that the Spanish church's own revenues and power would have been immeasurably enhanced, because the market system was inconsistent with the ideology of post-Inquisition Spain.[4]

There have been some attempts to reconcile the (arguably) efficient workings of the market (intuited by Smith and demonstrated formally by Arrow, Debreu, and others) with the rise and decline of economically and militarily powerful states. Olson (1982) offers an explanation for growth and decline outside the pure market, based on the interaction of political self-interest and political institutions. In the early stages of a society's development, egoistic action creates wealth and welfare through the creation of jobs and goods for consumption.

However, as self-interested action becomes more routinized and established as "organized interests," and these interests can defend their position through the entrenched power of the state, growth slows and the economy becomes sclerotic and rigid. Ultimately, the society is destroyed from within unless some potent outside force, such as war, sweeps away the rigidities and allows new growth.

Though Olson's theory has been influential, it is far too mechanistic in its treatment of political ideologies and the idiosyncratic institutions they create. Different states can be expected to differ dramatically in their susceptibility to what Olson calls "institutional sclerosis," based on the capacity of the prevailing ideology to prevent destructive rent seeking. The problem Olson identifies can be cured, or at least mitigated, either by outside pressure or by direct moral suasion on ideological grounds.

Douglass North, in his two books *Structure and Change in Economic History* (1981) and *Institutions, Institutional Change, and Economic Performance* (1990) argues a much broader and comprehensive thesis. He claims that apparently small differences in the initial cultural and historical conditions of a society's genesis and development are the cause of its long-run growth and decline. Attitudes toward education, freedom, and the importance of the individual have enormous (though hard to predict) effects on the path of

---

4. As L. E. Harrison notes:

Spain is amply endowed with agricultural and mineral resources. Yet its economic development, burdened by mercantilist policies and institutions whose roots go back to the sixteenth century, was so slow—and so inequitable—that, as recently as 1950, it could reasonably have been labeled an underdeveloped country. (Harrison 1992, 53).

Harrison also notes the extreme, prideful egoism (*soberbia*) that is the caricature of mid-century Spain in an unattributed epigram: "For the Spaniard it is not enough to have Heaven guaranteed for himself; he must also have Hell guaranteed for his neighbor" (Harrison 1992, 55).

future growth. An essential feature of North's work is its recognition that ideologies, or intellectual organizing themes and principles, are the means by which group or societal imperatives and individual actions are related.

There are a number of important recent analyses of the relation among attitudes, ideas, and prosperity.[5] One of the most provocative is L. E. Harrison's *Who Prospers? How Cultural Values Shape Economic and Political Success* (1993). Harrison's thesis is that "culture" (defined as "a coherent system of values, attitudes, and institutions that influence individual and social behavior in all dimensions of human experience") is the *primary* explanation for why some nations prosper and others wither. That is not to say that differences in growth, prosperity, and welfare are inevitably caused by culture, as a primitive, irreducible concept. Rather, culture, for Harrison, is akin to the notion of institutions for North, and both cultures and institutions are, themselves, products of history, chance, and outside influence on the nation. What is important is that the humanly devised arrangements for organizing productive activity are optimizing responses to the institutional/cultural milieu. Different cultures, and different ideological systems, will evoke different optimizing responses, even among nations similar in population, resources, and size.[6]

For example, the political and economic culture of Spain has changed dramatically since about 1960. Before 1960 (for the previous 250 years!), Spanish culture had imposed severe limits on entrepreneurship, economic growth, and political change. The reason was complex, varying among post-Inquisition Catholic theology, the Iberian-Catholic norm of *soberbia*, the enervating external aspirations of the monarchy, and the security-fixated fascist dictatorship of Franco. However, after 1960 (and with Franco still in power), Spain revolutionized first its economy, and then its political system, changing from an impoverished dictatorship to a developed nation and a democracy in less than thirty years.

By this point, the theory has come quite far from Smith's original answer. We do not claim to have answered the questions posed at the beginning of this chapter, but we do hope to have persuaded the reader that the answers

---

5. See also Greif (1992); North (1993); Ordeshook (1992); Przeworski (1991); and Weingast (1993a, 1993b).

6. An interesting question, outside of the boundaries of our investigation, is the conditions under which political and economic systems are stable. Stability may have its own reasons for desirability, including reduction of uncertainty and promotion of investment through well-defined property rights. On the other hand, as North (1990a) points out, stability does not indicate, or require, optimality. A number of recent studies have investigated the properties of politico-economic systems that create stability, the properties that create desirable outcomes, and conditions under which the two are the same. In particular, see Bates (1983); Greif (1992); North (1993); Ordeshook (1992); and Weingast (1993a, 1993b).

must lie with a theory that accounts for ideology. The task that remains is to argue that a theory of ideology should be expressed using the metaphor of spatial competition.

Why Use Spatial Theory to Represent Ideology?

The classical formal model of politics has a venerable heritage. The application of that model to political interaction between candidates and voters has afforded us much of our understanding of the underlying logic and structure of policy and platforms. The original spatial model of politics derives from the economic approach of Hotelling and Smithies, who conceived of competition in a simple market as taking place based on location, rather than on price and output. All else (price, quality) equal, consumers would choose the supplier who was closest. Traveling in some way to obtain the good or service being supplied, or else paying for the good to be delivered, represented an identifiable component of marginal cost. Firms would compete in reducing these costs by choosing positions on a two-dimensional map whose axes were North-South and East-West. From here it was a short, though important, step to conceiving of distance as a metric for expressing not just cost, but preferences more generally.

The approach of using "closeness" as a measure of satisfaction in choosers had an obvious application in politics. Downs began to exploit this approach for voters, or "mass publics," and Black focused the power of this model on "committee" voting. The models in these two settings are similar, except for two things: (1) committee members are assumed to be fewer, and to have better information about alternatives, and about the preferences of others, than are citizens, or members of the mass public; (2) committee members choose among alternatives that they themselves propose, while citizens choose among candidates who represent large bundles of policies in voters' minds.[7]

The classical spatial model of politics flowered in the 1960s and 1970s. Davis, Hinich, Kramer, McKelvey, Ordeshook, Plott, Rabinowitz, Riker, and Schofield, separately, and in several combinations, elaborated and corrected the early results. They showed that the model could account for the turnout decision, abstention either through alienation or indifference, and weighted, rather than simple, Euclidean distance metrics to express preference.

The results of the classical model can be separated into two sets of theorems. First, it was shown that, under its assumptions on information, goals, and strategies, the classical spatial model implies that stable equilibria

---

7. For more on the distinction between committee and mass voting, see Black (1958) and Enelow and Hinich (1984a).

will be observed only when certain highly restrictive conditions are forced on the spatial arrangement of voter preferences. Since stability exists only as a special case in this model, it implies profound and pervasive instability in policy. Candidates, in choosing positions to improve their chances of reelection, given a fixed set of known voter preferences, were predicted to cycle over the available alternatives with no equilibrium or stopping point.

Second, and in spite of this pervasive instability, there appears to exist a centralizing tendency in the competitive forces that drive political platform choice. Just as in the classical economic spatial model, the basic dynamic force in the spatial model of politics is toward the center of the distribution of voter preferences. Attempts to make this notion of centrality more precise have led to such arcana as "core," "pareto set," "yolk," and "median in all directions." The complex debate over the correspondence among these sets, and their utility as solution concepts to various types of electoral contests, is oriented toward a conclusion. In spite of the chaos results in electoral games, platforms far from the center of the distribution of voter preferences are less powerful than those close to the center in majority rule systems.

We have spent so much time in this book considering spatial models because the paradigm of spatial competition is uniquely capable, among the methods applied to analyze political phenomena, of representing both voter choice and candidate strategy. The other major approach, the psycho-social or "Michigan" model, has proven its value in explaining voter behavior and predicting choices among exogenous alternatives. But it makes no pretense of explaining where platforms come from, for it has no means of doing so. The spatial model makes endogenous predictions on platform, given the spatial representation of exogenous voter preferences. The theorems of spatial theory are general with respect to voter preferences: because the work applies to all preference configurations, it applies to any special set of preferences.

The difficulties in the classical spatial model lie not in the logic of the model itself, but in the metaphor motivating the application to politics. In particular, there are three problematic notions underlying the spatial model. First, voters are assumed to know the implications of all policy choices for their welfare, and to make decisions based on this knowledge. This assumption was originally (and plausibly) restricted to the setting of committee voting, but has since been extended by an osmotic, rather than conscious, intellectual process to the study of the mass public. It may be plausible to believe that voters have preferences over their own welfare. It is quite incredible, however, to require (as classical spatial theory does) that voters clearly understand the relation between national-level policy and their own situation. Ignorance and uncertainty, for very different reasons, force voters to fall back on simple principles and symbolism in making political choices.

The second problematic notion in applying the classical spatial model is the costs of negotiating and enforcing agreements between voters and political candidates. That is, even if voters did know what policies they most preferred, there is no reason that they would consider the promises of candidates to provide those policies as anything other than cheap talk. In making promises, candidates face the challenge not just of informing, but also of committing. Because the performance of the candidate is separated in time from the action he requests from the voter (i.e., voting for the candidate), the voter has no means of enforcing the agreement. Obviously, the interaction of the commitment problem with the information problem is enormous. If we acknowledge that the voter can only with great difficulty discover whether the candidate-cum-office-holder has carried out his promise, the problem of prior commitment becomes insurmountable in the classical model. The voter either does not understand the candidate's promises, or does not believe them, and chooses (at least in terms of the voter's welfare) randomly.[8]

The third problematic notion in applying the classical model is the role of the campaign. If candidates choose platforms, and then voters choose candidates, the campaign seems like a useless exercise. The spatial model has had great difficulty incorporating interest groups and campaign spending. It allows no role for persuasion and communication through simple symbolic representations and commitment to abstract principles. It is important to emphasize that the campaign has a focus other than commitment, which was the subject of the second problem above, though campaigns are surely also about commitment. To a far greater extent, however, campaigns are about the competition between simple, easy to understand principles, conformity to which it is possible to judge without much cost.

In the campaign, voters are asked (*a*) to place themselves in a hierarchically inferior role by handing over to the candidate the coercive powers that define government, and (*b*) to accept that this hierarchical relationship will exist long enough that the candidate will make decisions on issues, with implications for citizens' welfare, that are uncertain or even quite unknown.

This critique of the classical model is designed to suggest that the metaphor of spatial competition, and the interpretation of the results of spatial theory, should be modified, not that the theory should be discarded. The original insight of Downs was that the spatial model of political competition was different from the economic model, because of the problems of informing and committing. This insight was lost over time, as the political spatial model became indistinguishable from the economic model. Though we have made

---

8. If voters choose based on how telegenic the candidate is, or how well-dressed or pleasant-looking, and these characteristics are uncorrelated with how well the candidate performs in office, the choice is random, from the perspective of rationality, even if it is quite predictable from candidate characteristics.

the same assumption that economists make about human behavior (viz., that it is purposive), the means by which political man accomplishes his goal of maximizing satisfaction is quite different from economic man's approach.

We have harkened back to Downs's fundamental point, that economic theory does not apply to the polis, at least not directly. Fortunately, we have thirty-five years of social science hindsight on which to build. In the next section, we will review the boundaries within which a successful theory of purposive political choice must find its foundation.

Establishing the Boundaries for a Theory of Purposive Choice

> *Opinion is ultimately determined by the feelings, and not by the intellect.*
> —Herbert Spencer, *Social Statistics*, part 3, chapter 30

Modern social science has established a set of conditions for what a successful theory of political choice must be. These have taken the form of theoretical approaches that can be ruled out as inconsistent or illogical, and assumptions about behavior that are contradicted by observation. It is useful to summarize these boundaries for theorizing here.

1. The "economic" representation of preferences. The focus of much of the work of economists on democratic decisions has begun with the following (usually implicit) question: what if political choice works like a market? This question would be much more interesting if it were asked about the results of a theory of political choice, rather than advanced as the basic assumption for a starting point of that analysis. Political choice turns out to be *somewhat* like a market, and some market metaphors may be powerful in analyzing politics. The problem with this approach is that it is contradicted by an important set of theoretical results, published by Denzau, Parks, and Slutsky in the middle and late 1970s. If we begin with "economic" preferences on private goods, and proceed to analyze public sector preferences induced by those preferences on private goods, the public sector preferences do not generally inherit the properties (monotonicity, etc.) commonly assumed for them, unless, in addition, a strong form of separability is assumed.

Consequently, the spatial theories of political choice are not "economic," and are not derivable from economic principles or reasoning. Formal political theory has (unreflectively) adopted a very different set of principles for representing preferences; they provide a different way of representing preferences. The assumptions about the form of spatial preferences required for advanced spatial theory are not heroic, amounting, for the most part, to concavity of the upper contour sets. Still, they are different from the additively separable preferences required for treating these utility functions as economic. Thus, if political choices are, in any important way, to be like choices made in a market, such a likeness has yet to be shown. There is no reason to believe that political choices are "like" anything; they are important enough in human behavior to justify a new kind of modeling.

2. The theorems of classical spatial theory (*a*) show when we can expect stability, or instability, and (*b*) suggest that the broader solution concepts, such as the core or the pareto set (when they are not empty), are the sets of possible platforms from which successful policy promises may be chosen. More simply, platforms outside the pareto set (for example) are not sustainable; some kind of centrality, as defined by classical spatial theory, is a survival characteristic for a platform.

3. A variety of empirical work, from several perspectives, reveals a surprising and consistent regularity: the "space" in which political decision making takes place is of low dimensionality. Compared to the specific and detailed space of policies, these latent dimensions, revealed by factor analysis or multidimensional scaling, are few in number. What the data are telling us—and it must be emphasized that this is a wholly empirical result—is that, though the policy space citizens care about is enormously complex, differences over these policies tend to cleave along lines that are highly correlated across issues. The basic principle or judgment that dictates one's opinion on child care has high predictive content for health care, welfare reform, and educational policy. A successful theory must therefore recognize that the relevant space for political strategizing is not the policy space, with its high dimensionality, but a simple space, with latent or recovered dimensions.

Parallel to the purely empirical (and largely unrelated) results in part 3 above, there is emerging in the social sciences a unified cause for a variety of human actions that, until now, have been perceived as unrelated. Emphasis on culture, moral codes, and altruism have until recently been defined as beyond the purview of economics and political science. But there are new and important theoretical reasons why the use of simple principles, rules of thumb, and "culture" explain human action better than a narrow focus on individual self-interest. We reviewed these theories at some length in several chapters, but it is useful to briefly reprise them here.

(*a*) The physical process of human cognition, though only beginning to be understood, appears to quite severely limit the number of pieces of information that can be understood and related to one another. A platform that can be communicated to voters simply and coherently has a competitive advantage. (*b*) The costs of enforcing an agreement on what the platform is, once it is made, are very large. If it is impossible to commit to an agreement that can be enforced, all political rhetoric will simply be dismissed by citizens as cheap talk. (*c*) Political interaction is subject to profound and irreducible uncertainty about the likely decisions that political leaders, once chosen, must make. Further, voters are being asked to place themselves in a hierarchically inferior position to the politician-who-wants-to-be-ruler. Recent work on the private sector by David Kreps suggests that uncertainty and hierarchy make organizational "culture" valuable. By culture, Kreps means the creation of, and adherence to, a few simple and widely applicable principles for monitoring and enforcing agreements. (*d*) Societies exist to prevent anarchy. The means by which cooperation is achieved (or not achieved) in different societies influence the long-run growth and survival of that way of life. The basis of "community" in the work of Taylor is a shared set of norms and knowledge about one another that derives from experience. Schofield has suggested that this notion of community, though sufficient for achieving cooperation, may not be necessary, to the extent that common knowledge, in the technical sense, can be created by members of a society larger than a community.

It has been our thesis in this book that ideology answers all of these questions, and satisfies all of these conditions, better than any alternate approach. Further, since ideology can be modeled formally using the spatial model of politics, we bring to bear a powerful theoretical perspective entirely within the boundaries that circumscribe the conditions for a successful theory outlined above. We now turn to a very brief restatement of the central points and features of the theory.

A Restatement of the Theory and Results

We have claimed that ideology answers the questions and difficulties raised by other approaches. The simplest definition to be given for an ideology is a simple set of statements, more or less internally consistent, that have implications for (*a*) what is ethically good, (*b*) who gets what, and (*c*) who rules. Ideologies may not have implications for all three of these, but these are the questions that any society must have some answer for, if it is to avoid anarchy. Further, the lack of implication may simply suggest consensus. If two political parties with opposing ideologies do not disagree about (for example) "who rules," it is because both accept the existing means of selecting leaders and are working within the system to make sure that that choice is one of their members.

We have set out a preliminary theory of the origin and maintenance of ideologies as collections of ideas that derive from their utility in resolving disputes quickly, predictably, and (in the eyes of the disputants) legitimately. Whether an action is perceived as ideological may depend on the observer, as in the example of the thugs in the forest: are they thugs, or are they Robin Hood's Merry Men?

This notion of ideology as a set of ideas with policy implications can be formalized in a spatial model. The precise correspondence between ideological position and the policy platforms voters associate with that position is complex. Politicians depend on the historical relation of others who have claimed their ideological affiliation, and on the subsequent actions of those others, to create the correspondence in voters' minds. Each campaign influences this correspondence, to some extent, but the whole value to the voter is in not having to relearn the meaning of political language. Rather, each voter carries in his mind an individual, idiosyncratic expectation of what political messages mean.

We extend this simple model of correspondence between ideologies and policy in two ways. First, we use probabilistic voting, which allows for abstention, and uncertainty about the deterministic decision rule that voters use to evaluate candidates. Second, we incorporate interest groups and campaign contributions into the model, and can analyze not just the election, but also the campaign.

The implications of the results of the model are not very optimistic. If voters use ideology to judge candidates, and choose among candidates based on expected utility where candidate positions are uncertain, candidates have incentives to use negative advertising to distort voter perceptions of the other candidate. But since each candidate has access to the technology of negative advertising, and any viable campaign has access to funds from interest groups, the result is not Pareto optimal. Candidates spend large amounts of money on negative advertising in exchange for favors to interest groups, but the candidates receive little electoral gain. Voters are less certain about their choices, but spending in the campaign is unlikely to change the outcome.

Most important, the individual incentives facing candidates conflict with the common knowledge, cooperative goals of the society. By distorting the correspondence between ideology and policy, a party behind in the polls may improve its chances to win. Yet, by doing so, it attenuates the political capital of the society, built up over time in voters minds, about this correspondence. If ideologies are really what make large societies able to act like communities, this destructive aspect of political competition is a means by which order can be replaced by chaos, and an effective political system brought down.

Ideology and the Practice of Social Science

> *It is not the consciousness of men that determines their existence, but on the contrary it is their social existence that determines their consciousness.*
> —Karl Marx, *Critique of Political Economy*, 1859, ii

Separate from the consciousness that he thinks men have, Marx posits (in several writings) the existence of an objective, rational perspective, or "true consciousness." This worldview is normatively superior to, and, in economic terms, more efficient than, a society ruled by "false consciousness." The best-known example of false consciousness is, of course, religion; few have never heard Marx's famous remark, in the *Critique of the Hegelian Philosophy of the Right*, that "Religion . . . is the opium of the people" (1844, 3). But as Robert Higgs points out in *Crisis and Leviathan*, Marx "in effect branded as ideology the social thought of all those who did not fully share his views.[9]

With hindsight, we can paraphrase Marx's theory of ideology as the barrier that prevents the masses from taking their rightful place in society as follows: (*a*) citizens *should* act collectively to pursue their interests; (*b*) ideologies are (mendacious) means of preventing this; (*c*) societies that are not ideological, but encourage true consciousness, are morally superior to societies stupefied by ideological galimatias; (*d*) most important, societies that are not ideological will win the evolutionary efficiency contest, and will overwhelm those that do not rid themselves of ideology. The goal of much of Marx's, and Marxist, thought is, then, to strip away this flummery so that the "new man" can achieve his destiny. Those who pursue this project are liberators, seeking an end to the series of squabbles and disagreements over dogma that form human history.

The definition of ideology as false consciousness was, no doubt, rhetorically useful to Marx, but it provides a tenuous basis for social science. The false consciousness, or nonrational, view of ideology has largely been accepted into social science, without reflection or good reason. Higgs (1987) claims that, because modern political economists have ignored or ridiculed ideology as an analytic concept, "The oft-lamented failure of the social sciences to provide guidance for 'solving' [social] problems is actually unavoidable" (37).

We agree. Ideology is not nonrational, it is not a residual or random component of conscious human decision making. So long as social science does not take ideology into account, it cannot make claims either to descriptive accuracy or to theoretical closure. This disagreement goes to the very heart of the study of human behavior. The question of what ideology is, and how it should be modeled, will occupy the best minds of the next generation of scholars; the resolution to the controversy will determine the very form of political and economic discourse for the foreseeable future. The "question" we refer to is really two: (*a*) Is political and social life possible without ideology? (*b*) Even if it is possible, is such a life desirable?

The answers given to these two questions in most of the social science literature today is yes and yes. Our answer to the first question is no; obviously the answer to the second question is, therefore, moot. Every political

---

9. By contrast, "true" consciousness was, for Marx, the single-minded focus on class, defined as the relation to the ownership of the means of production, and the consequent imperative toward revolution by the workers, who have no title over capital.

position *must* be ideological. Group identity, the understanding of labels such as "left," "conservative," or "Christian Democrat," indeed, the very essence of political communication, requires ideology, and cannot exist without it. These ideologies themselves rely on sets of statements about ethical norms, and different ideologies differ, by definition, on the appropriate set of ethical norms to apply. By selecting one set of norms over others, consciously or unconsciously, societies, in effect, choose their growth paths and the distribution of welfare among their citizens.

In this book, we have barely scratched the surface in mining the rich lode of theories about ideology and their implications for studying and understanding human behavior. In closing, let us emphasize that there are two separate sets of tasks to which we have addressed this work. The first is to persuade the reader that existing theory is simply incapable of expressing, much less understanding, the set of questions that can be asked and answered by the complex concept we have defined as "ideology." The second task is to suggest how ideology might be embodied in a rigorous, formal model. Clearly, the first goal is the more important one. If some reader is moved to extend, correct, or wholly replace the theoretical perspective we have proposed, but does so in a way that accounts for the importance of ideology, our work will have been worthwhile. An obvious objection is worth noting immediately, because it is of distinguished vintage already.[10] Barry (1970) points out:

> There is [an] objection to the use of values as explanations which is so important and fundamental that it must be examined. . . . It undercuts all [other criticisms and defenses] by saying: suppose you have established a causal connection, so what? Values are at best the last link in the chain of causation before behavior itself. They are not independent variables. A good explanation may incorporate values as intervening variables, but then the values themselves must be explained. (Barry 1970, 96)

A first answer might be that this is *just* what we have tried to do. Instead of taking the "values," usually called preferences, as primitives, and allowing all possible preference profiles, we have claimed that there are certain configurations of preference that (*a*) derive from a coherent worldview based on ethical principles, and (*b*) are shared (more or less) by large groups of citizens in any functional political system. Thus, future researchers may be led back up the chain of causation to more fundamental concepts in cognitive psychology, or to some as yet unguessed new approach. We hope that the notion of ideology we have advanced proves useful as a step along this chain.

Artists often intuit results that the ponderous progress of science takes

---

10. We thank Eric Mlyn for pointing out the quotation from Barry (1970).

decades to even imagine. William Butler Yeats's first stanza from "The Second Coming," in *Michael Robartes and the Dancer* (1921), is such an artistic leap. In this one brief verse, Yeats seems to recognize everything we have claimed is important about ideology, communication, and society:

Turning and turning in the widening gyre
The falcon cannot hear the falconer;
Things fall apart, the center cannot hold;
Mere anarchy is loosed upon the world,
The blood-dimmed tide is loosed, and everywhere
The ceremony of innocence is drowned;
The best lack all conviction, while the worst
Are full of passionate intensity.

References

Alchian, Armen. 1950. Uncertainty, evolution, and economic theory. *Journal of Political Economy* 58:211–21.

Aldrich, John. 1975. Voting in two U.S. presidential elections: An analysis based on the spatial model of electoral competition. Ph.D. diss., University of Rochester.

———. 1980. *Before the convention: Strategies and choices in presidential nomination campaigns.* Chicago: University of Chicago Press.

———. 1994. *Why parties?* Chicago: University of Chicago Press.

Alesina, Alberto, and Alex Cukierman. 1987. The politics of ambiguity. Carnegie-Mellon-GSIA Working Paper.

Alesina, Alberto, and Howard Rosenthal. 1989. Partisan cycles in congressional elections and the macroeconomy. *American Political Science Review* 83:373–98.

Almond, Gabriel. 1960. *The politics of the developing areas.* Princeton, NJ: Princeton University Press.

Alt, James, and Kenneth Shepsle, eds. 1990. *Perspectives on positive political economy.* New York: Cambridge University Press.

Anderson, Theodore W. 1984. *An introduction to multivariate statistical analysis.* 2d ed. New York: John Wiley and Sons.

Aranson, Peter, and Melvin Hinich. 1979. Some aspects of the political economy of election campaign contribution law. *Public Choice* 34:435–61.

Ardrey, R. 1970. *The social contract: A personal inquiry in the evolutionary sources of order and disorder.* New York: Atheneum Press.

Arrow, Kenneth. 1963. *Social choice and individual values.* 2d ed. New Haven: Yale University Press.

Arrow, Kenneth, and Gerard Debreu. 1954. Existence of an equilibrium for a competitive economy. *Econometrica* 22:265–90.

Arrow, Kenneth, and Frank Hahn. 1971. *General competitive analysis.* San Francisco: Holden-Day.

Austen-Smith, David. 1981. Voluntary pressure groups. *Economica* 48:143–53.

———. 1987. Interest groups, campaign contributions, and probabilistic voting. *Public Choice* 54:123–40.

———. 1990. Information transmission in debate. *American Journal of Political Science* 34:124–52.

Austen-Smith, David, and Jeffrey Banks. 1988. Elections, coalitions, and legislative outcomes. *American Political Science Review* 82:405–22.

Aylmer, G. E. 1963. *A short history of Seventeenth-century England: 1603–1689.* London, England: Blandford Press, Ltd.

Baier, K. 1958. *The moral point of view: A rational basis of ethics*. Ithaca, N.Y.: Cornell University Press.

Banks, Jeffrey. 1990. A model of electoral competition with incomplete information. *Journal of Economic Theory* 50:309–25.

———. 1991. *Signalling games in political science*. Chur, Switzerland: Harwood Academic Publishers.

Banks, Jeffrey, and J. Sobel. 1987. Equilibrium selection in signalling games. *Econometrica* 55:647–61.

Barnes, Samuel H. 1967. *Party democracy: The internal politics of an Italian socialist federation*. New Haven: Yale University Press.

Baron, David. 1989a. Service-induced campaign contributions and the electoral equilibrium. *Quarterly Journal of Economics* 104:45–72.

———. 1989b. Service-induced campaign contributions, incumbent shirking, and reelection opportunities. In *Models of strategic choice in politics*, ed. Peter Ordeshook, 93–120. Ann Arbor: University of Michigan Press.

Barr, J. L., and Otto Davis. 1968. An elementary political and economic theory of the expenditures of local governments. *Southern Economic Journal* 33:149–65.

Barro, Robert. 1973. The control of politicians: An economic model. *Public Choice* 14:19–42.

Barry, Brian. 1978. *Sociologists, economists, and democracy*. Chicago: University of Chicago Press.

Barzel, Yoram, and Eugene Silberberg. 1973. Is the act of voting rational? *Public Choice* 16:51–58.

Bates, Robert. 1983. *Essays on the political economy of rural Africa*. New York: Cambridge University Press.

Bauer, Raymond; Ithiel de la Sola Pool; and Lewis Dexter. 1963. *American business and public policy: The politics of foreign trade*. New York: Atherton Press.

Becker, Gary. 1983. A theory of competition among pressure groups for political influence. *Quarterly Journal of Economics* 98 (3): 371–400.

———. 1985a. Public policies, pressure groups, and dead weight costs. *Journal of Public Economics* 28:329–47.

———. 1985b. Special interests and public policies. The Frank E. Seidman Distinguished Award in Political Economy, Acceptance Paper, Rhodes College. Memphis: P. K. Seidman Foundation.

Bental, Benjamin, and Uri Ben-Zion. 1975. Political contribution and policy: Some extensions. *Public Choice* 24:1–12.

Bentley, Arthur. 1908. *The process of government*. Chicago: University of Chicago Press.

Ben-Zion, Uri, and Zeev Eytan. 1974. On money, votes, and policy in a democratic society. *Public Choice* 14:19–42.

Bergson, Abram. 1938. A reformulation of certain aspects of welfare economics. *Quarterly Journal of Economics* 52:310–34.

Bergstrom, Theodore, and R. P. Goodman. 1973. Private demand for public goods. *American Economic Review* 63:280–96.

Bernhardt, M. Daniel, and Daniel E. Ingberman. 1985. Candidate reputations and the incumbency effect. *Journal of Public Economics* 27:47–67.

Black, Duncan. 1958. *The theory of committees and elections*. Cambridge, England: Cambridge University Press.

Blau, J. H. 1972. A direct proof of Arrow's theorem. *Econometrica* 40:61–67.

Borcherding, Thomas, and Robert Deacon. 1972. The demand for the services of non-federal governments. *American Economic Review* 62:891–901.

Boulding, Kenneth. 1964. *The meaning of the twentieth century*. New York: Harper and Row.

Brady, Henry. 1988. Multidimensional scaling in political science. University of Chicago.

Brady, Henry, and Paul Sniderman. 1985. Attitude attribution: A group basis for political reasoning. *American Political Science Review* 79:1061–78.

Brown, Donald J. 1975. Aggregation of preferences. *Quarterly Journal of Economics* 89:456–69.

Bruner, Jerome S. 1957. On perceptual readiness. *Psychological Review* 64:123–51.

Buchanan, James. 1965. An economic theory of clubs. *Economica* 32:1–14.

Buchanan, James, and Gordon Tullock. 1962. *The calculus of consent*. Ann Arbor: University of Michigan Press.

Burnham, Walter D. 1970. *Critical elections and the mainsprings of American politics*. New York: Norton.

Cahoon, Lawrence S. 1975. Locating a set of points using range information only. Ph.D. diss., Carnegie-Mellon University, Pittsburgh.

Cahoon, Lawrence; Melvin J. Hinich; and Peter C. Ordeshook. 1978. A statistical multidimensional scaling method based on the spatial theory of voting. In *Graphical representation of multivariate data*, ed. P. C. Wang, 243–79. New York: Academic Press.

Calvert, Randall. 1985. The value of biased information: A rational choice model of political advice. *Journal of Politics* 47:530–55.

———. 1986. *Models of imperfect information in politics*. New York: Harwood Academic Publishers.

———. 1989. Political decision-making with costly and imperfect information. *Mathematical and Computer Modelling* 12:497–509.

———. 1992. Leadership and its basis in problems of social coordination. *International Political Science Review* 13:7-24.

Cameron, Charles, and James M. Enelow. 1992. Perceptual asymmetries, campaign contributions, and the spatial theory of elections. *Mathematical and Computer Modelling* 15:71–89.

Cameron, Charles, and Rebecca Morton. 1992. Elections and the theory of campaign contributions: A survey and critical analysis. *Economics and Politics* 4:79–108.

Campbell, Angus; Phillip Converse; Warren Miller; and Donald Stokes. 1960. *The American voter*. New York: John Wiley and Sons.

Chappell, Henry W. 1988. Information, advertising, and spatial voting. University of South Carolina, Department of Economics Working Paper.

Clarke, Edward H. 1971. Multipart pricing of public goods. *Public Choice* 11:17–33.

Congleton, Roger. 1991. Ideological conviction and persuasion in the rent-seeking society. *Journal of Public Economics* 44:65–86.

Congleton, Roger, and Viktor Vanberg. 1992. Rationality, morality, and exit. *American Political Science Review* 86:418–31.

Conover, Pamela. 1984. The influence of group identifications on political perception and evaluation. *Journal of Politics* 46:760–87.

Conover, Pamela, and Stanley Feldman. 1981. The origins and meaning of liberal/conservative self-identification. *American Journal of Political Science* 25:617–45.

———. 1982. Projection and the perception of candidates. *Western Political Quarterly* 35:228–44.

———. 1984. How people organize the political world: A schematic model. *American Journal of Political Science* 28:95–126.

———. 1986. The role of inference in the perception of political candidates. In *Political cognition*, ed. R. R. Lau and D. O. Sears, 79–102. Hillsdale, N.J.: Lawrence Erlbaum.

———. 1989. Campaign perceptions in an ambiguous world. *American Journal of Political Science* 33:912–40.

Converse, Phillip E. 1964. The nature of belief systems in mass publics. In *Ideology and discontent*, ed. David Apter, 219–41. New York: Free Press.

———. 1966. The problem of party distances in models of voting change. In *The Electoral Process*, ed. M. Kent Jennings and L. Harmon Zeigler, 105–31. Englewood Cliffs, N.J.: Prentice-Hall.

Coughlin, Peter. 1986. Probabilistic voting models. In *Encyclopedia of social sciences*, ed. S. Kotz and N. Johnson. 7:204–10.

———. 1990. Candidate uncertainty and electoral equilibria. In *Advances in the spatial theory of voting*, ed. James Enelow and Melvin Hinich, 202–19. New York: Cambridge University Press.

Coughlin, Peter, and Melvin Hinich. 1984. Necessary and sufficient conditions for single-peakedness in public economic models. *Journal of Public Economics* 25:323–41.

Coughlin, Peter; Dennis Mueller; and Peter Murrell. 1990. Electoral politics, interest groups, and the size of government. *Economic Inquiry* 28:682–705.

Coughlin, Peter, and S. Nitzan. 1981. Electoral outcomes with probabilistic voting and Nash social welfare maxima. *Journal of Public Economics* 15:113–22.

Cox, Gary. 1984. An expected utility model of electoral competition. *Quality and Quantity* 18:337–49.

———. 1987. Electoral equilibrium under alternative voting institutions. *American Journal of Political Science* 31:82–108.

———. 1990. Centripetal and centrifugal incentives in electoral systems. *American Journal of Political Science* 34:905–35.

Cox, Gary, and Mathew McCubbins. 1993. *Legislative leviathan: Party government in the House*. Berkeley: University of California Press.

Cox, Gary W., and Michael C. Munger. 1989. Contributions, expenditure, turnout: The 1982 U.S. House elections. *American Political Science Review* 83:217–31.

Crawford, Vernon, and Joel Sobel. 1982. Strategic information transmission. *Econometrica* 50:1431–51.

Cukierman, Alex. 1986. Central bank behavior and credibility: Some recent theoretical developments. *Federal Reserve Bank of St. Louis Review* 68:5–17.

Cukierman, Alex, and Allen Meltzer. 1986. A theory of ambiguity, credibility, and inflation under discretion and asymmetric information. *Econometrica* 51:1099–1128.

Daalder, Hans. 1955. Parties and politics in the Netherlands. *Political Studies* 3:12–13.

Dahl, Robert. 1961. *Who governs? Democracy and power in an American city.* New Haven, Conn.: Yale University Press.

Davis, Otto, and Melvin Hinich. 1966. A mathematical model of policy formation in a democratic society. In *Mathematical applications in political science II*, ed. J. Bernd, 175–208. Dallas, Tex.: Southern Methodist University Press.

———. 1967. Some results related to a mathematical model of policy formation in a democratic society. In *Mathematical applications in political science III*, ed. J. Bernd, 14–38. Charlottesville, Va.: University of Virginia Press.

Davis, Otto; Melvin Hinich; and Peter Ordeshook. 1970. An expository development of a mathematical model of the electoral process. *American Political Science Review* 64:426–48.

Davis, Otto A.; Morris H. DeGroot; and Melvin J. Hinich. 1972. Social preference orderings and majority rule. *Econometrica* 40:147–57.

Dawkins, R. 1976. *The selfish gene.* New York: Oxford University Press.

Debreu, Gerard. 1959. *The theory of value: An axiomatic analysis of economic equilibrium.* New Haven, Conn.: Yale University Press.

Denzau, Arthur, and Robert Mackay. 1981. Structure-induced equilibria and perfect foresight expectations. *American Journal of Political Science* 25:762–79.

Denzau, Arthur; Robert Mackay; and Carolyn Weaver. 1979. Spending limitations, agenda control, and voters' expectations. *National Tax Journal* 32:189–200.

Denzau, Arthur, and Michael Munger. 1986. Legislators and interest groups: How unorganized interests get represented. *American Political Science Review* 80 (no. 1):89–106.

Denzau, Arthur, and Robert Parks. 1975. The continuity of majority rule equilibrium. *Econometrica* 43:853–66.

———. 1977. A problem with public sector preferences. *Journal of Economic Theory* 14:454–57.

———. 1979. Deriving public sector preferences. *Journal of Public Economics* 11:335–52.

———. 1983. Existence of voting market equilibria. *Journal of Economic Theory* 30:243–65.

Domhoff, William. 1983. *Who rules America now?* Englewood Cliffs, N.J.: Prentice-Hall.

Dougan, William, and Daphne Kenyon. 1988. Pressure groups and public expenditures: The flypaper effect reconsidered. *Economic Inquiry* 26:159–70.

Dougan, William, and Michael Munger. 1989. The rationality of ideology. *Journal of Law and Economics* 32:119–43.

Downs, Anthony. 1957. *An economic theory of democracy.* New York: Harper and Row.

Duverger, Maurice. 1951. *Political parties: Their organization and activity in the modern state.* London: Methuen.

———. 1972. *Political parties and pressure groups: A comparative introduc-*

tion. New York: Thomas Y. Crowell Company. (French edition published in 1968.)

Edgeworth, F. 1928. *Papers relating to political economy.* New York: MacMillan.

Enelow, James. 1986. Measuring the linkage between predictive dimensions and candidate issue positions: An examination of group differences. *Political Behavior* 8:245–61.

Enelow, James; James Endersby; and Michael Munger. 1993. A revised probabilistic spatial model of elections: Theory and evidence. In *An economic theory of democracy in comparative perspective,* ed. Bernard Grofman, 125–40. Ann Arbor: University of Michigan Press.

Enelow, James, and Melvin Hinich. 1981. A new approach to voter uncertainty in the Downsian spatial model. *American Journal of Political Science* 25:483–93.

———. 1982a. Ideology, issues, and the spatial theory of elections. *American Political Science Review* 76:493–501.

———. 1982b. Nonspatial candidate characteristics and electoral competition. *Journal of Politics* 44:115–30.

———. 1983. On Plott's pairwise symmetry condition for majority rule equilibrium. *Public Choice* 40:317–21.

———. 1984a. *The spatial theory of voting.* New York: Cambridge University Press.

———. 1984b. Probabilistic voting and the importance of centrist ideologies in democratic elections. *Journal of Politics* 46:459–78.

———. 1989a. The location of American presidential candidates: An empirical test of a new spatial model of elections. *Mathematical and Computer Modelling* 12:461–70.

———. 1989b. A general probabilistic spatial theory of elections. *Public Choice* 61:101–14.

———. 1989c. The theory of predictive mappings. In *Advances in the spatial theory of voting,* ed. James Enelow and Melvin Hinich, 67–78. New York: Cambridge University Press.

———. 1993. Voter rationalization of candidate issue positions and its consequences for empirical spatial theory. *Public Choice.*

Enelow, James; Melvin Hinich; and Nancy Mendell. 1986. An empirical evaluation of alternative spatial models of elections. *Journal of Politics* 48:675–93.

Enelow, James, and Michael Munger. 1993. The elements of candidate reputation: The effect of record and credibility on optimal spatial location. *Public Choice* 77:757–72.

Ensminger, Jean, and Andrew Rutten. 1991. The political economy of changing property rights: Dismantling a pastoral commons. *American Ethnologist* 18:683–99.

Feldman, Stanley, and Pamela Conover. 1983. Candidates, issues, and voters: The role of inference in political perception. *Journal of Politics* 45:810–39.

Ferejohn, John. 1986. Incumbent performance and electoral control. *Public Choice* 50:5–25.

Ferejohn, John, and Morris Fiorina. 1974. The paradox of not voting: A decision theoretic analysis. *American Political Science Review* 68:525–36.

Ferejohn, John, and James Kuklinski, eds. 1990. *Information and democratic processes*. Urbana: University of Illinois Press.

Fiorina, Morris. 1977. *Representatives, roll calls, and constituencies*. Lexington, Mass.: Lexington Books.

Fiorina, Morris P. 1981. *Retrospective voting in American national elections*. New Haven, Conn.: Yale University Press.

Fiske, Susan T., and Shelley E. Taylor. 1984. *Social cognition*. Reading, Mass.: Addison-Wesley.

Frank, Robert. 1988. *Passions within reason*. New York: W. W. Norton.

Friedman, Milton. 1953. *Essays in positive economics*. Chicago: University of Chicago Press.

Gauthier, David. 1986. *Morals by agreement*. Oxford: Clarendon Press.

Gibbard, A. 1973. Manipulation of voting schemes: A general result. *Econometrica* 41:587–602.

Goertzel, Ted. 1992. *Turncoats and true believers: The dynamics of political belief and disillusionment*. Buffalo, N.Y.: Prometheus Books.

Grafstein, Robert. 1994. Ideology and Rationality. University of Georgia Department of Political Science, Athens, Ga.

Greif, Avner. 1992. Cultural beliefs and the rise of the west. Stanford University, Stanford, Calif.

Grier, Kevin B., ed. 1993. *Empirical studies of ideology and representation in American politics: A special issue of Public Choice*. 76:1–172.

Grier, Kevin B., and Michael C. Munger. 1991. Committee assignments, constituent preferences, and campaign contributions. *Economic Inquiry* 29:24–43.

———. 1993. Comparing corporate, labor, and trade association contributions to House and Senate, 1978–1986. *Journal of Politics* 55:615–43.

Grier, Kevin; Michael Munger; and Brian Roberts. 1991. The industrial organization of corporate political participation. *Southern Economic Journal* 57:727–38.

———. 1992. PAC it or leave it: An analysis of corporate campaign contributions to the U.S. House of Representatives. Paper presented at the meetings of the Midwest Political Science Association, Chicago, Ill., April 1991.

Grofman, Bernard. 1985. The neglected role of the status quo in models of issue voting. *Journal of Politics* 47:230–37.

Grofman, Bernard, and Barbara Norrander. 1990. Efficient use of reference cues in a single dimension. *Public Choice* 64:213–27.

Grondona, Mariano. 1992. *The triangle of development*. Buenos Aires: Editorial Sudamericana.

Groves, Theodore. 1973. Incentives in teams. *Econometrica* 41:617–31.

Groves, Theodore, and John Ledyard. 1977. Optimal allocation of public goods: A solution to the 'free rider' problem. *Econometrica* 45:783–809.

Hardin, Russell. 1971. Collective action as an agreeable n-person prisoner's dilemma. *Behavioral Science* 16:472–81.

———. 1982. *Collective action*. Baltimore: Johns Hopkins University Press.

Harrison, Lawrence E. 1992. *Who prospers: How cultural values shape economic and political success*. New York: Basic Books.

Heberle, Rudolf. 1951. *Social movements*. New York: Appleton-Century-Crofts.

Hibbs, Douglas. 1977. Political parties and macroeconomic policy. *American Political Science Review* 71:1467–87.

———. 1987. *The political economy of industrial democracies*. Cambridge: Harvard University Press.

Hicks, John R. 1946. *Value and capital*. Oxford: Clarendon Press.

Higgins, E. Tory, and Gillian King. 1981. Accessibility of social constructs: Information processing consequences of individual and contextual variability. In *Personality, cognition, and social interaction*, ed. N. Cantor and J. F. Kihlstrom, 187–94. Hillsdale, N.J.: Erlbaum.

Higgs, Robert. 1987. *Crisis and leviathan: Critical episodes in the growth of American government*. New York: Oxford University Press.

———. 1991. Eighteen problematic propositions in the analysis of the growth of government. *Review of Austrian Economics* 5:3–40.

Higgs, Robert, and Charlotte Twight. 1987. National emergency and the erosion of private property rights. *Cato Journal* 6:747–73.

Hinich, Melvin. 1977a. A model for campaign contributions. In *American Reevolution*, ed. Richard Auster and David Sears, 124–31. Tucson: Department of Economics, University of Arizona.

———. 1977b. Equilibrium in spatial voting: The median voter result is an artifact. *Journal of Economic Theory* 16 (2): 208–19.

Hinich, Melvin; John Ledyard; and Peter Ordeshook. 1972. Nonvoting and the existence of equilibrium under majority rule. *Journal of Economic Theory* 4:144–53.

———. 1973. A theory of electoral equilibrium: A spatial analysis based on the theory of games. *Journal of Politics* 35:154–93.

Hinich, Melvin, and Michael Munger. 1989. Political investment, voter perceptions, and candidate strategy. In *Models of strategic choice in politics*, ed. Peter Ordeshook, 49–68. New York: Cambridge University Press.

———. 1992. The spatial theory of ideology. *Journal of Theoretical Politics* 4:5–27.

Hinich, Melvin, and Peter Ordeshook. 1970. Plurality Maximization vs. vote maximization: A spatial analysis with variable participation. *American Political Science Review* 64:772–91.

Hinich, Melvin, and Walker Pollard. 1981. A new approach to the spatial theory of electoral competition. *American Journal of Political Science* 25:323–41.

Hotelling, Harold. 1929. Stability in competition. *Economic Journal* 39:41–57.

Hume, David. 1760. Essay on parties. In *Essays: Moral, Political, and Literary*. Indianapolis: Liberty Classics, 1985 edition.

Inglehart, Ronald. 1990. *Culture shift in advanced industrial democracy*. Princeton, N.J.: Princeton University Press.

Jovrasky, David. 1970. *The Lysenko affair*. Cambridge, Mass.: Harvard University Press.

Kadane, J. B. 1971. On division of the question. *Public Choice* 13:47–54.

Kahneman, D., and A. Tversky. 1973. On the psychology of prediction. *Psychological Review* 80:237–51.

———. 1979. Intuitive prediction: Biases and corrective procedures. *TIMS Studies in Management Science* 12:313–27.

Kalt, Joseph, and Mark Zupan. 1984. Capture and ideology in the economic theory of politics. *American Economic Review* 74:279–300.

———. 1990. The apparent ideological behavior of legislators: Testing for principal-agent slack in political institutions. *Journal of Law and Economics* 33:103–31.

Kant, Immanuel. 1976. *Foundations of the metaphysics of morals*. Indianapolis, Ind.: Bobbs-Merrill Company. (German edition published in 1785.)

Katzner, Donald. 1970. *Static demand theory*. New York: MacMillan.

Kau, James; D. Keenan; and Paul Rubin. 1981. *Congressmen, constituents, and contributors*. Boston: Martinus Nijhoff Publishing.

———. 1984. Economic and ideological factors in congressional voting. *Public Choice* 44:385–88.

Kelley, Stanley; Richard Ayres; and William Bowen. 1967. Registration and voting: Putting first things first. *American Political Science Review* 61:359–79.

Kemp, M. C., and Y.-K. Ng. 1976. On the existence of social welfare functions: Social orderings and social decision functions. *Economica* 43:59–66.

Key, Vladimir O. 1955. A theory of critical elections. *Journal of Politics* 17:3–18.

———. 1961. Public opinion and the decay of democracy. *Virginia Quarterly Review* 37:481–94.

———. 1964. *Politics, parties, and pressure groups*. 5th ed. New York: Crowell.

Kinder, Donald. 1982. Enough already about ideology: The many bases of American public opinion. Paper presented at the annual meetings of the American Political Science Association, Denver, Colorado, August 25–28.

Knight, Frank. 1921. *Risk, uncertainty, and profit*. New York: Harper and Row.

Koford, Kenneth. 1989. Dimensions in congressional voting. *American Political Science Review* 83:949–62.

———. 1993. The median and the competitive equilibrium in one dimension. *Public Choice* 76:273–88.

Kramer, Gerald. 1972. Sophisticated voting over multidimensional choice spaces. *Journal of Mathematical Sociology* 2 (2): 165–80.

Kreps, David. 1990. Corporate culture and economic theory. In *Perspectives on positive political economy*, ed. James Alt and Kenneth Shepsle, 90–143. New York: Cambridge University Press.

Kreps, David, and Robert Wilson. 1982. Reputation and imperfect information. *Journal of Economic Theory* 27:253–79.

Krosnick, Jon. 1988. Psychological perspectives on political candidate perception: A review of research on the projection hypothesis. Paper presented at the meetings of the Midwest Political Science Association, Chicago, Ill. April 15–17.

Ladd, Carll Everett, and Charles Hadley. 1973a. *Political parties and political issues: Patterns in differentiation since the New Deal*. Beverly Hills, Calif.: Sage.

———. 1973b. Party definition and party differentiation. *Public Opinion Quarterly* 37:21–34.

Ladha, Krishna. 1991. A spatial model of legislative voting with perceptual error. *Public Choice* 68:151–74.

Lakoff, George. 1987. *Women, fire, and dangerous things*. Chicago: University of Chicago Press.

Lancaster, Kevin. 1966. A new approach to consumer theory. *Journal of Political Economy* 74:132–57.

Lasswell, Harold. 1934. *Psychopathology and politics*. Chicago: University of Chicago Press.

Latham, Earl. 1952. *The group basis of politics: A study of basing-point legislation*. Ithaca, N.Y.: Cornell University Press.

Laver, M., and N. Schofield. 1990. *Multiparty governments: The politics of coalition in Europe*. Oxford: Oxford University Press.

Lazarsfeld, P. F.; B. Berelson; and H. Gandet. 1948. *The people's choice: How the voter makes up his mind in a presidential campaign*. 2d ed. New York: Columbia University Press.

Ledyard, J. 1984. The pure theory of two candidate elections. *Public Choice* 44:7–41.

Lichtenstein, Sarah, and Paul Slovic. 1971. Reversals of preference between bids and choices in gambling decisions. *Journal of Experimental Psychology* 89:46–55.

Lindahl, Erik. 1939. *Studies in the theory of money and capital*. New York: Rhinehart. (Swedish edition published in 1929.)

Lodge, George C. 1976. *The new American ideology*. New York: Knopf.

Lott, John. 1986. Brand names and barriers to entry in political markets. *Public Choice* 51:87–92.

———. 1987a. Political cheating. *Public Choice* 52:169–86.

———. 1987b. The effect of nontransferable property rights on the efficiency of political markets: Some evidence. *Journal of Public Economics* 2:231–46.

———. 1989. Sorting and shirking in a political market with finite-lived politicians. *Public Choice* 61:75–96.

Lott, John, and Robert Reed. 1989. Shirking and sorting in a political market with finite-lived politicians. *Public Choice* 61:75–96.

Lupia, Arthur. 1992. Busy voters, agenda control, and the power of information. *American Political Science Review* 86:390–403.

McCormick, Robert, and Robert Tollison. 1981. *Politicians, legislation, and the economy*. Boston: Martinus-Nishoff.

McCubbins, Mathew, and Thomas Schwartz. 1984. Police patrols and fire alarms. *American Journal of Political Science* 28:165–79.

Macdonald, Stuart, and George Rabinowitz. 1987. The dynamics of structural realignment. *American Political Science Review* 81:775–96.

———. 1990. Direction and uncertainty in a model of issue voting. Paper presented at the 1990 meetings of the American Political Science Association, San Francisco, Calif., August 29–September 1.

———. 1993. Ideology and candidate evaluation. *Public Choice* 76:59–78.

McKelvey, Richard 1979. General conditions for global intransitivities in formal voting models. *Econometrica* 47:1085–1111.

———. 1986. Covering, dominance, and institution-free properties of social choice. *American Journal of Political Science* 30:283–314.

McKelvey, Richard, and Richard Niemi. 1978. A multistage game representation of sophisticated voting for binary procedures. *Journal of Economic Theory* 18:1–22.

McKelvey, Richard, and Peter Ordeshook. 1976. Symmetric spatial games without majority rule equilibria. *American Political Science Review* 70:1172–84.

————. 1985a. Elections with limited information: A fulfilled expectations model using contemporaneous poll and endorsement data as information sources. *Journal of Economic Theory* 36:55–85.

————. 1985b. Sequential elections with limited information. *American Journal of Political Science* 29:480–512.

————. 1986. Information, electoral equilibria, and the democratic ideal. *Journal of Politics* 48:909–37.

————. 1987. Elections with limited information. *Mathematical Social Science* 14:77–99.

McKenzie, Lionel. 1959. On the existence of general equilibrium for a competitive market. *Econometrica* 27:38–51.

MacRae, Duncan, Jr. 1958. Dimensions of congressional voting. *University of California Publications in Sociology and Social Institutions* 1 (3): 203–390.

————. 1965. A method for identifying issues and factions from legislative votes. *American Political Science Review* 59 (4): 909–26.

————. 1970. *Issues and parties in legislative voting: Methods of statistical analysis*. New York: Harper and Row.

Macridis, Roy C. 1980. *Contemporary political ideologies: Movements and regimes*. Cambridge, Mass.: Winthrop.

Magee, Stephen; William Brock; and Leslie Young. 1989. *Black hole tariffs and endogenous policy theory: Political economy in general equilibrium*. Cambridge, Mass.: Cambridge University Press.

Margolis, Howard. 1982. *Selfishness, altruism and rationality: A theory of social choice*. New York: Cambridge University Press.

Marshall, Alfred. 1961. *Principles of economics*. 9th ed. London: MacMillan.

Matthews, Donald R., and James W. Prothro. 1966. Dimensions and measurement of attitudes. In *The electoral process*, ed. M. Kent Jennings and L. Harman Zeigler, 132–49. Englewood Cliffs, N.J.: Prentice-Hall.

Milgrom, Paul, and John Roberts. 1982. Predation, reputation, and entry deterrence. *Journal of Economic Theory* 27:280–312.

Minsky, Marvin. 1975. A framework for representing knowledge. In *The psychology of computer vision*, ed. P. H. Winston. New York: McGraw-Hill.

Mitchell, William, and Michael Munger. 1991. Economic models of interest groups: An introductory survey. *American Journal of Political Science* 35:512–46.

Moe, Terry. 1981. *The organization of interests*. Chicago: University of Chicago Press.

Mueller, Dennis. 1977. Allocation, redistribution, and collective choice. *Public Finance* 32:225–44.

————. 1989. *Public choice II*. New York: Cambridge University Press.

Mueller, Dennis, and Peter Murrell. 1986. Interest groups and the size of government. *Public Choice* 48:125–45.

Nelson, Douglas, and Eugene Silberberg. 1987. Ideology and legislator shirking. *Economic Inquiry* 25:15–25.

Neumann, Sigmund, ed. 1956. *Modern political parties*. Chicago: University of Chicago Press.

North, Douglass. 1981. *Structure and change in economic history*. New York: Norton.

―――. 1990a. *Institutions, institutional change, and economic performance*. New York: Cambridge University Press.

―――. 1990b. A transactions cost theory of politics. *Journal of Theoretical Politics* 2:355–67.

―――. 1990c. Economic development in historical perspective: The Western world. Political Economy Working Paper, Washington University, St. Louis.

―――. 1993. Institutions and credible commitment. *Journal of Institutional and Theoretical Economics* 150:421–38.

North, Douglass, and Barry Weingast. 1989. The evolution of institutions governing public choice in Seventeenth-century England. *Journal of Economic History* 49:803–32.

Norton, Anne. 1988. *Reflections on political identity*. Baltimore, Md.: Johns Hopkins University Press.

Olson, Mancur, Jr. 1965. *The logic of collective action*. Cambridge: Harvard University Press.

―――. 1982. *The rise and decline of nations: Economic growth, stagflation, and social rigidities*. New Haven, Conn.: Yale University Press.

Ordeshook, Peter. 1992. Constitutional stability. *Constitutional Political Economy* 3:137–86.

O'Rourke, P. J. 1989. *Parliament of whores*. New York: Atlantic Monthly Press.

Owen, Guillermo. 1982. *Game theory*. 2d ed. New York: Academic Press.

Page, Benjamin. 1976. *Choices and echoes in presidential elections*. Chicago: University of Chicago Press.

Palfrey, Thomas, and Keith Poole. 1987. The relation between information, ideology, and voting behavior. *American Journal of Political Science* 31:511–30.

Palfrey, Thomas R., and Howard Rosenthal. 1985. Voter participation and strategic uncertainty. *American Political Science Review* 79:62–78.

Pareto, Wilfredo. 1971. *Manual of political economy*. Trans. by Ann S. Schwier. New York: Augustus M. Kelley.

Parks, R. P. 1976. An impossibility theorem for fixed preferences: A dictatorial Bergson-Samuelson welfare function. *Review of Economic Studies* 43:447–50.

Peltzman, Sam. 1976. Toward a more general theory of regulation. *Journal of Law and Economics* 19 (August): 211–40.

Plott, Charles. 1967. A notion of equilibrium and its possibility under majority rule. *American Economic Review* 57:787–806.

―――. 1976. Axiomatic social choice theory: An overview and interpretation. *American Journal of Political Science* 20:511–96.

Poole, Keith. 1981. Dimensions of interest group evaluation of the U.S. Senate, 1969–1978. *American Journal of Political Science* 25:49–67.

Poole, Keith, and R. S. Daniels. 1985. Ideology, party, and voting in the U.S. Congress. *American Journal of Political Science* 75:373–99.

Poole, Keith, and Thomas Romer. 1985. Patterns of political action committee contributions to the 1980 campaigns for the U.S. House of Representatives. *Public Choice* 47:63–112.

Poole, Keith T., and Howard Rosenthal. 1984a. The polarization of American politics. *Journal of Politics* 46:1061–79.

———. 1984b. U.S. presidential elections 1960–1980: A spatial analysis. *American Journal of Political Science* 28:282–312.

———. 1985. A spatial model for legislative roll call analysis. *American Political Science Review* 29:357–84.

———. 1991. Patterns of congressional voting. *American Journal of Political Science* 35:228–78.

Pryce-Jones, David. 1991. *The Closed Circle: An Interpretation of the Arabs*. New York: Harper-Collins.

Przeworski, Adam. 1991. *Democracy and the market*. New York: Cambridge University Press.

Rabinowitz, George. 1974. *Spatial models of electoral choice: An empirical analysis*. Chapel Hill, N.C.: Institute for Research in Social Science.

———. 1978. On the nature of political issues: Insights from a spatial analysis. *American Journal of Political Science* 22:793–817.

Rabinowitz, George, and Stuart Macdonald. 1989. A directional theory of voting. *American Political Science Review* 83:93–121.

Rader, Trout. 1963. The existence of a utility function to represent preferences. *Review of Economic Studies* 30:229–32.

Reichley, James A. 1981. *Conservatives in an age of change: The Nixon and Ford administrations*. Washington, D.C.: Brookings.

Riker, William. 1958a. The causes of events. *Journal of Philosophy* 54:57–69.

———. 1958b. The paradox of voting and congressional rules for voting on amendments. *American Political Science Review* 52:349–66.

———. 1963. *The theory of political coalitions*. New Haven, Conn.: Yale University Press.

———. 1980. Implications from the disequilibrium of majority rule for the study of institutions. *American Political Science Review* 74:432–46.

———. 1982. *Liberalism against populism: A confrontation between the theory of democracy and the theory of social choice*. San Francisco: W. H. Freeman and Company.

———. 1989. Why negative campaigning is rational: The rhetoric of the ratification campaign of 1787–1789. Paper presented at the annual meeting of the American Political Science Association, Atlanta, Ga., September 1989.

Riker, William, and Peter Ordeshook. 1968. A theory of the calculus of voting. *American Political Science Review* 62:25–42.

Roberts, K. W. S. 1977. Voting over income tax schedules. *Journal of Public Economics* 8:329–40.

———. 1980. Possibility theorems with interpersonally comparable welfare levels. *Review of Economic Studies* 47:409–20.

Rosch, Eleanor. 1978. Principles of categorization. In *Cognition and Categorization*, ed. E. Rosch and B. Lloyd, 51–69. Hillsdale, N.J.: Erlbaum.

Rosenthal, Howard, and Subrata Sen. 1977. Spatial voting models for the French Fifth Republic." *American Political Science Review* 71:1447–66.

Rubinfeld, Daniel. 1977. Voting in a local school election: A micro analysis. *Review of Economics and Statistics* 59:30–42.

Rusk, J., and Herbert Weisberg. 1972. Perceptions of presidential candidates. *Midwest Journal of Political Science* 16:388–410.

Samuelson, Paul. 1954. The pure theory of economic expenditure. *Review of Economics and Statistics* 36:386–89.

———. 1977. Reaffirming the existence of 'reasonable' Bergson-Samuelson Social welfare functions. *Economica* 44:81–88.

Sartori, Giovanni. 1969. Politics, ideology, and belief systems. *American Political Science Review* 63:398–420.

———. 1976. *Parties and party systems*. Cambridge: Cambridge University Press.

Satterthwaite, M. A. 1975. Strategy-proofness and Arrow's conditions: Existence and correspondence theorems for voting procedures and social welfare functions. *Journal of Economic Theory* 10:187–218.

Schattschneider, E. E. 1935. *Politics, pressures, and the tariff*. New York: Prentice-Hall.

———. 1960. *The semi-sovereign people*. New York: Prentice-Hall.

Schofield, Norman. 1975. A game theoretic analysis of Olson's game of collective action. *Journal of Conflict Resolution* 19:441–61.

———. 1980. Generic properties of simple Bergson-Samuelson welfare functions. *Journal of Mathematical Economics* 6:316–31.

———. 1985a. Anarchy, altruism, and cooperation: A review. *Social Choice and Welfare* 2:207–19.

———. 1985b. *Social choice and democracy*. Heidelberg: Springer-Verlag.

———. 1992a. Political competition in multiparty coalition governments. Washington University Center in Political Economy, Working Paper #164, January 1992.

———. 1992b. A theory of coalition government in a spatial model of voting. Washington University Center in Political Economy, Working Paper #162, January 1992.

Schwartz, Thomas. 1981. The universal-instability theorem. *Public Choice* 37:487–501.

Searing, Donald; Joel Schwartz; and Alden Lind. 1973. The structuring principle: Political socialization and belief systems. *American Political Science Review* 67:415–32.

Seliger, M. 1976. *Ideology and politics*. London: Allen and Unwin.

Sen, Amartya K. 1970. *Collective choice and social welfare*. San Francisco: Holden Day.

Shapiro, Perry. 1973. Representation, voting, and public goods. *Journal of Public Economics* 4:21–36.

Shepsle, Kenneth. 1972. The strategy of ambiguity, uncertainty, and competition. *American Political Science Review* 66:551–68.

Shepsle, Kenneth, and Barry Weingast. 1981. Structure-induced equilibrium and legislative choice. *Public Choice* 37:503–19.

Simon, Herbert. 1982. *Models of bounded rationality*. 2 vols. Cambridge, Mass.: MIT Press.

———. 1985. Human nature in politics: The dialogue of psychology with political science. *American Political Science Review* 79:293–304.

Slutsky, Steven. 1975. Abstentions and majority equilibrium. *Journal of Economic Theory* 11:292–304.

———. 1977a. A characterization of societies with consistent majority decision. *Review of Economic Studies* 44:211–25.

———. 1977b. A voting model for the allocation of public goods: Existence of an equilibrium. *Journal of Economic Theory* 14:299–325.

———. 1979. Equilibrium under α-majority voting. *Econometrica* 47:113–25.

Smith, Adam. 1776. *An inquiry into the nature and causes of the wealth of nations.* Reprint, 1972. New York: Basic Books.

Smithies, A. 1941. Optimum location in spatial competition. *Journal of Political Economy* 49:423–39.

Sniderman, Paul; Richard Brady; and Philip Tetlock, eds. 1991. *Reasoning and choice: Explorations in political psychology.* New York: Cambridge University Press.

Snyder, James. 1990. Campaign contributions as investments: The U.S. House of Representatives. *Journal of Political Economy* 98:1195–1227.

———. 1992. The dimensions of constituency preferences: Voting on California ballot propositions, 1974–1990. University of Chicago.

Sowell, Thomas. 1987. *A conflict of visions.* New York: William Morrow Publishers.

Stark, William, ed. 1954. *Jeremy Bentham's economic writings.* London: George Allen and Unwin.

Stigler, George. 1988. *Chicago studies in political economy.* Chicago: University of Chicago Press.

Stokes, Donald. 1963. Spatial models of party competition. *American Political Science Review* 57:368–77.

Stone, Deborah. 1986. *Policy paradox and political reason.* San Francisco: Scott-Foresman.

Strauss, R. P., and G. D. Hughes. 1976. A new approach to the demand for public goods. *Journal of Public Economics* 6:191–204.

Tajfel, Henri. 1981. *Human groups and social categories: Studies in social psychology.* Cambridge: Cambridge University Press.

Tajfel, Henri; M. Billig; R. Bundy; and C. Flament. 1971. Social categorization and intergroup behavior. *European Journal of Social Psychology* 1:149–78.

Tajfel, Henri, and A. Wilkes. 1963. Classification and quantitative judgement. *British Journal of Social Psychology* 54:101–14.

Taylor, Michael. 1976. *Anarchy and cooperation.* London: Wiley.

———. 1982. *Community, anarchy, and liberty.* Cambridge: Cambridge University Press.

Taylor, S. E., S. T. Fiske; N. L. Etcoff; and A. J. Ruderman. 1978. Categorical bases of person memory and stereotyping. *Journal of Personality and Social Psychology* 36:778–93.

Tenbarge, Joseph. 1990. Ideology and social categories: A review. University of Texas, Department of Political Science.

Tideman, Nicholas, and Gordon Tullock. 1976. A new and superior process for making social choices. *Journal of Political Economy* 84:1145–59.

Truman, David. 1952. *The governmental process*, New York: Alfred A. Knopf.

Tullock, Gordon. 1981. Why so much stability? *Public Choice* 37:189–202.

van Schur, Hendrik. 1984. *Structure in political beliefs: A new model for stochastic unfolding with application to European party activists.* Amsterdam: CT Press.

Vickrey, W. 1960. Utility, strategy, and social decision rules. *Quarterly Journal of Economics* 74:507–35.

Von Mises, Ludwig. 1981. *Epistemological problems of economics.* Trans. by George Reisman. New York: New York University Press. (German edition published in 1933.)

Walras, Leon. 1954. *Elements of pure economics.* Homewood, Ill.: Irwin. (French edition published 1874–1877.)

Weber, Max. 1947. *The theory of social and economic organization.* New York: Oxford University Press.

———. 1950. *The Protestant ethic and the spirit of capitalism.* New York: Scribner.

Weingast, Barry. 1993a. The economic role of political institutions. Hoover Institution, Stanford University, Stanford, Calif.

———. 1993b. The political foundations of democracy and the rule of law. Hoover Institution, Stanford University, Stanford, Calif.

Weingast, Barry, and William Marshall. 1988. The industrial organization of Congress; Or, why legislatures, like firms, are not organized as markets. *Journal of Political Economy* 96:132–63.

Weisberg, Herbert. 1968. Dimensional analysis of legislative roll calls. Ph.D. diss., University of Michigan, Ann Arbor.

Weisberg, Herbert, and Jerrold Rusk. 1970. Dimensions of candidate evaluation. *American Political Science Review* 64:1167–85.

Welch, William. 1974. The economics of campaign funds. *Public Choice* 20:83–97.

Wicksell, Knut. 1958. A new principle of just taxation. In *Classics in the theory of public finance,* ed. Richard Musgrave and Alan Peacock, 24–49. New York: St. Martin's Press. (Swedish edition published 1896.)

Wildavsky, Aaron B. 1959. A methodological critique of Duverger's political parties. *Journal of Politics* 5:303–18.

Wittman, Donald. 1973. Parties as utility maximizers. *American Political Science Review* 67(June): 490–98.

———. 1977. Candidates with policy preferences: A dynamic model. *Journal of Economic Theory* 14 (February): 180–89.

———. 1983. Candidate motivation: A synthesis of alternative theories. *American Political Science Review* 77:142–57.

———. 1991. Contrasting economic and psychological analyses of political choice. In *The economic approach to human behavior,* ed. Kristen Renwick Monroe, 65–89. New York: Harper-Collins.

Wolfinger, Raymond, and Steven Rosenstone. 1980. *Who votes?* New Haven, Conn.: Yale University Press.

Zeckman, Martin. 1979. Dynamic models of the voter's decision calculus. *Public Choice* 34:297–315.

Name Index

255

Subject Index